Exploring and Understanding Careers in Criminal Justice

Exploring and Understanding Careers in Criminal Justice

A Comprehensive Guide

Matthew J. Sheridan and Raymond R. Rainville

ROWMAN & LITTLEFIELD
Lanham • Boulder • New York • London

Published by Rowman & Littlefield
A wholly owned subsidiary of The Rowman & Littlefield Publishing Group, Inc.
4501 Forbes Boulevard, Suite 200, Lanham, Maryland 20706
www.rowman.com

Unit A, Whitacre Mews, 26-34 Stannary Street, London SE11 4AB

British Library Cataloguing in Publication Information Available

Library of Congress Cataloging-in-Publication Data

Rainville, Raymond R., 1943- author.
 Exploring and understanding careers in criminal justice : a comprehensive
guide / Raymond R. Rainville and Matthew J. Sheridan.
    pages cm
 Includes bibliographical references and index.
 ISBN 978-1-4422-5430-5 (cloth : alk. paper) — ISBN 978-1-4422-5431-2
(electronic) 1. Criminal justice, Administration of—Vocational guidance—
United States. 2. Law enforcement—Vocational guidance—United States. I.
Sheridan, Matthew J., 1948- author. II. Title.
 HV9950.R35 2016
 364.024'73—dc23
                                                              2015026494

∞™ The paper used in this publication meets the minimum requirements of
American National Standard for Information Sciences—Permanence of Paper
for Printed Library Materials, ANSI/NISO Z39.48-1992.

Printed in the United States of America

DEDICATION BY MATTHEW J. SHERIDAN

For Mom; Lynda, my wife; and McKenzie, my daughter, who have provided love, encouragement, and support. For my father, who would have loved to have seen this.

For Ron Sopenoff, who gave me my first college position. For Don Halsted, who encouraged me to write and is no longer with us to see one task come to fruition. For the many who have been beacons of light when there was darkness.

For every student who sat before me and taught me what they needed to know. Hopefully, every student who now reads this book will be helped toward a successful career.

DEDICATION BY RAYMOND R. RAINVILLE

For Pat, my wife, support, and friend. For Pat, who walked with me for over fifty years. We had a long journey together, starting during my undergraduate days, through good times and bad times. She always supported me, was always patient through graduate school—not once, but twice—five children, and 100,000 miles, and we are still together. Without her help, this book would not be. For Pat, who always allowed me the time to be me.

For Gerald Shattuck, a graceful guide to Fordham. I went into the doors of Fordham University and out into the world with changed views and attitudes. What a spectacular professor, mentor, and lifelong friend.

For all the friends, coworkers, professors, supervisors, and students who have helped me develop into the person I am today.

Contents

Preface

We have spent countless hours listening to students talk about their career aspirations and what they believe are the steps to entering the profession. We believe that *Exploring and Understanding Careers in Criminal Justice: A Comprehensive Guide* is a critical and much-needed book for students preparing for college and who are beginning their pursuit of a criminal justice career. We have heard the comments of fellow faculty members who field the myriad questions asked by students of their experiences and of the students' reactions to their presentation of work and duties that they previously did not comprehend. This book is also for faculty/advisors of students. Unfortunately, we have also encountered students who have labored through their studies, received excellent grades, and then during their internships in the third or fourth year, discovered that their career choice was poorly considered. With that said, this book is also for guidance counselors and others who would discuss the various career opportunities in criminal justice with students. The pursuit of a degree in criminal justice, as a stepping-stone to a career, will help the student to make choices that will not limit him/her to the more commonly considered occupations in criminal justice. This guide will better prepare students for the many career opportunities to be encountered as a career unfolds.

Exploring and Understanding Careers in Criminal Justice: A Comprehensive Guide is designed to be a road map through the quagmire of choices that face the new career employee by suggesting that they plan their career in increments through the acquisition of additional education and skills to meet the needs of a changing world. Certainly, since 9/11, the work of criminal justice and the employment opportunities in this area have undergone revision, if not drastic changes.

Exploring and Understanding Careers in Criminal Justice: A Comprehensive Guide will help students expand their focus and intensify their preparation through the understanding that a career is part of their lives and that proper planning will result in greater satisfaction and achievement. There is more to life than a career. However, careers do play a major role in life satisfaction. In addition, other considerations go beyond the career that affect the life plan. This book will help the student and the advisor to evaluate those life choices.

Exploring and Understanding Careers in Criminal Justice: A Comprehensive Guide will help students assess their career aspirations. The authors wish all students a successful career through good planning.

Acknowledgments

We are only as successful as those we have behind us. Family represents our strength and motivation. Many circumstances also guide us, and our students have served as beacons of light. We hope that those seeking careers in this profession will be better at it than we were—choosing, advancing, and looking back with a sense of accomplishment.

We thank our colleagues at Rowman & Littlefield, beginning with Kathryn Knigge, who did not know our original intentions for the book but saw them in the prospectus and suggested the way we should proceed. She did not know that our original vision was greater than we actually suggested. Kathryn, you also suggested steps we did not foresee, and those were improvements on our design.

1

Introduction: Why Another Book on Criminal Justice Careers?

Crime and criminals intrigue and capture not only our attention but our imagination. Newspapers, TV, and radio reporting typically begin with the latest and most graphic, sensational criminal event. The more extraordinary the crime, the sooner someone writes a book about it, and the names of the judge, the cop, the prosecutor, or the offender become household names. Some of the more popular TV shows today are centered on crimes and criminals. One show has a serial killer solving other crimes by serial killers; others are about criminal profiling, and one is even about probability theory as a means to solve and prevent crime. Of course, forensics, homeland security, and terrorism have grabbed their share of viewers' attention, as well, and have become all the rage. New college courses and majors have appeared in colleges and universities centered around featured professions such as federal marshals, crime scene investigators, medical examiners, forensic scientists, FBI agents, criminal profilers, and others.

Many were glued to their televisions, waiting to see what secrets would be revealed when Geraldo Rivera opened the lost vault of Al Capone. Viewers were equally disappointed to see that it was empty. Many of the better actors, from Humphrey Bogart and Jimmy Cagney to Clint Eastwood, Robert DeNiro, Al Pacino, and Denzel Washington, have cemented their reputations by starring in criminal roles that depict someone, real or fictional, in the field of criminal justice. Literature, both adult and juvenile, from Sherlock Holmes to the Hardy Boys and Nancy Drew to the novels of James Patterson, are rife with crime, crime-solving, and superior criminals sought after by superior crime solvers.

Many who have had an experience with the criminal justice field, including offenders, victims, wardens, correctional officers, judges, police officers, federal agents, medical examiners, and others, have written their personal stories. College and university criminal justice programs became and remain the fastest-expanding programs and the largest departments on their respective college campuses. New majors, such as Homeland Security, appear all the time to keep pace with events and demand in the criminal justice profession.

Criminal justice is more than a profession, however; it is a vast industry that for prisons alone has a combined national annual budget that "eclipses the GDP (Gross Domestic Product) of 133 nations." Estimates of the national cost of prisons is about $74 billion.[1] However, that figure may actually underestimate the cost of prisons when we take into account the cost of California prisons at $7.9 billion,[2] Texas at $3.3 billion,[3] and Michigan at about $2 billion.[4] These figures also do not take into account the cost of municipal and county jails. In addition, these figures do not take into account other costs that are subsumed by departments other than the departments of corrections. New Jersey serves as an example. The cost of vehicles for the New Jersey Department of Corrections is found in the Department of Treasury budget. If we take into account this information, then in all likelihood the cost of incarcerations in the United States exceeds $100 billion.

Some of the industry that caters to the criminal justice field is even listed on the New York Stock Exchange. Crime has gone public. State and federal governments and private companies manage criminal justice operations. For-profit corporations and nonprofit agencies operate private prisons, halfway houses, and day reporting centers. They also manage the medical, psychological, and social services needs of both convicts and ex-convicts and provide for technology (including upgrades and maintenance), food for the prisons, and more.

The U.S. Congress and each of the state legislatures have committees that specifically address crime and crime control issues. On a daily basis, new legislation is passed that affects the criminal justice system and generates jobs and products. Prisons are specifically located and built where they will improve the economic situation of local communities.

THERE IS SO MUCH INFORMATION AVAILABLE, SO WHY ANOTHER BOOK?

Students tend to see the criminal justice system through rose-colored glasses and are often myopic as they plan their futures. The authors have each been practitioners for more than thirty years. They also have been in academics for more than twenty years, beginning while they were working and continuing after retirement from their careers. As practitioners, they became painfully aware of the lack of preparation new employees brought to the field. As members of the academic community, they became more painfully aware that students had been poorly and even inappropriately advised about career opportunities in this field. In addition, there is the recognition that students oftentimes have to rely upon faculty who in a former life were practitioners.

There is, perhaps, no one more influential to a student than a dynamic professor who has also had a fulfilling and involved career. However, that wonderful professor may be speaking about his/her specific niche in the criminal justice field while unsuspectingly overlooking not only other aspects of the field but what it takes to be successful in the criminal justice field overall, or unfortunately, what might be a better fit for a student asking questions about a career.

The intrigue of the criminal justice profession, the depth of potential employment, and the multitude of career opportunities cannot be adequately covered in any one course. Some colleges and universities now offer courses that specifically address jobs in the criminal justice profession. Professors teaching these courses rely on several texts that have been developed for other courses. *Exploring and Understanding Careers in Criminal Justice: A Comprehensive Guide* will serve as a text for these courses as well as a resource for the administrators of criminal justice programs as they guide students through their undergraduate studies in academic tracks that meet their needs.

There is no single book or site that lays out the breadth and depth of working in the criminal justice field, and too little is included in criminal justice curriculums to describe all the career opportunities in criminal justice. Furthermore, there is little to no guidance that explains how an individual is to conduct himself or herself in the profession in terms of advancing one's career or changing careers. A person's career is a journey.

Bo Orichowsky (see his profile in Appendix 1) is an excellent example of someone who broke into the criminal justice profession, took advantage of opportunities to advance, and then landed a position that has provided him with career satisfaction. Then, there is the end of the career to consider—retirement.

All too often, retirement and the future are barely mentioned, thought of, or consequently planned for in the early career stages. The early days of a career are potentially the most productive time during which to begin planning for retirement and one's personal economic future well-being. The past decade has seen severe challenges to retirement plans and medical benefits. Successful retirement requires early planning.

A common theme from those who have generously supplied their profiles for this book is what they would have done differently if they could go back to the beginning of their careers. This book will not ameliorate those issues, but hopefully it will at least minimally address them so that students and even those employed in the profession can begin to think about improving the manner in which they manage their careers—from the moment of hiring to their separation from the job.

While TV shows and movies serve to glorify the criminal justice field, television commercials for private technical schools play up the personal benefits of working in the field. They advertise that their courses of study will provide students with the training they need to qualify. In reality, such training may actually be of little use. The criminal justice profession has its own training academies, and especially for those vocations in law enforcement, the specialized academies are rigorous. Generally, students know little of how to prepare for the academy of their choice. Therefore, academy preparation is included in this book.

CAREER PROFILES

Career profiles are a special feature of this book and have been collected from many professionals in the criminal justice field. Each professional has shared what he or she has thought to be important about their career and has attempted to highlight not only what has made them successful but also what enabled them to develop as a professional. Perhaps they, too, serve to glamorize the field. However, our intention is that they represent a sampling of the breadth and depth of experiences that are to be found in the criminal justice career. These successful practitioners attempt to highlight both the opportunities they were fortunate to have taken advantage of and the missteps that interfered with their entrance into the criminal justice field.

This book was primarily written for anyone who wishes to have a career in the criminal justice field. The book has also been written for those who would counsel high school and college students about career opportunities in criminal justice. Finally, there are those who are curious about criminal justice and have relied upon the media for guidance. Unfortunately, the media's primary purpose is entertainment and not accurate information. This book will provide a better understanding of the field of criminal justice and how its components relate to one another. There are many who do not know which questions should be asked, simply because they lack knowledge about the depth and breadth of the profession. Part of the uniqueness of *Exploring and Understanding Careers in Criminal Justice: A Comprehensive Guide* is that it tries to anticipate not only concerns that are commonly expressed but others that are less commonly expressed. Please use the subject index as you explore your career choice for the inclusion of information about topics that can be found in other chapters. Many questions of students and others will require a broader treatment than would be possible for the scope of this book. To help resolve this deficiency, a bibliography of suggested readings and websites has been included in Appendices 9 and 10. Specific questions about the components that comprise the criminal justice field may be more appropriately answered in courses such as Introduction to Criminal Justice, Policing, The Courts, Corrections, Juvenile Justice, or Criminology. Nevertheless, as a career in criminal justice is considered, your ability to explore personal questions and obtain appropriate answers to your questions is critical. This book will provide greater clarity about the pursuit of a career in criminal justice and what may be the more appropriate career choice for you.

THE INDEX

You may wish to use the index as you consider whether you are clear about the answers to your questions. That is, the index provides a reference to other places in the book where such information may additionally be discussed. For example, examine the following questions. They have begun to be addressed in this chapter, and the questions are more completely answered in other chapters. Some important questions that may be asked are:

- What are the three primary areas of criminal justice in which there are career opportunities?
- What are the differences between the three principal components of the criminal justice field?
- Are the job requirements different in federal, state, and local employment?
- What are the benefits of a career in criminal justice?
- What are the risks of a career in criminal justice?
- What are the ethical issues to consider in a criminal justice career?
- Is there a minimum or maximum age to start employment in a criminal justice career?
- Is there a maximum age at which you must terminate your employment?
- Are there a maximum number of years you can work in a specific career in criminal justice?
- What options are available upon retirement from a career in criminal justice?
- Does age affect which pension system you can join?
- Does age affect when you can retire?

Perhaps these questions have already entered your mind. Perhaps you now have additional questions. You should develop your own questions (and we suggest that you write them down—questions not retained get forgotten quickly) as you read through *Exploring and Understanding Careers in Criminal Justice: A Comprehensive Guide*. When those questions arise, you need to get answers. Speak with a professor or an advisor. This book cannot answer all possible questions about the field of criminal justice, but it will serve as a guide to discovering satisfactory answers to many questions.

THE APPENDIX

To further assist your exploration, particularly if you are investigating a career that is somewhat less commonly discussed, you will find websites listed in the back of the book that will help you achieve a comprehensive understanding of your choice of career. In addition, there are sections in the appendices that will help you along the way, including such items as sample résumés, a networking guide, civil service exam preparation materials, and interview advice.

BIBLIOGRAPHY OF REFERENCES AND SUGGESTED READINGS

The bibliography in this guide has been created to provide the inquiring student with a broad range of sources from which he/she can pick and choose to learn about their potential profession. All professions have a downside as well as an upside. Students should not ignore the downside when selecting a chosen profession in which they are likely to spend twenty, twenty-five, or thirty, or more years. For example, under policing, *Serpico* is referenced. The author of this book, Frank Serpico, was a New York City police officer who helped to uncover massive corruption in the police force. Under corrections, the student may wish to read *Newjack* by Ted Conover. Conover was an investigative reporter who was denied access to a corrections training academy. He discusses his application process, his academy training experience, and his assignment to Sing-Sing Correctional Facility. Other books on the list cover the careers of ministers, educators, correction officers, and wardens.

The number of and type of positions in the criminal justice field is constantly changing. There is a great likelihood that criminal justice will require different specializations as we go forward because of the burgeoning numbers and the necessity to change because the cost has become intolerable, because of the development of new technology, and because the failure rates are unacceptable. For example, in the past decade we have seen such innovations as day reporting centers added to the area of community corrections. Nevertheless, criminal justice will remain a large field of employment that requires a well-educated, well trained, and well-informed workforce. Good luck in your search for a successful career path and in your understanding of what that career entails.

Feel free to contact the authors with your experiences and questions. We hope to expand this primer as we go forward to provide the most informed source of material for those aspiring to a criminal justice career. We invite students, counselors, and career professionals alike to provide us with their comments and suggestions to make this book a valuable resource for all.

Some information is repeated in different sections, as it applies to information in that section. We do not wish to be repetitive, but we recognize that some will not read the entire book. Therefore, we have repeated certain information so that important details relative to a specific topic are not missed.

2

Exploring Careers in Criminal Justice

A BRIEF REVIEW OF THE CRIMINAL JUSTICE SYSTEM

The criminal justice system is comprised of three components: law enforcement, corrections, and the courts. Generally, but not always, they operate separately from each other. In addition, there are distinctions in operations from state to state, and there may be jurisdictional issues between federal government agencies and the states as well as within state agencies at both the state and local levels. Together, they represent a complex array of agencies that may or may not interact with one another. In addition, the operations and responsibilities of state and federal agencies often overlap, and they may come into conflict with each other as they attempt to determine jurisdiction.

CAREERS AND PROFESSIONALS

There is a wide breadth of careers in criminal justice; however, not all careers require that the individual be a professional, have a college degree, or even be involved in law enforcement. Some careers are clearly more professional than others, and some have specific law enforcement requirements. That is not said to downplay one career versus another. Within the field of criminal justice, many career paths intersect, and when they work together, there is a greater likelihood for success and accomplishment within the field. Of course, when they fail to cooperate, then there is the likelihood of breakdowns in operations and even failure to successfully complete some assignments.

THE CRIMINAL JUSTICE ENVIRONMENT

Each component of the criminal justice system has unique environmental factors that should be considered by the student or job seeker. The criminal justice environment is distinctive because of its daily interactions with those who have violated the law or are suspected of violating the law, as well as tragic events and problems that often lack acceptable solutions. Similarly, each position in the criminal justice field has the upside potential of making contributions to society (most commonly defined as "making society safer") and unraveling the specific challenges to discover "what works."[1] At times, some of the more problematic circumstances, such as domestic violence or ensuring the care and well-being of children, are best served when persons from the criminal justice field and others from different career paths, such as social services, work together to find acceptable solutions. The current hot topic, terrorism, helps to illustrate criminal justice professions at their best when it comes to working together. The 9/11 tragedy saw professionals from many criminal justice career paths come together to provide assistance, comfort, counseling, reassurance, and more to help a nation overcome great loss. A more recent notable example was the cooperation between many law enforcement agencies to resolve the bombing incident that occurred during the Boston Marathon of 2013.

Negotiating problems and developing potential solutions require such elements as having good people skills, being well-trained, anticipating difficulties, developing good organizational skills, and thinking outside the box. To be sure, jobs in criminal justice require the successful employee to look at problems and situations differently to discover unconventional problem-solving approaches. Many times employees will only discover how successful they may be when they are actually on the job facing real-life circumstances. Some discussion of the environments in which criminal justice personnel work will be helpful to the prospective employee to understand the value of introspection and soul searching to discover whether their personality and skills match the job. Obviously, a quality education with an emphasis on criminal justice is the first step to making an appropriate career decision.

THE COURTS

Courts, with the exception of the juvenile court, are open to public scrutiny. Juvenile courts, to put it simply, operate behind closed doors to preserve confidentiality for the accused juvenile. The vast majority of court cases are routine, and the daily operation of the court is in actuality a management chore. However, the more higher profile the case, the greater the media and social attention paid to it. The nature of the case—whether it involves issues of wealth (Bernie Madoff), impropriety (Barry Bonds), race (O.J. Simpson), celebrity (Martha Stewart), or politics (Rod Blagojevich)—influences the audience. In addition, the nature of the case is important, and each of the above-mentioned defendants has caught the attention of different facets of the criminal justice profession. To be sure, these cases may also add to the confusion, controversy, and uncertainty that exist about the role of the courts in modern society.

High-profile court cases have considerable social implications that may then be reflected in changes of legislation (Megan's Law) and rules (testing for steroids), considerations for legal representation (Johnnie Cochran's declaration that "if the glove don't fit, you must acquit"), or selection for recognition (Pete Rose's lifetime ban from baseball for gambling following his conviction and prison time).

The focus on the actors in high-profile cases has resulted in considerable controversy. Heretofore, there was little challenge to the competency of a judge, prosecutor, defense attorney, or others in specific criminal justice capacities. (Some examples include Judge Ito's rulings in the O.J. Simpson trial and Marcia Clark's change of appearance for the courtroom cameras, or Mark Fuhrman's neglect of protocol in handling the evidence.) The majority of cases brought before the court are ordinary and even mundane, involving circumstances in which the primary actors follow procedures, day in and day out, from which there is little deviation.

The actors in the courtroom play roles and assume duties that, to the untrained observer, may seem to contradict what is in the best interest of the public. For example, public defenders and defense attorneys may appear to be helping obviously guilty parties avoid penalties for their actions (such as making motions for dismissal because of improper procedures followed in obtaining evidence or a confession). Overzealous prosecutors may seem to be acting in the best interest of the public safety by bending the rules (such as by withholding evidence from defense attorneys) to ensure a guilty determination and thus remove an offender from the streets. And judges may seem to ignore important issues, prevent testimony or evidence from being presented, or instruct juries to ignore evidence that has been presented that would ensure a successful prosecution.

The point is that each actor in the criminal justice system must follow certain rules in their specific roles if the integrity of the criminal justice system is to be maintained. Defense attorneys are there to protect the rights of the accused, even if that protection means a supposedly guilty party is found not guilty. Prosecutors who violate constitutional protections (such as by submitting dry-labbing evidence)[2] are denying rights guaranteed to all citizens. Judges, on the other hand, are to act as referees who interpret constitutional issues to ensure and enforce the upholding of the rights of all defendants. They are not to support the actions of defense attorneys or prosecutors except as they act in accordance with the rules of the court and the constitution.

LAW ENFORCEMENT

Police officers are depended upon to provide protection and safety, and they do this while they are on and off duty. Police work is dangerous and results in frequent injuries. Stress is common to the profession and contributes to illness and at times bad judgment. Policemen and women are daily exposed to potential dangers, whether from those who would break the law or from other circumstances. Subsequently, police officers must maintain a heightened state of awareness and vigilance to respond to threatening or dangerous situations. Frequent injuries and death are associated with the daily routines of law enforcement (such as when they encounter accidents or respond to criminal events). Of course, among the more tragic and unfortunate events associated with on-the-job stress are the occurrence of suicide, divorce, and substance abuse. Careers in law enforcement are well-known for their negative effects on police officers and their personal lives. (Note: See Cop2Cop for a helping agency that responds to police stress in New Jersey.[3] Also see the profile in Appendix 1 of Bill Ussery, the founder of Cop2Cop.)

The work of law enforcement is generally scheduled around a forty-hour workweek, but there is the necessity for frequent overtime. Overtime is often the result of required written reports on the day's activities, the need for more police coverage at an event or incident, or the need to continue work because of having already responded to an incident. The more complex the incident, the more hours of overtime will be required. Investigations require extended hours of labor and complex arrangements of support to ensure not only the successful completion of the investigation but the protection and well-being of those involved. Police work is shift work, but duties must be performed around the clock seven days a week. The officer just emerging from the academy will undoubtedly pull the least-desirable shifts—nights, weekends, and holiday duty—and often the least-desirable locations to patrol.

Federal enforcement agents encounter different obstacles that obstruct what would otherwise be a normal lifestyle. Federal agents are called upon with little or no notice to travel. Travel may include protective services (especially for U.S. Marshals and Secret Service personnel), such as guarding judges during high-profile cases, or even the president of the United States; investigations (especially for CIA, FBI, or U.S. Treasury agents); or promotions in rank, such as assuming administrative duties in different locations with the BOP or the U.S. Parks Service. Some positions involve periodic transfers that may occur several times during the course of career. And to be sure, some postings and responses to incidents can place officers in the harsh conditions of inclement weather and other hazardous situations, such as the events of September 11, 2001.

The bulk of police work comes under the heading of "patrol," which involves the performance of a variety of routine tasks during daily assignments, many of which vary little from when they were initiated by Sir Robert Peel in London in 1829. Patrol primarily accomplishes three tasks:

1. Maintaining a police presence,
2. Providing availability for emergencies, and
3. Detecting and solving crimes.[4]

The face of law enforcement has undergone many changes since its humble beginnings. Great mystery stories, terrific movies, and TV episodes with intricate plots are filled with accounts of men and women who have a career in law enforcement or others who have left official law enforcement careers to pursue it privately. The plots are tense (find the kidnapped girl before she dies), dramatic (discover the shooter before he shoots you), exciting (breathtaking car chases with outrageous crashes, from which everyone inexplicably walks away), and filled with great lines, such as "Was it five shots or was it six?" that stimulate the imagination. While these images, made possible through the lens of the camera, are titillating, they are also exceptional and do not bear much resemblance to the everyday work of law enforcement personnel.

Unfortunately, law enforcement itself has also had its share of unsavory incidents, such as Abner Louima and Rodney King becoming the victims of police brutality, Mark Fuhrman's inappropriate actions in the O.J. Simpson case, and the scandalous corruption made known through *Serpico*. These incidents have all contributed to public perceptions of police officers acting at odds with the public good. Nevertheless, there are confused perceptions of the manner in which law enforcement must operate or be considered soft that have been promoted in novels and films such as *Dirty Harry*, in which the end justifies the means; that is, police officers must do whatever is necessary to apprehend the criminal, even if it involves committing crimes themselves or violating the constitutional rights of citizens. Police officers have bemoaned actions by the courts such as *Miranda v. Arizona*, which upheld the principle that suspects must be read their rights. At first, law enforcement considered this a hindrance to their ability to catch criminals, thinking it would lead to fewer convictions, but instead more effective police work has resulted in a sharp increase in convictions. Fortunately, the unsavory incidents that detail human failings are not characteristic of all who do the job. Unfortunately, however, such incidents do reflect on all who perform the job of law enforcement.

The changing face of law enforcement has brought with it increased responsibility and expanded involvement for professionals from an assortment of disciplines. The police psychologist, for example, was once a dreaded or even scorned professional, but he has in recent times emerged to play an ever-increasingly valuable role. Once limited to the examination of new recruits for fitness that could eliminate them from law enforcement or to conduct follow-up sessions with police officers after critical incidents that could relegate them to desk duty or relieve them from duty altogether, they now are seen as providing a beneficial and supportive role that might salvage a career or even a reputation. The psychologist, as often seen on television shows such as *Bones*, may also be critical to an investigation by providing advice about suspects or by developing a profile that leads to the apprehension of an offender.

CORRECTIONS

Corrections is probably the least-understood and the more confusing of the three components of criminal justice professions, because its operations are more hidden or masked by the tall walls that shield its actions from outsiders. In addition, corrections officers by far receive the greatest press and the most mention in textbooks and other sources, which almost entirely ignore civilians who work in such occupations as administrators, social workers, psychologists, human resources personnel, teachers, counselors, fiscal management counselors, public relations workers, grant managers, doctors, nurses, researchers, and other managers.

Corrections may also be the environment that on a daily basis is the most potentially hazardous. Ted Conover,[5] an investigative reporter and the author of *Newjack*, could not gain access to the New York Correction Officers Academy, yet he could apply for, gain acceptance to, and advance through the academy to become a correctional officer himself. Conover explored the manner in which corrections officers are trained and then how they fulfill their job assignments. Through Conover we get a glimpse into the conflicting if not confusing or contradictory expectations of the corrections business generally, and the work and environments of the correctional officer specifically.

The history of corrections has shown itself to exist in a capricious manner through its constantly shifting philosophical position from the humane intention to the retributive posture and the repetitive struggle to instill meaningful reforms. The environment is caught up in the dilemma of whether to punish or to treat—a debate that gains strong emotionally charged supporters for each side. All too often, the contrasting and conflicting goals of the penal sanction (retribution, incapacitation, rehabilitation, and deterrence—terms not always easily understood) are confounded by startling revelations that leave even the more conservative observer wondering about the role that prisons should play to punish offenders and safeguard society.

Extreme, extraordinary, and unusual events, such as shootings in California prisons, the Attica and New Mexico riots, abusive Arkansas prison farms, the mistreatment of prisoners in Abu Ghraib, the medical experiments in Holmesburg, and the case of Willie Horton, who absconded from prison and later committed a terrible crime—these all capture the headlines because of their notoriety, but they seem to be soon forgotten until the next tragedy occurs. These circumstances raise questions about ethical and appropriate conduct that challenge the purpose of the prison as a social institution and the roles that correctional officers, professional employees, and administrators are to serve.

Criminal justice environments are subject to constant scrutiny by the media and the legislature. The nature of the work is difficult to manage on a day to day basis and the nature of the client may require day-to-day adjustments. Their intentions, problems, needs and demeanors call into play complex decision making that often exceeds even the ability of the best trained person. There are sharp reactions to those who do the work that includes exceptional, if not unquestioning support to absolute suspicion and disbelief about the occupational work of being in a helping profession.

CIVILIAN VERSUS LAW ENFORCEMENT

Choosing to pursue a career in criminal justice is only the first step to landing that first position. There are three distinct career paths in criminal justice. There is the civilian track, the law enforcement route, and the private path. Your choice of the law enforcement, the civilian or the private path will affect your preparation process. Your personal aspirations will help you determine the strengths and weaknesses for you in each career path.

Careers in law enforcement, and primarily those in state and federal agencies, seem to attract the greater attention. After all, they are more likely to be the subject of media attention, as well as featured in TV shows and movies. However, civilian careers are much greater in number and cater to a notable diversity of skills. Some civilian career paths include administration, social work, psychology, human resources, teaching (both academic and vocational), counseling, fiscal management, public relations, grant management, doctors, nurses, researchers, and overall management. The choice of whether to pursue a sworn or a civilian position is personal and should be based on your own interests, your abilities, and the means for you to prepare. Something that should be kept in mind as you prepare for a career is that there are those who do switch from the law enforcement side to the civilian side or the private side and vice versa. Career changes and advancement occur over many years, perhaps even several decades. See the profiles of Lenny Ward (who went from parole officer to administrator)[6] and Bo Orichowsky (who went from social worker to parole officer) in Appendix 1 at the end of this book. Warden Bob Hood (also see Appendix 1), to be sure, provides one of the more interesting career profiles, as he advanced from a prison teacher to become the Warden of the Alcatraz of the Rockies—ADX, the federal supermax prison.

There are some common means of preparation for each position. Perhaps the most interesting thing about this preparation is that students will discover more about the criminal justice profession than they ever imagined, and in doing so they will begin to discover which may be the better personal career choice for them and how many options are available in each profession. There is also the likelihood that what begins as a desire to work on one side may change after greater exposure to the other side. That is, what initially interested you may lose ground to other aspirations that have greater potential for personal satisfaction and achievement as you explore the field and discover the variety of available positions in the criminal justice field. As your experiences with criminal justice professionals and the components of the criminal justice profession increase, your choice of career path may become more complex as you realize the depth of possible career opportunities and the requirements for each. The person interested in the criminal justice field owes it to themselves to understand the many opportunities that are available. That also includes inquiring about limitations or the downsides to one profession as opposed to another. Visiting criminal justice websites (see Appendix 10) and reviewing requirements for jobs will help you with this exploration.

THE ROAD TO CAREER SELECTION

Many aspects of the criminal justice system are readily available for review by interested persons. A phone call to an agency will help you to arrange a visit. When a phone call will not work, a professor may be able to open a door. Treat the visit like a field trip by adequately preparing yourself. Think about what questions you need to have answered. Ask your professors what you should look for and what questions they suggest you might ask. See if there is a website available for the agency. Hopefully, the visit will permit you to carry a notebook in which you will have listed your questions and where you will record the answers and your observations. Plan to dress professionally, and afterward send a thank-you note. First impressions are always important and they should never be ignored. Similarly, good manners are recommended and will be remembered by your host.

COLLEGE COURSES

While college may not be for everyone, neither is it a necessary requirement for all careers in criminal justice. However, a college degree in criminal justice will provide greater exposure to many facets of the criminal justice field. A college degree will also help prepare you for career advancement and possible changes in your career. Nevertheless, college courses, and specifically introductory courses, will provide overviews to many career possibilities while removing some myths and misunderstandings that develop as a result of media portrayals. Many college criminal justice programs are staffed by professors who have already completed a career in the criminal justice profession. See the profile of Dr. Robert Louden (provided in Appendix 1), who went from New York City police officer with the rank of the commander of the detective squad and hostage negotiator, to college professor, and finally to university criminal justice program director. During a college program you will have the opportunity to meet men and women who have served in both law enforcement and civilian careers. They represent not only informed persons but role models of success.

Certainly, one of the values of taking courses taught by experienced professionals is that they can pull a less-certain student under their wing to guide them and make suggestions that lead to a better, more-informed decision about their career path—they can answer questions that are of specific concerns to students. More importantly, they can provide introductions to professionals in the field with whom the student may serve internships, volunteer, or simply ask questions.

College courses—such as Introduction to Criminal Justice, Criminology, or Corrections—provide background information such as the structure of the courts; more specialized subject matter, such as crime scene investigation; and theoretical foundations, such as victimization. Oftentimes, the course selection will be influenced by what the student perceives their career choice to be. As the student becomes more certain of a potential career path, then a heavier concentration of courses in that area may be more appropriate. College courses are inclusive of all areas of criminal justice, but they are not inclusive of all work in criminal justice. For example, traditional undergraduate courses may not discuss the role of a psychologist in law enforcement or in corrections, or that of a business manager. To be sure, the role of the food service supervisor will be even further removed from the instructional curriculum. However, college courses will provide students with the opportunity to explore their personal interests in criminal justice and thus consider what may become their ultimate career choice.

A SAMPLE COLLEGE CURRICULUM

Undergraduate programs, and specifically two-year college degree programs, are generally more focused on the practitioner's functions in the criminal justice profession. Oftentimes, college departments will offer what are called tracks, options, certificate programs, or specializations, in which the courses are even more sharply focused on the specific profession. The examples below provide a track for Law Enforcement and another for Corrections.

LAW ENFORCEMENT CURRICULUM

- Introduction to the Criminal Justice System
- Police in the Community

- Criminal Law
- Police Administration
- English Composition I and II
- History of Western Civilization I or II
- Concepts of Health and Fitness
- Introduction to Psychology
- Introduction to Sociology or Social Problems
- Computer Concepts
- Criminology
- Human Communication or Public Speaking
- History elective
- Political Science elective
- Mathematics elective
- Laboratory Science elective
- Criminal Justice elective
- Criminal Justice Internship
- Free electives

CORRECTIONS CURRICULUM

- Introduction to the Criminal Justice System
- Introduction to Corrections
- Community Corrections
- Juvenile Justice
- English Composition I and II
- History of Western Civilization I and II
- Concepts of Health and Fitness
- Introduction to Psychology
- Computer Concepts
- Introduction to Sociology
- Introduction to Social Problems
- Multiculturalism
- Criminology
- History elective
- Mathematics elective
- Political Science elective

- Laboratory Science elective
- Human Communication or Public Speaking
- Criminal Justice Internship
- Free electives

This is in sharp contrast to four-year colleges or university degrees that begin with introductory courses and then progress to more theory-based or criminological studies. An example is provided below. The prospective student will note that in each case there are standard course offerings, such as English and Math. These courses seek to round out a student's education and should not be neglected—they will be needed on the job. Free electives provide students with opportunities to take courses, such as in psychology or social work, that are outside their primary field of inquiry. Students would be well-advised not to neglect these opportunities with which they can explore other interests or even take a minor (as discussed below).

FOUR-YEAR DEGREE AND UNIVERSITY STUDY

- Introduction to Criminal Justice
- Criminology
- Police Work
- Correctional History and Philosophy
- Crime and Public Policy
- Criminal Procedure
- Law and Politics
- Criminal Justice Research Methods
- Introduction to Political Science Methods
- Quantitative Methods in Psychology
- Introduction to Social Research
- Computer Analysis of Social Science Data
- Introductory Statistics for Business
- Ethics
- Social Deviance
- Independent Study
- Internship

Coursework provides opportunities for students to do research. Research may cover literature searches—explorations of what others have done in a specific area. Research may also include opportunities to interview persons in the criminal justice field—excellent occasions to ask those questions that have not yet been answered in the course material. Interviews are a great opportunity to ask questions and obtain answers from someone who is actually doing the work. In addition, a more exciting prospect would be the opportunity to visit sites where work in the criminal justice field is taking place, such as a local or state police station, a courthouse, or a correctional facility. Students would be well-advised, prior to interviewing or visiting a site, to search its specific web page for background information about the site to be visited. Of course, for the student more inclined toward the criminology side of the criminal justice curriculum, the four-year college or university may offer greater opportunities for hands-on criminological research currently being conducted by professors.

Students will find themselves more and more being directed to enroll in and take online courses. While this is beneficial for colleges, the student may not find them as beneficial for meeting their goals. Please see Appendix 6, in which the benefits and downsides of online education in a criminal justice career are discussed.

We live in a rapidly changing world and the field of criminal justice is changing along with it. For example, since the tragedy of 9/11 many colleges now offer undergraduate majors and graduate degrees in Homeland Security and Forensics. Another growth area in criminal justice is that of private security. The complexity of corporations, especially of those involved with technology, has required them to develop their own in-house private security components, which are not only responsible for site protection but also for the welfare of scientists and other workers. These highly skilled professionals develop cutting-edge technological advances that must be guarded and protected from such events as cybercrime, otherwise the corporation risks losing billions of dollars.

While colleges offer the opportunity for students to specialize in a specific area as a major, they also allow students to select a minor course of study. The value of carefully selecting a minor cannot be understated. The minor will provide a different perspective about areas of interest. They expand versatility in the workplace. They may increase opportunities for promotions or even for a change in career, or a change from one area of criminal justice to another. And there is another value to the minor, although the student may miss it at this career planning stage of their life. The minor may provide the way to a new career or perhaps an avocational interest either during or upon retirement from a career. Some minors, such as sociology, psychology, chemistry, and others, combine nicely with the field of criminal justice. Of course, a minor may also simply provide the student with the opportunity to pursue a personal interest such as cooking or archaeology. The point is, college preparation does not have to be limiting; instead it may be the means to explore and master some other personal interest or skill.

There are several ways that career exploration can be undertaken proactively. The professional criminal justice career will require a well-educated, well-trained individual. The better-educated and the better-trained worker will make wiser choices and be more qualified for advancement. Three primary avenues to gain exposure to the criminal justice profession include college and other educational courses, internships, and volunteering. Each has its own advantages.

YOUR SELECTION OF COLLEGE
COURSES AND THE INTERNSHIP

Many college courses are required and thus preselected according to your curriculum; that is, you have no choice about taking them. However, degree curriculums also leave room for electives and minor courses of study. College courses frequently excite and stimulate interest for students in many areas, and the internship may be *the stuff* that ultimately cements for the student the fact that they are making the right decision. Of course, there is also the possibility that the internship may show a side of a profession that dissuades students from further consideration of that job for a career. This may seem terrible—as if the career aspirant has just had their hopes and dreams crushed. But, the better news is that this is actually an opportunity. Now that the student has been exposed to what their career would really have been like, he or she can refocus their goal; that is, make different choices for a successful and rewarding career for themselves. While internships are generally limited to second-year students at a community college, or to third- and fourth-year students at four-year colleges and universities, another means of field exploration is available to the curious student prior to that time—volunteering.

INTERNSHIPS AND VOLUNTEERING

Colleges generally require internships prior to graduation to help students explore their career choices. Internships are generally assigned college credit whereas, volunteering is not. Internships or volunteer work in criminal justice frequently require a criminal justice background check. Many students cannot wait for the internship to begin; they want to go out and experience the field for themselves. Frequently, the internship is a positive experience that affirms for students that they have made the right choice in their career preparation. In some cases, too, the internship provides exposure to other aspects of the career, which they can now explore as their primary career choice. Essentially, the internship ensures that the uninitiated have chosen wisely. The successful internship enables the student to begin the next and official steps for entering the career field.

Unfortunately, a frequent lament that comes from students during the internship takes place when they discover elements of the job (such as the volume of paperwork that accompanies it) that were not emphasized during the courses or of which they had been unaware. Unexpected events or environmental conditions can affect students' consideration of a position as their career choice. When this happens, the more extreme reaction is to change one's major to a different career path. However, another way of reacting to this would be to reexamine the original career choice and find a more personally acceptable role for one's career.

The primary source of exposure to law enforcement is through the media. Law enforcement is portrayed as active, busy, challenging, and at times dangerous. In these capacities heroic rescues are being made, offenders are being captured, and complex investigations are undertaken and solved. Inasmuch as most police work is patrol, it fails to resemble any of the descriptions just mentioned. When students wait too long to begin their internships (such as waiting until the year in which they graduate), their other degree requirements may already be completed. If they discover that the job of which they have dreamed is somehow not a good fit for them, or that they may not qualify, then they find themselves in a bad position. Emotionally there is letdown and bewilderment about what to do with their hard-earned education and how to adapt their preparations to a different career choice. Too often this disheartening situation also signals a change of curriculum/major. The consequences of such a change at a late date usually include needing to take additional courses, even adding on semesters along with the additional tuition expenses for a new major.

There are practical solutions to this dilemma. Participation in a combination of activities will help students make rational informed decisions before the final year of their degree work, preferably in the early stages of college preparation. Our electronic age makes a wealth of information available through the Internet. Few students get through high school without becoming quite proficient at Internet searches. Virtually all criminal justice agencies have their own websites. After an initial search of these websites, more specific searches can be conducted.

Volunteering is another doable experience. When done early, volunteering may facilitate the timely discovery of new career options within a field of interest—or a non-fit for a career. When this becomes evident, a change of focus is less traumatic. Three activities (visiting, volunteering, and interviewing) will help the student with the decision-making process by clarifying what seems to be the better path to follow.

We strongly suggest that college be one of the ways you use to prepare for a career. Similarly, you can prepare for your college internship by engaging in a few pursuits such as reviewing potential agencies available for your internship. Dorothy Taylor[7] has written a book that can help you with your internship preparation and guide you through the internship so that you get the most from it. It will help to ensure that you successfully coordinate your efforts with your college professor/advisor. Often there are internship requirements for your college degree that must be completed. Taylor's book can help you to understand the many tasks you must adhere to. For example, her second chapter will help define the goals of the internship, and Chapter 8 the "Evaluation of the Field Placement Experience," will help to lay out what you must do to comply with your criminal justice department's requirements.

VOLUNTEERING

Volunteering entails the least risk and potentially the greatest gain for the student. The advantages of volunteering vastly outweigh the disadvantages. Some of the advantages include real work experience, real person interaction, references, knowledge, on-the-job training, an entry for the résumé, and availability to changes and openings in the field as they occur. If you are accepted as a volunteer, you will do the work and you will watch others doing it as it happens or needs to be done. This is often somewhat different from the general job description. Volunteers are assigned specific tasks, but as other events or projects come up, the volunteer may be shifted to provide assistance and gain a broader view of the career potential.

By volunteering, you may discover whether or not this work is for you. If the work is different from your expectations, you don't have to stay; you are a volunteer. You can move on and try something else. Volunteering is time well invested. If nothing else, you have gained an experience. You may also come to realize that there are other aspects of criminal justice you had not previously considered, which may be more attractive to you for a career choice.

Volunteering and oftentimes internships are unpaid experiences. But the smart intern or volunteer treats the experience as if it were a paid job. Dress appropriately, arrive on time, do the work assigned to you. You can request greater responsibility and ask questions about what you see and do. If your immediate position does not bring you into contact with what you are interested in, you can ask. Most employers and employees understand the position of the intern/volunteer as a learning experience and are very willing to extend themselves and their staff to provide fulfilling opportunities.

CAREER GOALS

Selecting a career and preparing for it are only the first steps of a career. As a student, it is not too early to make some preliminary decisions about how you would like to advance in a career and what you would like to do as your career comes to a close. College is an excellent time to prepare for a life course, a time to plan. You can devise a five-year plan, a ten-year plan, and a twenty-year plan. This does not suggest that once you have made these choices, you are stuck with them. Just like the initial preparation, you are beginning to determine where, or to put it another way, how far you might go. This preparation will prevent stagnation, that is, remaining forever in one position. Preparation begun early will set you up to be organized and ready to take the next steps when opportunities, such as eligibility for promotion, present themselves.

One important preparation you can make at this time is to understand the requirements for promotions. Once you have identified those promotions, you can begin to explore the means to achieve them. Career advancement requires more than doing a good job. You can anticipate changes in departments, and you can prepare yourself through ongoing personal development.

You may think that any consideration of graduate school is somewhat premature at this point. But graduate school is an investment. Graduate school degrees can be the deciding factors when it comes to promotions. You should not ignore the fact that a graduate degree can open doors for other opportunities, such as teaching at a training academy. There is one last thing to consider about when to start work on a graduate degree; in a word, you should start *immediately*. We often hear from students that they want a break after completing their undergraduate degree, or that they are tired of school and will soon return. Unfortunately, life can and will get in the way. Taking a job can mean facing a transfer, and more serious life events such as marriage and children alter the way we think about everything. We would suggest that if you can, do not delay—go get your graduate degree as soon as possible. We will discuss more on this later.

CHANGING CAREERS

Your career need not be a static experience. That is, where you begin is not necessarily where you have to finish or where you actually will finish.[8] What is important is the personal preparation needed to advance, transfer, or even change fields. Some people do grow out of their careers or find that they have accomplished all that it will allow them to do. Unfortunately, this may happen long before the person's eligibility to retire. Staying in a career that is not satisfying or that no longer provides a sense of personal worth is not healthy. The best choice may be to change jobs or careers. How easily that is accomplished will depend on what was done prior to starting your career and after the career has begun. Hopefully before your career takes off, you have had the opportunity to build a solid foundation. Some career shifts are made from the civilian side into law enforcement (see Bo Orichowski's profile in Appendix 1), while others move from law enforcement to a civilian career (see Len Ward's profile in Appendix 1). Some simply leave the criminal justice profession altogether.

If the need for change is experienced, there are a variety of questions that may be asked at that time. They would include:

- What do you want to do?
- What are you capable of doing?
- What are you qualified to do?
- How can you obtain the credentials and experience to make the move?
- Is there funding available (such as scholarships or grants) to assist you?

This last question is addressed in Appendix 10, "Paying for College." These questions are also appropriate for the individual who is terminating a career for any reason. If you have been engaged in personal development, you may have already completed all or some of the work necessary to make a change. If not, and you are unsure of how to proceed with the change (and it may well be life-altering), then professional assistance may be required. Colleges and vocational schools generally offer counseling help, and perhaps they could provide you with an assessment inventory that would identify your strengths and weaknesses in certain areas related to your career.

LEAVING THE CRIMINAL JUSTICE
PROFESSION (RETIREMENT OR TRANSITION)

At some point down the road you will leave your career. We discuss this in depth in Chapter 9. At this point, what we want you to consider is that the decisions you make now will affect how you prepare for your retirement. You cannot begin your preparation for retirement too early. The question is, what do you want to do after you retire? What you can do in retirement will be determined by your experiences, your colleagues, your preparation, and your financial status. Warning: Do not neglect your financial status! Believe it or not, the time to begin your financial preparation for retirement is now. Criminal justice and law enforcement careers come to an end for many at a relatively young age. You may retire earlier than expected with a pension and benefits that open up a wide range of choices for what you could do next. Or, more unfortunately, you could become disabled and need to leave your career and take a disability pension. We strongly suggest that you make a quick but not a careless decision. That is, the longer you are out of the workforce, the more difficult it may be to return. If you are fortunate and have prepared well, you should have the means to live very productively in your retirement years. But if you have not, you can expect to have to work until much later in life.

For some, retirement provides the opportunity to do what they have always wanted to do but could not because of their career path. Retirement opens the door. The question is, have you set yourself up to move on? Retirement can open the door for a second career or the opportunity to pursue an avocational interest. Those options hold the potential to be rewarding: professionally, personally, and financially.

THE CONFLICTS IN CRIMINAL JUSTICE

The criminal justice profession has a well-documented history of persons and agencies that find themselves embroiled in conflicts and controversies. Understanding why conflicts occur may help with your level of satisfaction on and off the job. Each of the components of the criminal justice system has specific tasks that seek to accomplish specific goals. A few examples will help to illustrate the depth of those conflicts and controversies.

Willie Horton was released from a Massachusetts prison on a community release program. He absconded, committed a violent offense, and fingers were pointed. The governor was accused of being soft on crime. In reality, the governor had very little to do with internal programming but because of the magnitude of the event, he was forced to withdraw from the presidential primaries. There is much more to this story, and the curious or astute observer of criminal justice can explore the complexities further through several websites. The Willie Horton story is an interesting criminal justice and criminological conundrum that demonstrates the sometimes unhappy mix of politics, the media, and expectations from the correctional/criminal justice system.

The mass of get-tough legislation that began in the mid-1970s caused prison populations to skyrocket. States were not prepared for these increases, and they suffered great financial hardship as a result. Due to cutbacks and massive overcrowding, which in many prisons exceeded 50 percent, reductions were made in programming. The complexity of the problem also resulted in increased violence and other events publicized in recent years.

Your criminal justice career will bring you into contact with the goals of sentencing. While the goals of sentencing are defined, they are not always clear to everyone or understood by them. The goals that the courts attempt to achieve through adjudication and sentencing are incapacitation, deterrence, retribution, and rehabilitation. While these things are desired by the courts, they are not as straightforward when aspects of law enforcement and corrections attempt to fulfill their tasks. Other goals include restoration and restitution. For example, there is some expectation that once the offender has served his sentence, he has then paid his debt. Restoration is very difficult for the offender to achieve when he/she encounters the myriad civil penalties, often referred to as "collateral consequences."[9] For example, family reunification is challenging when the ex-convict is denied public housing. Collateral consequences often involve lifetime exclusions. On every front, restitution is a commonsense criminal justice objective. Unfortunately, the ex-convict will usually have difficulty finding employment that permits even a poor standard of living, and if someone cannot find a job, they cannot make good on restitution. Understanding these goals may add clarity to the manner in which you will conduct yourself during your career.

Stating the goals is easier than either achieving them or even understanding how they work together. We should also note that how the criminal justice system operates, with the goals in mind, may shift according to prevailing political contentions, philosophical dispositions, social events and trends, as well as other affairs that often influence practical considerations for operations. Clearly, an analysis of the goals will illustrate how they are in conflict and frequently confound attempts to implement them. Perhaps the most severe example is the death penalty. We all abhor certain criminal activities that are death-penalty eligible. However, if we carry out the death penalty, then there is no room for rehabilitation. A counterargument for the imposition of the death penalty is that it ensures incapacitation, or public safety. Less clear to those unfamiliar with judicial functions are the ideas of incapacitation and retribution when the sentence is probation. Most introductory corrections and criminal justice textbooks provide detailed discussions of the debates and controversies that surround these goals. *American Corrections*,[10] by Clear, Cole, and Reisig, for example, provides an excellent discussion of the difficulties of achieving the goals and common confusions about the goals.

Criminal justice is often referred to as a system. Unfortunately, it is more of a collection of parts that actually have very little coordination between them. An oversimplification is that the police arrest, the courts adjudicate, and the corrections officers carry out the punishment—usually involving some deprivation of liberty. Police officers wonder why judges grant probation after they have worked so hard to catch the wrongdoer. The courts are often frustrated by a lack of available options. Corrections facilities, due to a massive incarceration policy in the United States, suffer extreme overcrowding and a poor budget allowance with which to provide programs that meet the specific needs of offenders. Students who wish to enter the field of criminal justice would do themselves justice (no pun intended!) to become familiar with all aspects of the criminal justice fields, their limitations, and their ability and the restrictions with which to interact. Chapter 8 serves as an introduction to the ethical dilemmas encountered in criminal justice careers.

CIVILIAN AND LAW ENFORCEMENT INTERACTION

Law enforcement has much greater interaction on a daily basis with civilians than either of the other criminal justice components. Corrections, in many ways, discourages civilian access to prisons in order to maintain custody and security. The rules of the courts specify what involvement civilians may have, and in the case of the juvenile courts, civilians may not observe the proceedings unless they have some direct connection to the case under consideration.

On another level, the involvement between civilian employees in the criminal justice system may have roles that complement or conflict with law enforcement functions. In some cases, civilians report directly to law enforcement personnel, and in other cases law enforcement may report to or be accountable to civilians.

SUMMARY

Exploring and Understanding Careers in Criminal Justice: A Comprehensive Guide will help you to realize the depth of the criminal justice field. Generally, the more correct the initial career choice is, the more likely it will be that you will enjoy success in your career because you have been able to prepare properly. Related to that, the more successful you are in your career, the more opportunities you will have during your career, and this will create greater opportunities in retirement. Whether you are still in your career or you have completed it, you want to have achieved satisfaction. Looking ahead and asking, "What else is possible?" and, "What do I need to do?" will assist you to achieve that status. There are many avenues with which to explore and prepare yourself for employment. Your future is in your hands.

3

Careers in Law Enforcement

Entrance into the law enforcement profession is a formal and complex process that continues to become more rigorous in its requirements. This chapter will primarily be concerned with the law enforcement side of policing as it exists on the state level, in local policing, in the state police or highway patrol, and for the sheriff's officers.

The aspiring officer should search their state's websites to assess the available agencies that employ police officers in that state. The point is to find an agency that is hiring, for which you have/can meet the requirements, and that does the work or has a position that interests you. If that sounds a little complicated, perhaps what follows will help to explain.

In police officer Michael Di Lieto's book, *How to Become a New Jersey Police Officer or State Trooper*,[1] the author examines his personal struggle to become a police officer and what he learned in order to be successful in that effort. While his book is specific to New Jersey, there are many helpful hints and suggestions that may be generalized to policing anywhere. For example, he lists the "13 things you can do to be the best candidate" for a position as a police officer:

1. Have a college degree.
2. Have a specialization from a vocational school.
3. Be fluent in a foreign language (Spanish is usually an agency's preferred choice).
4. Have alternate route certification.

5. Become a police officer special II.
6. Become a police officer special I.
7. Become a county deputy sheriff.
8. Become an auxiliary police officer.
9. Have experience in police dispatching.
10. Have experience with police explorers.
11. Have certification in first aid and an EMT-B.
12. Have experience as a firefighter.
13. Become a charity or community group volunteer.

Officer Di Lieto explains the importance of each of these in his book, and in some cases he provides accompanying information that further emphasizes their value.

For example, New Jersey has more than 550 law enforcement agencies throughout the state, which range from municipal police departments to college and university police departments. If you anticipate an interview with a department (see Appendix 3 for "A Guide to Interview Questions"), it is always in your best interest to learn as much as possible about the specific agency and the areas of responsibility for the position. Most police agencies have their own websites, and this would be a good place to begin. For example, you could familiarize yourself with the philosophy of the specific agency that interests you. Some basic questions for exploring a police department would include: How large is the local population that it serves? How large is the geographic territory? How many departments (sometimes called "bureaus") does it have? What are its specialized units, such as public morals (vice) narcotics, juvenile, detective, and patrol divisions, as well as public/community relations? What are the starting salaries? Do they have their own training academy, or is there a county academy? Who pays for academy training? What impresses you the most about the department?

These 550 law enforcement agencies in New Jersey deliver tremendous diversity in programs and policing activities throughout the state. While there is a similarity in the requirements for each, the hiring methods may be different (civil service versus municipal positions), and the primary focus may be specialized to the local department in which the force has jurisdiction. Small departments often have what is referred to as a "chief's test," specific to the local community.

All law enforcement personnel in New Jersey are governed by the New Jersey Statutes Annotated (N.J.S.A.) 52:17B-98, which established the Criminal Justice Act of 1970. A careful review of the Criminal Justice Act of 1970 for New Jersey, therefore, would be informative. Other states have promulgated their own criminal justice legislation to regulate law enforcement.

JOB POSTINGS FOR LAW ENFORCEMENT OFFICERS

Openings for police officer positions may be found in a variety of places. You will need to check several sources regularly for these positions. Oftentimes postings are listed for a specific time period, which means there is a cutoff date after which no more applications will be accepted. Among the places to look for postings are specific police department websites, the state department of personnel listings, newspapers, and postings placed on bulletin boards at the local college and unemployment agencies.

Obviously, when you see a posting, you need to carefully review the hiring requirements to ensure you meet the minimum standards. If you do not and a posting is in a department for which you are interested, you should take action to meet the minimum requirements before the vacancy is posted again.

THE APPLICATION PROCESS

Once you have begun to make decisions about where and which departments you will focus on for law enforcement officer employment, you should prepare yourself for the application process. There are several steps you should take in this regard. The next sections will briefly describe these steps of preparation.

DOCUMENTATION: THE APPLICATION PORTFOLIO

Assemble all of your original documents into a single file (see the Document Portfolio Checklist in Appendix 7). These should minimally include a birth certificate, a Social Security card, your high school diploma, any certificates of training, your college or graduate school diploma(s), other skill certifications, your driver's license, your health insurance card, your voter registration card, your passport, a military ID, any Selective Service registration ID, your firearms ID, any awards you have received, and other pertinent pieces of documentation. Hopefully, the departments with which you will file applications will have websites that list what is required, as well as other suggested documentation. Do not assume that a listed document or certification is minor and thus irrelevant. Such documents may include certifications for lifeguarding, scuba diving, EMT training, CPR, or first aid. These documents may also be helpful in the pursuit of a college degree, which will be explained later.

Once you have assembled your documentation, make a minimum of two copies of the file. The point is that you never want to send or give away an *original* document. However, to complete some applications you may have to appear in person with the original document/record for the department to copy. *ALWAYS MAKE SURE THAT YOUR DOCUMENTS ARE RETURNED!* Once you have your documents returned to you, be sure to place them back in the appropriate file.

REFERENCES

The issue of references requires careful consideration. (See Chapter 6 for additional information on references.) Draft a preliminary list of potential references. Review this list and organize it in an order that ranges from most to least important. Many hiring applications will require about three references. Your personal list should be longer.

Now that you have assembled the list, take the time to speak to each person on it. You should come away from each meeting with a pretty good idea of what that person will say about you. For example, let's say you completed a course and received an A from a dynamic professor who had a distinguished career in law enforcement. This, in your opinion, is someone who has name recognition and would give you an excellent reference because of your grade. The reality is that when someone gives a reference, they are extending their own reputation to the one for whom they give the recommendation.

A college course typically lasts fifteen weeks, and interactions with professors are often quite limited. While the professor may attest to your grade or even that you turned in an excellent paper, they may be unwilling to say much more about you. The time period for which they have known you is quite short. In addition, because of class size, the professor may not even remember you. Unfortunately, many professors have taught classes with more than 125 students. Such classes leave little opportunity to interact with and remember individual students. However, this not the time for you to take a shot in the dark; be certain of what your reference will say about you. It can and will affect the image you portray to prospective employers.

Let's tackle one more example, with the same potential reference, only this time the professor knows you well. The problem in this case is something much different: You need to know whether the reference himself is in good standing with the department to which you are applying.

Throughout our careers, we often encounter situations and persons with whom we have had difficult relationships. In this case, your reference may have had some unfortunate circumstance take place with the chief of the department to which you are applying. Perhaps your reference, because of that circumstance, is either unwilling to write a letter to that department, or they decide to write a letter on your behalf, but it has little meaning to the department because of the bad circumstance, which had nothing to do with you. You are then caught in the middle. It would be in your best interest not to include this person as a reference. Go back to your list and select another. This should help explain why it is important to talk to your reference prior to submitting their name on an application.

You should always ask your reference to send or provide you with a copy of their letter. This way there will be no surprises if the letter is brought up during an interview. More importantly, if you know what is in the letter, you can prepare responses for the interview to cover points which have been made in the letter. You may wish to make this part of your "ten-point preparation," discussed in Appendix 3, "A Guide to Interview Questions."

THE INTERVIEW

You can and should thoroughly prepare for your interview. While your résumé and application will get you in the door, the interview is the time to sell yourself. Begin by asking yourself, *What do I have to sell? What makes me special? What do I have to contribute?*

These may appear to be simple questions, but there are others that may not be so simple. I think one of the toughest questions to answer is, "What do you see as your two weakest points?"

Such a question is intended to discover first, whether you have done sufficient self-reflection to be aware of your weakest points; in other words, how well do you know yourself? However, when someone is asked about a second weak point, this may be the interviewer's attempt to discover how well you think on your feet. Your preparation for this is to reflect on the question and prepare a response in advance: always write out your responses to such potential questions before any interviews.

Many years ago, I was asked to appear on a television show that had listeners call in to ask questions or make comments. While I think well on my feet, I was also prepared. I put together what I call "My Ten Points." These were relatively generic answers to any of a variety of questions. Such preparation means that you will not be stumbling around to think about the best answer before responding. A little hesitation is good during an interview; it suggests you are reflective. However, a longer period of dead air indicates that perhaps you do not know the subject matter or are not adequately prepared. Remember, the questions that you are asked are probably the questions that other interviewees will also be asked. (See the section in Appendix 3 entitled, "A Guide to Interview Questions." This guide discusses in some detail the preparation of the "My Ten Points." You can begin to develop your Ten Points on the chart at the end of this section.)

TESTS, REQUIREMENTS, AND OTHER QUALIFICATIONS

The process of entering a career in law enforcement will require the applicant to pass a variety of tests and to meet several other requirements. Minimally, the applicant must meet the age and education requirements and be a U.S. citizen. In some jurisdictions, there may be a residency requirement; that is, the applicant will have to establish a state or local residence. Generally speaking, the minimum age requirement is eighteen, and the maximum age is thirty-five. In some cases, the applicant may register for tests or submit an application prior to their eighteenth birthday, as long as the applicant turns eighteen by the date of hire. This is a critical piece of information to keep in mind. Those states or positions that require civil service tests may offer the test sporadically or on a less-than-annual basis. Review the state's personnel or human resources sites for testing dates. You may be able to apply before you reach your eighteenth birthday.

Among the tests and examinations will likely be a written test, a physical examination, which includes vision and hearing tests, as well as tests of agility and stamina. (To review samples of test packages, see the list of prep manuals found in Appendix 8.) The applicant will also be examined for physical abnormalities or other characteristics that could render them unable to bear up to the strenuous duties of police work. There will also be a psychological evaluation (often both written and oral), a criminal and personal background check, a drug test, a polygraph test, a B-PAD (Behavioral Personnel Assessment Device) test, and perhaps an oral board exam.

The B-PAD test is sometimes referred to as the Video Simulation Exercise, and it represents an effort by law enforcement to enhance its hiring practices. It is a standardized test. This may be its sole source of detraction because there are those who simply do not test well. Otherwise it is well-recognized for its fairness. In many cases it has replaced the oral board because of its reported reliability. Among the strengths of the B-PAD test are that it:

- Assesses individual ethical determination;
- Assesses the ability to work effectively with the public;
- Assesses problem-solving abilities; and
- Assesses interpersonal skills.

There are websites that provide information about the B-PAD and that also provide test-taking tips to help you obtain a higher score. See especially those websites that provide test scenarios and advice, such as using a logical sequence of answers for a higher score. Visit the listed websites for many helpful suggestions for taking the B-PAD.

While the information in the previous paragraph applies only to one specific test, there are many available books or manuals that can help you plan a regimen for test-taking and academy preparation. See the recommended readings at the end of this book for some of these book titles and manuals.

ACCESS TO ACADEMY TRAINING

There are more than six hundred police training academies in the United States as well as other alternatives for academy training. You would be well-advised to check your state's approved/accredited alternatives to formal police academy training. The first likely step is to be hired on by a police department. This is the more financially attractive alternative to official academy training. The hiring police department may pay the cost for the academy and pay you a salary at the same time.

Another alternative is for you to pay for your academy training prior to acceptance by a police agency. However, many academies will accept only those who have been accepted as official candidates for law enforcement positions. In addition, prior academy training may not be as helpful as you intended it to be. Some hiring agencies will not accept prior academy or private training and will require you to complete their own "academy training." What is often true is that you must have a certificate of training completion from the private entity if a police department is to accept such alternate training. Finally, academy training in one state may not be accepted in another state. This also holds true if the applicant has prior experience as a law enforcement officer in a different state. In this case, the applicant may be required to complete the academy training for the new state in which they are applying.

Police officer jobs are highly prized, and generally there are far more applicants than there are openings. The aspirant should not be discouraged by their position on a hiring or civil service list. Applicants tend to advance quickly on lists. Every academy session shortens it, and some applicants may not wait and will accept other employment. Those who accept other jobs will then skip academy training because they now have a different job. Some will not pass the psychological examination. Some cannot meet the physical requirements. Some will (believe it or not) fail the drug tests or will have acquired a criminal conviction that renders them ineligible. Of course, there are also those who will not pass the academy tests or will realize through the academy training that law enforcement is not for them. The point is that the list *will* shorten, and if you are serious about gaining a position in law enforcement, be patient and your turn will come.

EDUCATION REQUIREMENTS

Education requirements to become a law enforcement officer vary from state to state and from locality to locality. Almost all police agencies require a minimum of a high school diploma, and others require one or two years of college or even the completion of a bachelor's degree (see "degree requirements" in Chapter 2). Nevertheless, there are departments that may hire you even without your ability to fulfill the degree requirement. In this case, the department may require that you complete the degree requirement in a specified time.

We cannot emphasize strongly enough the value of a criminal justice degree from a college or university. Through the course work, students gain knowledge about the interconnectedness of criminal justice components, police/law enforcement history, legal issues, and technological applications to police work and more, which increases their general knowledge base. Through internships, students gain exposure and experience, which enables them to apply theoretical concepts to police practice. To be sure, those persons who have attained the criminal justice degree almost always do better on civil service/law enforcement examinations.

While completing a degree is not required for all agencies, it is becoming more and more desirable and thus is recommended for several reasons. The law enforcement profession has become more complex, and as a result, more technical expertise has become essential. A degree in criminal justice will provide you with a wealth of general knowledge about many aspects of the field, including the courts and corrections, as well as specific information about performance expectations and a theoretical foundation in law enforcement. In the event that you may have already completed your academy training but have not achieved a degree, the academy training courses may be worth credits toward a degree. Some colleges assess academy training and award a specific number of credits. In addition, many colleges offer reduced tuition for members of law enforcement and those who have served in the military and are seeking employment in law enforcement.

Some states also give extra credit on exams or in the civil service application process for having completed the criminal justice degree. In many cases, the degree need not be in criminal justice or law enforcement; other fields of study are acceptable and in many cases valuable. The degree may also be of assistance to obtain a variety of positions in law enforcement once you are hired. For example, you may be asked to teach in the academy. The degree also may be a means to transition to larger police departments or to a federal agency such as the FBI, DEA, or other specialized lines of policing employment.

Physical fitness is a necessity for entering the law enforcement profession. The inclusion of physical education and sports participation during college should not be ignored and is an affirmation of your physical ability. Fitness activities will help prepare you for your academy training by increasing your stamina, flexibility, and competitiveness, and it is an indication that you are a team player. Sports participation can be listed on your résumé where you describe your degree and major.

Most academy training includes not only daily physical fitness activities but requires that you demonstrate fitness by passing prescribed requirements that are considered essential to job performance. There are differences in the physical fitness requirements for men and women (see Appendix 13 for a specific example—the Vermont Police Training Academy). A review of these standards will help the serious law enforcement applicant to prepare for the academy.

The ability to write and write well cannot be overemphasized. As a member of law enforcement, you will be required to write numerous reports. These reports are official documents and can become court records. Such reports are critical when you testify in court. Oftentimes court testimony comes long after the arrest is made and the charges are filed. The report is your official record of the events, and the accuracy of your report is essential. A well-written report is crucial when the case comes to court—sometimes months in the future. The report is a tool to stimulate recall for both the preparation for testimony and for the actual testimony before the court. Poorly documented information or any indication that the officer is confused about his testimony can damage the court case.

ACADEMY TRAINING

Classes for academy training are routinely scheduled to fill the ongoing need for qualified police personnel. Occasionally, academy sessions may be scheduled when unusual circumstances present a greater need for sworn law enforcement officers. Depending upon the specific requirements for an agency, applicants may be required to remain at the academy for the duration of their training and are mandated to adhere to the rules and regulations of the academy during their training. The duration of academy training is anywhere from six to eight months depending upon jurisdiction.

The training academy curriculum is a well-thought-out experience of academic and physical tests designed to transform the recruit into a well-rounded officer who is competently prepared to fulfill the duties of law enforcement. In 1970, the Commission on Accreditation for Law Enforcement Agencies (CALEA) was established to accredit police departments, and in 2002 to accredit training academies. CALEA establishes standards and ensures consistency of training requirements established by state agencies. CALEA accreditation provides quality assurance to the administration of the academies and for the police departments for whom it trains its personnel.

The curriculum is generally a legislatively mandated requirement that has been overseen and developed by an agency to meet that need. For example, many adhere to the Peace Officer Standards and Training (POST) Councils or another agency. In New Jersey, the Police Training Commission approves curriculum, reviews course content for consistency with changes in law or practice, and mandates changes to curriculum to maintain legal currency. Many police academies now include very specific ethics training as a consequence of legal challenges and court rulings. Officers must stay current with changes in the law, and the academy trains officers to come into compliance with new legislation and court holdings.

A practical case in point was *Miranda v. Arizona*, which produced the Miranda warning. The Miranda warning was first seen as an impediment to police work because it was viewed as the means for a defendant to avoid questioning. That is, the suspect, upon realizing that they might be charged with a crime, could request an attorney, which meant the investigating officer had to terminate questioning until an attorney was provided.

This gives the appearance of hampering an investigation and causing delays. However, ultimately, the Miranda warning resulted in better, more conscientious police work that produced both increased convictions and fewer reversals upon appeal.

Through the six to eight weeks of academy training, training is divided into classroom experience followed by on-the-job training, in which the officer-to-be or recruit job-shadows a sworn officer. This allows the recruit to see firsthand the distinctions between training in the academy and the realities of the job.

Academy trainers are generally active duty police officers who have passed additional training that certifies them as academy trainers and subject matter experts. For example, New Jersey's Police Training Commission requires Methods of Instruction (MOI) training to ensure that instructors are prepared to deliver high-quality classroom instruction. That is, the instructor, through MOI certification, has shown that he or she is competent at teaching others the skills needed to be an accomplished police officer. During the training session, recruits are also subject to a variety of guest speakers, such as persons from the prosecutor's office, experts on ethics from the attorney general's office, representatives from drug enforcement, and others from the gang identification and management unit. Recruits will also get an introduction to their union representatives.

Completion of academy training is a cause for celebration. The recruit has successfully passed each phase of his training and demonstrated his competence to perform law enforcement duties and the responsibilities that accompany the badge. The applicant will be certified or sworn in as a law enforcement officer. A long tradition at this time has included the pinning of the badge on the recruit by a family member or other sworn law enforcement person who has had a strong influence in the life of the recruit. Depending upon the state and the jurisdiction, the certification may be a lifetime certification or it may have to be renewed periodically.

The swearing-in ceremony and the tossing of the hat, however, is not the completion of training. Now comes the learning of the practical side of the job—on-the-job training (OJT). The newly sworn officer will generally be paired up with a veteran who will augment the academy training with actual life experiences of being a police officer.

Portrayal of this part of becoming a police officer has included illustrations that the recruit may place their senior partner in jeopardy. *Dirty*

Harry movies suggest that the recruit not only hampers the seasoned veteran, but can even result in their own death. In other renderings the recruit is not respected because they are "new" and lack practical know-how. In reality, however, recruits are not just thrown into the mix; the on-the-job training is designed to teach them not only how to best perform the job, but also how to stay safe. Oftentimes, recruits will bring to the job certain specializations that they have acquired elsewhere, such as in the military, through university training, or through some other source of instruction. In reality, and in the best of all possible worlds, the employing police department will be aware of individual special talents and call upon that person when circumstances require that proficiency.

THE BENEFITS OF LAW ENFORCEMENT

There are many benefits to work in law enforcement. The first is the satisfaction that comes with doing worthwhile work protecting communities and improving life for many citizens. Another is that salaries are comparatively good, with a potential for increases. However, the starting salary for many police officers just coming out from the academy may be comparatively low. There are many ways to offset low salaries. Overtime is often offered for staff shortages, special events, or other off-duty policing needs in the private sector. A college degree can be a plus for attaining many higher-level off-duty work assignments (which usually pay better). If you pursue graduate school, a master's or doctorate degree will open doors for promotions or to lecture as an adjunct professor or program director/chair in a college. This will be discussed later on in Chapter 9. (See the profile of Dr. Robert Louden in Appendix 1.)

If you are already working as a police officer or in another law enforcement capacity, you should inquire with any local colleges whether they will provide you with credit for your completed academy and other specialized training, as well as on-the-job experience. Some colleges provide law enforcement personnel with generous credit allowances and reduced tuition as an incentive to return to school to complete a degree. This may include graduate studies. In many cases, law enforcement agencies will also provide monetary assistance for college. Generally, these grants require that you receive grades above a C and maintain a certain grade-point average. The granting agencies may also require that you remain in service for a specified period of time as payback for the monetary assistance. If either the grade is not achieved or the grade-point average drops, they may discontinue funding or refuse to provide reimbursement. The opportunity for ongoing education is a benefit with great potential. While most who enter policing are young and the notion of retirement seems too far off to require immediate action, nothing could be further from the truth. The right undergraduate degree or an advanced degree can help supplement your pension. More importantly, the degree or an advanced degree frequently sets the individual up for satisfying activity in retirement. This is discussed in greater detail in Chapter 9.

Law enforcement need not be static employment. There are many opportunities for promotions and transfers either within departments or to other departments. Law enforcement is becoming more and more specialized, and opportunities are available for those who have the credentials.

The day of the average cop who just walks a beat on patrol may have come to a close. There is so much need for distinctive areas of expertise that the generalist may find himself reduced to an almost irrelevant status. While those assigned to patrol are more likely to arrive on the scene first, they may have little to do except to contain and protect the integrity of the site. Television shows portray the more graphic and elaborate degrees of specialization that exist, but they do not mention all. Some of the more forgotten or ignored of these, which would be utilized in larger police departments, include the public information officer, who responds to the press and/or limits the dispersal of information while satisfying the right of the public to know. Another area of specialization often neglected in these discussions is the range officer. While all officers need to demonstrate proficiency with weapons, the range officer must requalify with their weapons at least annually if not more often. The range officer is an expert in weaponry and its uses, and he ensures that the many functions to take place at the range are satisfactorily completed. First, he makes sure that police officers qualify, that is, know how to use their weapons proficiently. In addition, this officer is responsible for range safety and the suitability of the weapon.

There are many diverse assortments of weapons available to law enforcement. Many are only to be utilized in the most unusual of circumstances. In such cases only those qualified in the use of the weapon will be allowed to engage it. Of course, the range officer is also responsible for the paperwork that certifies each officer as qualified in the use of weapons.

Specializations may allow the officer to utilize particular skills in which the officer is already proficient, scuba diving or computer programming for example. Of course, the vast array of specialized training now taken advantage of by police agencies, whether on a state or federal level, may allow the officer to explore personal interests that heretofore were unavailable. For example, the officer may wish to learn forensics. Once certified, those talents will likely be utilized by the police department and, in times of emergency, by other departments.

There are various specialties in policing that may cater to your interests. Those specialties include domestic violence, organized crime, electronic surveillance, cybercrime, juvenile crime, internal affairs, homeland security, SWAT teams, hostage negotiations (see Bob Louden's profile in Appendix 1), and many others.

THE POLICE BENEVOLENT ASSOCIATION (PBA) AND THE FRATERNAL ORDER OF POLICE (FOP)

The PBA and the FOP are national organizations (or, unions) that represent police officers. Every police department elects some of its members to serve as union representatives. The unions are supported by the dues that are paid by the police officers. The PBA and FOP organizations work tirelessly to ensure that officers are adequately compensated. They ensure that officers are fairly represented in disciplinary and court proceedings, and they will file suit when officers are unfairly treated. Unfortunately the risks of the profession sometimes become a reality, and in times of loss, they help to provide support to officers' families and dependents. Some of the local and the national organizations may also offer scholarships for officers and their dependents. You should not neglect to inquire upon hiring whether the local PBA will assist you to finance additional education.

MEDICAL AND RETIREMENT BENEFITS

When choosing the law enforcement profession, you should not ignore medical and retirement benefits. There are excellent health benefits that provide coverage for the officer and his or her family. Benefits, in addition to medical insurance, may include dental and vision coverage, as well. Generally, earlier retirement is allowed than what is available in other professions, and a generous pension, and medical benefits for life, is usually part of the package. There are also opportunities for other preparations for retirement, such as deferred compensation plans. In some cases eligibility for retirement comes after only twenty years on the job. However, early retirement means that you need to be prepared for the many decades to come after your career in law enforcement has ended.

MULTICULTURALISM IN LAW ENFORCEMENT

There is greater and greater emphasis on multiculturalism in law enforcement. As you pursue your education, you may wish to consider learning another language. Fluency in a second language, both verbal and written, is a valued specialty. Certainly, a second language is a plus in diverse communities, but if you have aspirations of entering the federal service, then it is definitely a positive point on a résumé. The future law enforcement officer should not ignore one other benefit of proficiency in a second language—personal safety. Knowing a language may help you better understand the intentions of those with whom you must interact. That is, when they speak to another person in their native language, you can hear and understand what is being said. If harm is intended, you are more likely to be able to remove yourself from harm's way. Conversely, if you do not know a language, you cannot interpret the intentions of others and will not be forewarned if they have dangerous intentions.

ON THE JOB

The job of law enforcement seldom entails a forty-hour, nine-to-five workweek. Initially you should plan on afternoon, night, weekend, and holiday duty. As you gain seniority and promotions, this will change and more favorable shifts will become available.

Obviously, any detailed discussion of police work is much too involved for this writing. The interested student should refer to the bibliography of suggested readings for a more in-depth understanding of police work.

A NOTE ABOUT THE MILITARY POLICE

The men and women who serve as our military police are in many ways similar to others who serve in law enforcement. In short, they protect and serve. While their service is usually the enforcement of military laws and regulations regarding army personnel and property, they also perform duties similar to other police. Such tasks include patrol, traffic control, and writing tickets. Then there are the tougher tasks of policing, such as crime scene investigation, interrogation and interviewing witnesses, arrest and charging of suspects, and coming to the aid of those in need.

Military policing dates its history back to 1775, during the War for Independence. It has preserved its rich and noble history in the U.S. Army Military Police Corps Regimental Museum located at Fort Leonard Wood, Missouri. The museum is open to the public. Fort Leonard Wood also serves as the U.S. Army Military Police School.

There are many benefits to being a member of the Military Police Corps. Many of the required training courses that prepare and qualify a soldier as military police are certified by the American Council on Education (ACE) for college credits. In addition, during active duty in the military, college courses can be taken toward a degree. The military will provide full tuition, payment toward books and fees, payment of existing college loans, and a stipend for living expenses. In addition, there is the GI Bill, which supports education after your service is completed.

Military police training is similar to the preparation given to civilian police, and thus it has great transfer value from the service to civilian police. Many civilian police agencies will credit time served in the military police and recognize the importance of the military police training. The website www.wood.army.mil/usamps/MissionVision/MP Disciplines.PDF provides a list of both general and advanced training in the military police corps.

Anyone interested in a career in law enforcement will benefit from exploring the military police corps website at www.goarmy.com/careers -and-jobs/browse-career-and-job-categories/legal-and-law-enforcement/ military-police.html.

Brigadier General Mark Spindler, the Deputy Provost Marshal General of the Army Commanding General, United States Army Criminal Investigation Command, and Army Corrections Command has had a distinguished and decorated career in the U.S. Army. He is also a graduate of basic and advanced military police training. He has prepared a recommended reading list for those interested in service as a member the military police corps. See www.wood.army.mil/usamps/CMDTReadingList .pdf for more information.

There are many positive points to consider when advancing from the military to civilian law enforcement. Military police seeking to transition into the law enforcement profession may find themselves with several advantages over regular applicants. In many circumstances, the applications of servicemen and women may be fast-tracked, or there is incentive pay and points added to civil service or municipal applications. Military service time can count toward retirement. Do not neglect time served in the military, because to purchase retirement credit later on in your career can become very expensive. The person with military experience has had valuable experience and training desired by police departments; a disciplined officer who is well-trained to follow orders, familiar with weapons, and familiar with high-stress and dangerous surroundings is a valued asset for any law enforcement agency. Military personnel possess skills and experiences that the average new police recruit lacks.

SUMMARY

Law enforcement offers many varied career opportunities. The career may remain rooted in one department or have the potential to allow the officer to expand their interests and assume different roles as their skills and training increase. The law enforcement officer, in many ways, is only as limited as they fail to see themselves in other roles, and they have the ability to train, adapt, and prepare for other opportunities. The benefits of the law enforcement career are excellent and extend beyond early retirement, pension, and medical benefits. The law enforcement career can transition into a second career and the fulfillment of personal interests.

4

Careers in Corrections

Are we guards or correctional officers? . . . A "guard" is one who watches over, protects and prevents escapes, etc., but more than that, a "guard" is a technician trained to do a rather specific task, maintain security/custody. On the other hand, an "officer," by definition, is one who . . . is called "to minister," to serve. Specifically, a corrections officer is one who serves other people in a wholistic way, concerned about the total person . . . and the surrounding environment. They learn how to care for the physical health of a person, how to promote mental/emotional well-being, and how to lift the spirit by promoting self-esteem. They learn how to provide a safe and secure environment. Above all, they are respecters of persons, individuals and their rights.[1]

INTRODUCTION

The fifty states, the District of Columbia, and other U.S. territories are responsible for more than 1,800 correctional facilities[2] and another 3,200 local and county jails.[3] Prison systems continue to expand, and few prisons ever close. That number does not include juvenile or federal prisons, nor private prisons or private nonprofit community corrections centers.

"An estimated 6,899,000 persons were under the supervision of adult correctional systems at year end 2013."[4] About 2.2 million convicts[5] are in some form of confinement, and the remainder are supervised in some form of community corrections. The number of people under correctional supervision is not likely to decrease, and in all probability will increase although the ratio between confinement in prisons and jails and community corrections may experience a shift. Little by little legislators are recognizing that reliance on prisons and other forms of confinement has proven much too costly and ineffective.[6] That is, corrections has failed to serve the needs of either offenders or society in its ability to provide long-term public safety. Often this failure is expressed as recidivism, or as the crime rate (see UCR, or the Uniform Crime Report)[7]. Recidivism[8] has not decreased, and despite a booming prison population, neither has the crime rate been reduced as has been projected that it would during the past forty-five years of rapid prison expansion.

A career in corrections, like other fields in criminal justice, is comprised of both civilian and law enforcement positions at the federal, state, and local level. Private correctional enterprises, which include armed security, are also expanding. The huge increase in the number of people incarcerated in the past forty-five years has caused the ranks of correctional officers and parole officers (law enforcement) to expand beyond 474,000[9] positions nationally. Similarly, the ranks of civilian employees have likewise expanded to meet the needs of an increased correctional population. In addition, there has been a rise in the number of private companies that operate private prisons, as well as a variety of community corrections centers such as halfway houses, day reporting centers, resource centers, and other agencies. The current focus on the potential of community corrections has increased and will likely see additional need for the use of those centers. The intention is that such centers will affect more positive results in reduced recidivism and a diminished crime rate.

This chapter cannot answer all of your questions. However, your questions can be your guide to seek answers for your anticipated career path. Your search should not be difficult. Many answers can be found in college courses and are also readily available from various sources (including the Internet, textbooks, and professionals who work in the field). Write your questions down and then ask them of knowledgeable experts in the field!

INSTITUTIONAL CORRECTIONS

The median salary of a correctional officer is $39,000.[10] The posted salary for correctional officers will always be considerably less than what the correctional officer will actually earn, however. Salary is affected by several variables, which include a daily stipend for shift overlap. That is, one shift officer cannot leave until the next shift officer is in place—this is referred to as the shift differential and usually results in about fifteen minutes of overtime per day. The contracts for correctional officers also include different rates of compensation when overtime is worked. An officer may be contracted to earn a larger amount if he/she is required or has a mandatory assignment to work more than two shifts in a row. This may occur not only because a shift is shorthanded, but also because there are emergency circumstances. In addition, those who work holidays may receive an increased daily wage, and concomitantly if there is overtime on a holiday, then the compensation is larger than the normal rate for overtime. Therefore, correctional officers are guaranteed to earn more than the stated base salary.

LAW ENFORCEMENT

The law enforcement side of corrections includes correctional officers, juvenile correctional officers, sheriff officers or deputy sheriff officers (titles will change by jurisdiction), and parole and probation officers. There are some states in which probation officers have gained additional status as law enforcement officers through new provisions that permit them to be armed and sworn in as law enforcement personnel. Correctional officers, juvenile correctional officers, and sheriff officers operate federal and state prisons, county jails, and juvenile detention centers. Parole officers and probation officers provide community supervision of ex-convicts, offenders placed on probation, and juvenile offenders once they are released from confinement or have noncustodial sentences handed down by the court.

ARE THEY GUARDS OR CORRECTIONAL OFFICERS?

The correctional officer has sometimes been called a keeper, a night keeper, a jailer, a hack, a screw, a guard, and a turnkey, among other terms. Many of these terms are antiquated or are now viewed as derogatory, depending upon who is saying them and the context in which they are used. *Correctional officer* is the more recent term that has been used as a professional title, and it is distinguished from the other terms by virtue of training and standards of conduct both on and off the job. Correctional officers are sworn members of the law enforcement community. Correctional officers are trained to carry weapons and uphold the law, and in some jurisdictions they are dual-certified so that they are able to report to a patrol position if needed.

The prospective employee will apply to take a test and then be placed on a civil service or appointment list that can number in the hundreds of applicants. As mentioned in the previous chapter, the list of applicants will shorten quickly for many reasons. Those reasons include:

- Some candidates will not wait and will take other jobs.
- Some test takers will not pass the physical, psychological, or drug tests.
- Some applicants will not pass the academy.
- Some individuals will realize in the academy or shortly thereafter that they do not wish to work in corrections and will resign.
- Unfortunately, some applicants will commit felonies that will render them ineligible for law enforcement positions.
- Correctional officer ranks experience high turnover rates.

Departures from corrections careers occur for many reasons. Some officers cannot handle the stress. Other officers will leave for civilian positions. There will be terminations for incompetence or for inappropriate, unethical, and illegal conduct. Injury on the job will cause others to leave. And criminal behavior, both on and off the job, will result in dismissals.

There are many, of course, who complete their terms of service and honorably retire. Correctional facilities must be staffed twenty-four hours a day, seven days a week, and vacancies must be continually filled. Academy classes will be scheduled to fill the ranks of officers leaving, and they are needed to fill new positions or other correctional jobs. Academy classes for new recruits are scheduled on a regular basis to maintain and to restore to appropriate levels the number of officers required for adequate staffing (often called "post tricks") of correctional facilities.

You will find that once you are on the employment list, you will move up quickly, perhaps even sooner than you would think, and you will then receive a letter to report to the academy. This is when the real work begins, and you will be tested in many ways so that when you emerge, you will have earned the privilege to be called a correctional officer.

RISING THROUGH THE RANKS

The correctional officer's career provides opportunities for promotions, changes in assignment, and transfers to other, sometimes less desirable or perhaps more desirable duty. Generally, after a specified period of time, an officer may qualify for a promotion. Oftentimes, a test must be taken to qualify for a new position. A correctional officer advances through the ranks from officer to sergeant to lieutenant, then to captain and perhaps to chief. Depending upon the jurisdiction, the actual correctional titles may vary.

New Jersey is an excellent example of changing job assignments. When a position becomes available, it is posted. Eligible officers may bid for the job. Eligibility is based on seniority, or in some specified cases, other requirements such as education, special skills, or the possession of a Methods of Instruction (MOI) certification. The advantage of seniority is that over time officers will gain more desirable shifts and assignments. Officers usually begin their service on second or third shifts, that is, from 2 p.m. to 10 p.m. or from 10 p.m. to 6 a.m. These shifts are also likely to include weekends and holidays for the recruit.

The needs of a corrections department might mean that openings in other institutions become available. These openings may be closer to home or have more desirable work hours. In other cases, there may be openings in different divisions of the department that would permit the officer to transfer. These may include a move from a correctional institution to parole, which is often viewed as a more attractive duty inasmuch as it removes officers from the prison environment, which requires direct contact with convicts. The role of a correctional officer is seldom a static assignment and instead offers many opportunities for change and growth.

The Federal Bureau of Prisons offers an example of advancement from the custody ranks to civilian status. In this case, promotions are usually from within, and an officer may advance to become a warden. If there is an exception to this process, it is for the medical doctor or a hard-to-fill position. Warden Bob Hood (see his profile in Appendix 1) has emphasized that retirement is mandatory at fifty-seven and comes with "a nice twenty-year retirement package."

Promotions are the result of experience and preparation. Generally, there is a minimum time that must be spent in rank to qualify for a promotion. And then there is the test. The smart officer (or other correctional employee) should be aware that there is often a civil service test requirement, and the scores determine an officer's placement on a list. The exception to this is the person who has served in the armed forces and is a veteran. These people receive "veteran's status" and move to the top of the list. The final step for promotion is the interview. (See Appendices 2 and 8 for preparation guides for tests and interviews.) In addition, there are companies that provide assistance with preparation for promotional tests. They will, for a fee, provide the promotional aspirant with classes, books, and sample tests.

THE BENEFITS OF CORRECTIONAL EMPLOYMENT

There are tremendous benefits to working in corrections that should not be ignored. There is great similarity between the benefits for law enforcement and civilian employees. New Jersey, for example, provides a generous benefit package for correctional employees. They include:

- Twelve vacation days per year
- Fifteen sick days per year
- Three administrative leave days per year
- Vision care reimbursement
- Health and dental benefits
- Prescription drug plan
- Retirement plan
- Deferred compensation plan
- Life insurance
- Paid leave for annual military training

One of the areas of greatest difference between benefits for law enforcement and civilian employees is the number of years required to qualify for pension benefits. Some law enforcement officers can retire in twenty or twenty-five years with 65 percent of their salary, while civilian employees have a somewhat lower percentage and the scale is based on a combination of age and years in service. These benefits are under current review and may see revisions in the upcoming years due to fiscal concerns. Nevertheless, there remains great likelihood that these benefits will remain generous when compared to benefits in other, non-correctional employment.

CORRECTIONAL OFFICER JOB DUTIES AND RESPONSIBILITIES

Correctional officers are responsible for performing many tasks. The most common is, of course, working the tiers or galleries of cells. (The language of prisons may change slightly from state to state.) This assignment is usually worked regularly and may last a very long time. There are advantages to having officers regularly assigned to cell blocks. Most notably, as they get to know the convicts and the convicts get to know them, each comes to learn what they can expect from the other. For the prison administrator, this means consistency as well as a more intimate knowledge of the convicts, which helps the administrator to anticipate and prevent trouble. Similarly, should a convict have a problem, he knows the working officer and may turn to him in time of need. While the correctional officer will argue that he is not a social worker, he may need to refer convicts to medical, social, or psychological staff should problems become evident. This is important because it helps the prison to maintain conformity and thus improves the custody and security of the prison. Many convicts will not request such a referral, and only when the officers know those confined will they have a sense of trouble that they can act on and thus prevent possible disturbances or other unforeseen problematic occurrences.

Prisons may be likened to small, contained cities because of the numbers of persons involved and the diversity of work. Someone needs to work a mail room, supervise visits, oversee kitchen duty, perform intake of new convicts, work roving patrol around the perimeter of the prison, have yard duty, perform laundry services, and transport convicts to court or to other prisons. And there is probably the most lonely assignment— working the tower. Some assignments place the correctional officer in constant contact with the convicts or with the public, while a few place the officer in an isolated circumstance. Assignment to the training academy generally means a more reduced contact with the actual prison population. The life of the correctional officer is usually filled with a diversity of job assignments.

Advancement in rank has both advantages and disadvantages. An officer should be aware of both as well as any implications for their career. Perhaps a supervising officer may feel relief that they are no longer working the cell blocks, but be disappointed if the new assignment places them in an office pushing papers. Prisons operate with great bureaucracy. Some examples of the paperwork that is maintained includes the head counts to be taken and recorded several times a day, and reported incidents to be written up and perhaps investigated. Disciplinary matters begin with a charge, proceed to an investigation, and then culminate in a hearing and the appropriate corrective action assigned. Training never stops. There are policies and standard operating procedures to be reviewed and implemented as well as adapted to the working environment.

One of the more crucial duties of supervision is maintaining consistency of the staffing pattern. Recruits, fresh out of the academy, must transition from the ideal to the practical, to understand that interactions in the prison world are vastly different from those in the civilian world. It is important to remember that convicts are still people with real needs and real concerns just like everyone else. Someone has to show this recruit, the "newjack," the ropes and work with them to acquire the hands-on skills that allow prisons to operate with minimal difficulty.

INTERNAL AFFAIRS

Television and movies frequently portray the internal affairs officers as the bad guys of law enforcement because they go after their own. The truth of the matter is that the internal affairs office performs several vital law enforcement functions.

One of the more critical tasks is to do background checks. These checks are made for new hires (both civilian and law enforcement), volunteers, contract workers, and others who would enter or have involvement with the correctional field. Background checks serve to ensure that persons with inappropriate histories, including criminal histories, are made known to the hiring authorities to determine suitability for employment. A criminal history may exclude someone from the sworn law enforcement positions, but not for many civilian, volunteer, or other positions.

Internal affairs will conduct a variety of investigatory functions, such as allegations of unethical or criminal conduct by staff or misconduct by those in custody positions. These investigations serve to maintain the integrity of the organization, to ensure that allegations are valid or invalid, to advise the administration of the need for reviews of standard operating procedures (SOPs) based on incidents, or to prepare and refer cases to the prosecutor when the actions of the correctional employee are determined to be criminal. Corrections, like other areas of law enforcement, has been severely criticized for ethical breaches, cover-ups, and other inappropriate actions.

Internal Affairs will conduct investigations of disciplinary charges filed against convicts to make determinations of breaches of discipline within the prison or to refer it for prosecution. A well-run internal affairs office helps to maintain the integrity of the correctional organization by ensuring that all persons, both staff and those in custody, are not in violation of correctional laws, procedures, and other essential functions.

THE SHERIFF AND DEPUTY SHERIFF

The annual median salaries for sheriff careers are as follows:

- Sheriff: $100,512,[11]
- Deputy sheriff: $40,683,[12] and
- Sheriff's officer: $56,150.[13]

The idea of a sheriff may call to mind such characters as the sheriff of Nottingham from the Robin Hood tales; Sheriff John Stone from the Beach Boys' song "The Sloop John B"; Sheriff Andy Taylor of Mayberry; or the man who may be the most famous, albeit controversial, modern sheriff, the self-proclaimed *America's Toughest Sheriff* (his book title), Joe Arpaio.[14]

The history and the exploits of sheriffs generally make for good reading because of the exciting adventures and myths that have developed through interactions with more famous outlaws. An exploration of the position, as it developed in the United States, will extol its virtues as key to the establishment of order and civility in the Old West, but at the same time, there were some, due to a lack of accountability, who used the badge and the position to be as nefarious and threatening to public safety as those they were sworn to keep in check, arrest, or hold for prosecution. Just to stir the imagination of the reader, some famous names associated in this regard were Bat Masterson and Wild Bill Hickok. And while we all know that our first president was George Washington, what is lesser recognized is that his father held the office of sheriff.

The position of sheriff is unique when compared to other positions in law enforcement. The sheriff is regarded as the original law enforcement officer not operating in a military capacity. While almost all sheriffs are elected,[15] they are not required to have prior experience in law enforcement, and thus they may not have been through academy training. However, after being elected the sheriff, there may be a necessity to complete firearms training inasmuch as a sheriff, by nature of the position, has permission to carry a firearm. Sheriff's deputies, sometimes referred to as officers do receive academy training.

The position of sheriff originated in England prior to the tenth century and was called a *shire reeve*. The first part of the name refers to a geographic area and the second part loosely translates into "guardian." In time, the sheriff's duties increased from providing protective services to include the collection of taxes, delivering orders from the king, and keeping the suspect in jail until such as time as a sentence would be handed down by the court.

The American sheriff evolved into a different type of position that not only serves to protect but also to mete out punishment, including executions, public shaming, and whippings, which are now banned. The English sheriff responded to the king, whereas the American sheriff became more responsible to the citizens.

The duties of the sheriff and his subordinates (sheriff officer, or deputy sheriff) are perhaps the widest ranging of any member of the law enforcement profession. The duties can be separated into two categories: general and special. There are inconsistencies in the duties to be performed because the duties are determined by the state in which the sheriff will operate. General duties more closely resemble the responsibilities of a police officer. The sheriff officer/deputy sheriff officer's duties include:

- Executing warrants,
- Providing chaplain services,
- Responding to emergencies,
- Providing courtroom security,
- Investigating complaints,
- Promoting homeland security,
- Collecting of delinquent taxes,
- Conducting the sale of property,
- Performing evictions, and
- Arresting suspects on bench warrants.

SPECIAL FUNCTIONS OF THE SHERIFF'S OFFICERS AND/OR DEPUTY SHERIFFS

The more special functions of the sheriff include:

- Maintaining the security of the jail and the courthouse,
- Supervising the prisoners,
- Providing transportation for inmates, witnesses, and others between the jail and the courthouse, and
- Providing protective services to the courthouse, including admittance to the courthouse, security for the judge and those in attendance during a trial.

In accordance with courtroom functions, the sheriff will also serve warrants and execute civil actions, such as collecting delinquent taxes, serving evictions, and conducting sheriff's sales and repossessions. Officers also testify in court for both criminal and civil matters.

PAROLE AND PROBATION OFFICERS

Most states now require parole and probation officers to possess a bachelor's degree. In some states there are specific degree requirements, such as a criminal justice/social science major. Students interested in careers in parole and probation should check their individual state's requirements for education. A parole officer's median salary is $40,148,[16] and a probation officer's median salary is $38,616.[17]

PAROLE VERSUS PROBATION

Parole and probation officers are generally different positions with some similar duties and others that are unique to each position. In some jurisdictions there is little or no difference between parole and probation officers. Probation is generally under the control of the judiciary, and parole is generally within a state division such as corrections. Probation officers are more likely not to be armed, while parole officers are sworn law enforcement officers.

PAROLE OFFICERS

Parole officers (referred to as "agents" in some jurisdictions) were a late addition to the criminal justice profession. Parole officers work with convicts following their release from confinement. The requirements vary from state to state and the federal government. There are instances where the educational requirement is as minimal as a high school diploma, but other jurisdictions require a BS or BA degree, and in a few instances, a master of arts degree. Some parole jurisdictions stipulate that the officer have a specific degree, such as one in criminal justice.

The specific jurisdiction defines the extent of duties for the parole officer. In some instances there is divergence between the adult and the juvenile officers, specifically, the adult parole officer being more focused on the law enforcement function that ensures that the parolee maintains compliance with the conditions of their parole, while juvenile officers having an increased emphasis on rehabilitation, including social and educational services.

Employment prospects for parole officers remain positive through 2020. The U.S. Bureau of Labor Statistics for 2012–2013 Occupational Outlook Handbook[18] expects growth to remain steady at about 18 percent. Of course, as the parole officer starts out, he/she may expect to make considerably more than their starting salary due to overtime and holiday pay.

In addition, parole officers receive the same excellent benefits as other members of the law enforcement profession.

PAROLE TRAINING

The parole officer receives extensive academy training that may last from a few weeks to as many as sixteen weeks. Possible courses in a curriculum would include:

- Supervision,
- Counseling (such as drug and alcohol addiction),
- Weapons Qualifications,
- Excessive Force,
- Investigation,
- Policy and Procedure,
- Computer Skills,
- Legal Issues Related to Parole,
- Physical Fitness and Defensive Tactics (such as verbal judo), and
- Procedures of Arrest, Filing Warrants, and Report Writing.

Training and accountability are an ongoing part of a parole officer's life, just as it is for other members of law enforcement. The officers must minimally requalify with weapons and be advised of and often trained and retrained in statutory additions and changes. Parole officers are required to keep current with changes in the law and in policies and procedures. In some cases, such as the Interstate Parole Compact, officers must remain current with other states' requirements.

THE WORK OF PAROLE

The parole officer is responsible for supervising offenders who are released from prison on parole. Primary to the work of the officer is maintenance of the caseload. Just as prisons have become overcrowded, the caseloads of parole officers have grown, and in many cases they challenge appropriate levels of supervision and guidance.

Parolees released from prison have standard and special conditions to which they must adhere as part of their parole. The parole officer is responsible for accountability. Part of the parole officer's routine is to interview the parolee and assess willingness and openness to cooperate and to negotiate acceptance of available services following release. The purpose is to help the parolee establish stability upon return to their community.

A risk/needs assessment tool (such as the LSI, or Level of Service Inventory) may be administered to help prepare for the prisoner's release or upon release. These tools assess employment, education, medical, therapeutic, and other needs. These elements are generally referred to as *criminogenic factors* and are placed in two categories: static and dynamic. Static factors cannot be changed, such as an offender's age. Dynamic factors can be changed, such as the level of education that would make the offender more employable. The officer will identify resources as needed and stipulate that the offender comply with the provided services until such time as adjustment is apparent.

Some standardized supervisory functions would include increasing or decreasing the level of supervision for the offender. For example, a parolee starting out may be required to report in every other week. In time, reporting may be decreased to monthly, bimonthly, semiannually, or annually depending upon the severity of the sentence, the length of time the person will be on parole, and the parolee's adjustment. The officer must be a conscientious bookkeeper, collecting debts and fines and keeping accurate records. The officer will also be required to follow up on job, school, or other program attendance. There will be checks of accountability, such as ascertaining that the offender is maintaining an assigned curfew, staying away from undesirable persons, and adhering to restraint orders. Officers may conduct drug and alcohol screenings, recommend discharge from parole supervision, make arrests when violations occur, and file for parole revocations. These are only a few of the duties performed by parole officers.

More detailed examples of parole officer duties are discussed below.

ELECTRONIC MONITORING

Parole officers have a number of tools at their disposal to help them work with offenders who are perceived as representing the greatest risk.

Electronic monitoring devices are among the more recent innovations. Among the more frequently used devices are ankle or wrist bracelets. These devices are fairly simple to employ, and they rely on a telemetry signal that is sent to a central receiving station. In other cases, the parolee may be required to wear a backpack that has a programmable global positioning device. A GPS signal reports the parolees' location or sets off an alarm if the parolee either goes beyond approved borders or enters an area that is prohibited. To be effective, the system requires around-the-clock monitoring. Some drawbacks to GPS utilization include the high cost to implement and paying the salary of the person who does the monitoring. Parole officers currently monitor about 200,000[19] persons nationally on these instruments.

INTERSTATE PAROLE COMPACT

The management of the Interstate Parole Compact is an area of specialization for a parole officer. The officer will receive special training in their state and will attend frequent national conferences/trainings to remain current with changes in the Interstate Compact. This contract involves the transfer of parole supervision from one state to another or to a U.S. Territory other than that in which the person has been sentenced. This contract is made in accordance with the Interstate Commission for Adult Offender Supervision and other criminal justice concerns. The Interstate Compact is an agreement between each of the fifty states and the District of Columbia, Puerto Rico, and the Virgin Islands. At any one time, there may be thousands of offenders involved in the Interstate Compact. The officer in charge of the transfer must ensure that the laws of those states involved in the transfer are upheld. (For more information about Interstate Compacts, including common myths, visit www .interstatecompact.org/.)

The parole officer in charge of administering the state's Interstate Compact will ensure that the offender meets the requirements of both the sending and the receiving state. Those requirements include such criteria as time under supervision, demonstrated compliance with parole conditions, and a plan of supervision. In addition, the receiving state ensures that the offender will be able to comply with the receiving state's policies for supervision, including that the person has a visible means of support, such as employment or a promise of employment, and is or has been a resident of that state or territory or has family who has residency there.

Offenders do not have a right to transfer and may only be approved after the receiving state has done its investigation so that both the receiving and the sending state are in agreement. In addition, the receiving state may impose special conditions that were not ordered in the sending state, thus changing the conditions of parole for the offender. Similarly, the sending state may also attach special conditions to the parole status of the offender going to the receiving state. For example, the sending state may stipulate that the offender not return to the sending state without permission of both states during the specified time that the offender is on parole.

THE PROBATION OFFICER

The probation officer position is a combination of investigator, supervisor, social services coordinator, counselor, and enforcer. In each role, the officer's actions have a distinct impact on the lives of those with whom they interact. An example of each will help to illustrate how this happens and how it is important in the lives of the probationer, the protection of society, and the reduction of criminality—all of which are intertwined.

The investigative role helps determine suitability for a sentence of probation or a recommendation for incarceration. Presentence investigative reports examine many aspects of the client's life, including school, family, work, societal involvement, the current offense, its impact on victims and others, and prior instances of legal violations.

The role of the supervising officer ensures that the client meets the conditions of probation as determined by the court. The supervisory/counselor role may result in independent action by the probation officer to assess need and determine other avenues of service that will best help the probationer through his/her time of supervision. The probation officer maintains records of his involvement with the probationer, including reporting, adhering to conditions of probation, attitude, payment of fines, and personal effort to demonstrate responsible citizenship. The probation officer can recommend termination of probation for failure to be compliant with the conditions of probation or recommend revocation for new criminal offenses. In such cases, the officer may become a witness before the court whose testimony and records will be critical to judicial decisions.[20]

There are about 4 million persons[21] on probation at any given time for misdemeanors and felony offenses. More than half the states combine their probation and parole services into one agency. Probation is the most widely used sanction of the courts. The offenders' reporting schedule is determined by the probation officer. Probation services cost only a fraction of the cost of institutionalization. Nationally, the approximate cost of institutionalization per convict is about $30,000 per year,[22] whereas probation only costs between $700 and $1,000 per year.[23]

Probation officers may or may not be sworn members of law enforcement. Generally, probation officers report directly to the court.

Among the duties performed by probation officers are:

- Supervision of offenders,
- Holding offenders accountable for violations of probation conditions,
- Writing progress reports,
- Collecting fines or other court-ordered costs,
- Screening for drug use,
- Electronic monitoring,
- Conducting risk/needs assessments,
- Writing reports on progress,
- Conducting presentence investigations,
- Evaluating offenders' progress and determining necessary courses of treatment,
- Identifying resources for offender treatment and services, and
- Meeting with offenders and their family members, as well as others who are directly involved with the offender.

Probation officers are concerned with community safety. Officers work to ensure that the offender does not represent a risk to the community. Officers may work with either adults or juveniles. The pre-trial investigation seeks to determine whether an offender who is granted probation will represent a risk to the community. Probation officers present their reports to a judge with a written recommendation. Officers may also supervise those placed on bond awaiting trial or other adjudication.

The role of the probation officer has evolved. The officer may now be thought of as a community treatment specialist or a case manager. In these capacities officers will be concerned that probationers receive treatment, obtain employment, or perhaps return to school to complete their education as an enhancement for employment.

Probation officer caseloads vary in size. The American Probation and Parole Association (APPA) recommends a caseload of fifty cases per officer.[24] However, an officer may supervise several hundred persons in high-density urban areas, while in a more rural area the caseload may be as few as fifty. Frequently, an officer in a rural area will have to cover a larger geographic area, which will result in larger caseloads. Officers dealing with high-risk offenders or those who are assigned to special programs (drug court, domestic violence, sex offenders, etc.) may have reduced caseloads. Intensive supervision programs are often administered by the judiciary outside the regular probation divisions. These programs have small caseloads and more rigorous compliance, which, in turn, has a higher success rate than regular probation.

REQUIREMENTS FOR PROBATION OFFICER

The requirements for probation officer are very similar to those of other positions in criminal justice. A probation officer will usually be required to possess a bachelor's degree; have a record that is clear of criminal offenses; pass a written test (see Appendix 8 for more information on civil service tests), a psychological test, and a physical; and attend academy training. The duration of the academy training will be shorter than for other positions of law enforcement. There is a lower turnover rate of probation personnel than in other areas of criminal justice, although stress and burnout are not uncommon.

CIVILIAN CAREERS

The number of civilian staff members in all areas of criminal justice has increased greatly during the past three decades. This is especially true for corrections. Changes in programs and in treatment philosophy have been primary driving forces that have pushed these increases. Salaries of civilian staff may range from the mid 30,000-dollar range for entry-level positions to some that are well above $120,000 for administrators.[25]

There are any number of ways to classify the civilian workforce. A four-part breakdown of positions by work performed and their starting salaries would include:

- Coverage or client supervision,
- Treatment and counseling services,
- Support staff, and
- Management and administration.

The types of job descriptions for the many roles would include teachers, social workers, youth workers, business managers, accountants, administration/management personnel, classification officers, substance abuse treatment workers, public information specialists, ministers, human resource managers, nurses, doctors, psychologists and psychiatrists, food service coordinators (cooks, food preparers, and managers), storeroom managers, industry employees, architects, building compliance or code enforcement personnel, information technology experts, researchers, grant managers, and many others.

Entrance into the civilian/professional ranks may require education that ranges from a high school diploma to a graduate degree or a medical degree and/or possession of special certifications or credentials, such as substance abuse counselor or certified public accountant. Many positions are placed along what may be referred to as career paths; that is, only certain titles fall into these categories, and to advance the employee must have previous experience in a lower title. Of course, one of the premier tools for employment and advancement is the dreaded civil service test. The good news is that the more often you take these tests, the better you tend to score on them. There are prep courses available for civil service examinations. Advancement or employment may be affected in several different ways. There are open tests for these positions, assuming you meet the minimal qualifications. Then there are those position openings that fall under the heading of promotional examination. These are only open to those already in the career track who meet the qualifications. Of course, as part of your career planning, you will be considering what type of continuing education you should pursue that will best prepare you for promotional examinations and other opportunities to advance.

Civilian correctional positions can be found in institutions, community correctional centers, and private correctional enterprises, such as private prisons and halfway houses. As an example of the changing nature of the civilian profession, let's take a look at the correctional counselor, which has become an expanding career position. The correctional counselor may wear many different hats, including providing support to those having difficulty adjusting to institutional life, preparing convicts for release, performing risk/needs assessments, and providing assistance to those just released from institutions. The emphasis on community corrections has expanded from post-incarceration concerns to addressing the concerns the individual will face before leaving incarceration. This also includes such medical circumstances as an HIV-positive status. Some of these issues receive institutional focus, while others come from parole, and others yet come directly from the private and nonprofit community corrections providers. The reader is urged to go online and explore the topic of reentry. Job seekers for civilian positions may find employment announcements posted in newspapers or in state personnel, human resource, or other publications, such as *Corrections Today* magazine (see Appendix 15), or online sites such as indeed.com.

PRIVATE PRISONS AND COMMUNITY CORRECTIONS

Private prisons did not exist prior to the twentieth century. The emergence and rapid expansion of private prisons has been driven by at least four factors: overcrowding, exorbitant costs, expanding government, and the avoidance of lawsuits. As private prisons have emerged, controversy about this phenomenon has also surfaced. In its July/August 2011 issue, *Correctional News* published several articles about them and detailed some of the pros and cons. Among the more crucial issues are whether private groups can really operate correctional facilities less expensively than state equivalents, whether private correctional facilities can be operated safely, whether needed services can be provided to clients, and whether private correctional facilities are effective at what they purport to do. In each of these categories, the results have been mixed. In some states, such as Arizona, the cost seems to be less than the state expenditures, while in other states, such as California, the cost is greater. California, and at least five more states, are considering doing away with private prisons. According to the Bureau of Justice Statistics (2001), the cost savings of private prisons have generally been less than what was projected.[26]

There are a number of other issues that have come under scrutiny, such as the education and training of private prison employees, who are generally less well-educated or credentialed, as well as being less well-trained and consequently less well-compensated. Among the more vocal critics of privatized prisons and the issues just mentioned are unions such as the PBA or CCPOA that represent state and federal employees. Among the union arguments are that private corrections jeopardize public safety, the safety of their own employees, the professionalism of the profession, and the safety, well-being, and rehabilitation of offenders. On the positive side, privatized prisons are a growth industry that has increased its convict numbers in both state and federal prisons. Perhaps the more discouraging employment note is that the turnover rate in private prisons exceeds that in state prisons.[27] These arguments are not to suggest that the prospective corrections employee ignore employment opportunities in this newer field. The field of private corrections provides opportunities that range from getting that first job, to having a second career, to providing consultation for experienced correctional employees.

One theme for this book has been that the criminal justice career aspirant must plan for the future, and that that planning should begin as soon as possible. Corporations and nonprofits that operate private correctional facilities rely heavily on retired correctional employees from correctional officers to administrators. There are several reasons for this. Obviously the career professional has already been trained and is familiar with the environment and sound management practices. In addition, experienced correctional employees are already familiar with correctional problems, legal concerns, treatment issues, and more. Those who have retired from correctional administration have contacts and relationships with current correctional administrators who can help resolve issues between government and corporations. An additional incentive is that with a pension already in their pocket, going to work for a corporation provides another good salary (that may exceed either the pension or the salary from the career position), among other benefits.

JOB STRESS

A discussion about work in the correctional field must include information about job-related stress. Positions inside prisons are probably more stressful than those working the street. That is not to suggest that positions outside of prison are not stressful or that other settings, such as community corrections, lack stress. Anyone can be susceptible to job stress. The employee, and especially the correctional officer, must be vigilant and protective of his/her personal condition. Stress can be caused by long hours on the job and especially overtime, working nights and holidays that interfere with home and family life, as well as social and confrontational interactions associated with the job. Stress may often come from outside the work environment and then be carried over to the work site. The causes of stress may be financial, marital, or other life-affecting conditions, but any cause of stress should not be ignored.

The consequences of on-the-job stress are many and include alcohol and substance abuse, domestic violence, divorce, suicide, and other behavioral acts (including criminal acts) that have been identified as stress-related. Of course, stress also contributes to physical and mental illnesses such as depression.

Many correctional agencies provide various employee assistance programs that are confidential for the staff person seeking assistance. In addition, there are many other groups that offer assistance. In New Jersey, Cop 2 Cop (1-866-COP2COP [267-2267]) provides twenty-four-hour-a-day assistance and is law enforcement at its best looking after its own. (See the profile of Bill Usury found in Appendix 1) One message that comes across loud and clear from the many articles that have been published in recent years about job stress is that no one needs to be abandoned who needs help. Help is available, and lives and careers can be saved by asking for it.

COMMUNITY CORRECTIONS

Community-based corrections has evolved from its humble beginnings that include a Boston shoemaker volunteering to work with an offender who had a drinking problem: John Augustus—the father of probation.

Community corrections is made up of several types of operations: parole, probation, day reporting centers, halfway houses, assessment centers, information resource centers for ex-offenders, centers for substance abuse, and much more. As the emphasis on community corrections continues to grow, we can expect to see more and possibly different types of programming develop. One of the newer additions to the field of community corrections includes community or problem-solving courts. Drug Court is the better known of these courts. Service providers include both for-profit enterprises such as Correctional Education Centers (CEC), or nonprofit providers such as Volunteers of America. Many of these organizations are members of the International Community Corrections Association (ICCA), which promotes evidence-based practices.

Community-based corrections comprise an array of activities from pretrial diversion to intermediate punishments to post-incarceration supervision. In addition, there are treatment centers and others that provide education and job readiness preparation. Those involved in community corrections include individuals who have been charged with an offense and others who have been convicted.

Community Corrections is a combination of law enforcement activities such as those performed by parole and probation officers, and service provisions performed by social workers, substance abuse counselors, family counselors, and job readiness trainers. Each seeks to use the skills of their particular profession to assist offenders with the complex and often daunting tasks of reentry and reacclimation to society.

5

The Courts, Its Actors, and Its Functions

INTRODUCTION

The primary figures of the courts are the judge, the prosecutor, and the defense attorney. However, there are many other persons who perform a variety of roles that ensure the effective, efficient, and secure operation of the courts. Judges, prosecutors, and defense attorneys require advanced degrees. The process begins with the completion of an undergraduate degree (often in political science or criminal justice) and continues on to law school to obtain a JD, or Juris Doctor degree—the degree most common for persons serving in these capacities.

The operations of the court represent an array of opportunities for student internships. Internships for the courts provide students with exposure to special programs operated by the courts, the inner working of the courts and other agencies such as probation, and the complexities of a multifaceted arm of the criminal justice system. Internships with the courts are often viewed as prestigious in part because the internship is often limited to students who have excelled, have excellent recommendations, and who possess interests and talents related to the work of the court.

ATTORNEYS

Juris Doctor (JD)

The JD is a professional degree. While it takes about as much study or time in post-baccalaureate study as a master's or doctorate degree, there is no thesis requirement. JDs usually do not refer to themselves as doctors; instead and upon passing the bar exam they will place *Esq.* or *Esquire* after their name. The first JD was proposed at Harvard University in 1902,[1] but it did not become popular until about thirty years ago, when it replaced the LLB (Legal Laws Baccalaureate), or what was essentially a second bachelor's degree.

Roles of Attorneys

There are three principal roles for attorneys in the courts—the judge, the prosecutor, and the public defender. Private attorneys have the potential to make an excellent living; however, this is not always the case for criminal attorneys. Criminal attorneys engage clients who are often destitute, cannot make bail, and are without support. The defendant's case, especially when it is more serious, such as murder, may desperately require investigatory and other work to support a viable defense. Supporting defendants can be expensive if the case is to be successful. Clients, unfortunately, may be indigent. To put that another way, criminal justice clients/defendants may have poor or no resources with which to support their cases. Indigents must rely on the courtroom skills of their attorney. More complicated cases, such as those involving the death penalty or, to provide a specific example, the O.J. Simpson case, require incredible amounts of adjunct work to support the defendant. The late Johnnie Cochran[2] became famous for his brilliant defense in the O.J. Simpson case. However, as he initially remarked, "This case . . . is a loser."[3] Of course, Cochran could not have anticipated the advantages provided by the prosecuting attorneys, and particularly the glove that resulted in the now-famous closing statement by Cochran, "If the glove don't fit, then you must acquit." Cochran had seemingly done the background work. The prosecutors introduced the glove into evidence not knowing whether it would fit. They opened the door for the defense attorneys, who assumedly did their homework and were aware that the glove would not fit on Simpson's hand, and Simpson could not get the glove on his hand when so instructed.

Few criminal justice cases make it to trial. Almost all clients make a plea deal. The best hope for the client is that their public defender can make them a good deal.

JUDGES

Judges are the weakest link in our system of justice, and they are also the most protected.[4]

The United States is a federal republic comprised of fifty states, the District of Columbia, and other areas of U.S. protection. In other words, there are many jurisdictions, each with their own set of rules. Accordingly, the rules for the election or appointment of judges and other public officials and those that govern the legal process differ state by state—in accordance with the U.S. Constitution, which allows each state to establish its own court system as laid out in each specific state's own constitution.

The courtroom is the setting for the adversarial confrontation between the prosecutor and the defense attorney that is moderated by the judge. At the conclusion of the confrontation, there is an expectation that some truth will emerge in the quest for justice. The judge, in this formal, regimented environment, is referred to as "judge" or "your honor." There are a variety of other terms by which a judge might be referred, and these are generally the result of the jurisdiction in which the judge resides. For example, in the U.S. Supreme Court, judges are referred to more formally as "justices." In other instances, the term may be "surrogate," and in others it may be the "justice of the peace," magistrate, chancellor, arbitrator, or referee. In some very special circumstances the judge may be called a "master" or a "special master." In these cases, the "master" will be expected to review specific evidence, and his or her authority is determined by statute or the state or federal constitutions.

Curiously, not all judges are trained in law or are required to have a law degree. This is more common in situations where they are elected to the bench and are not career judges. While most judges in the United States are trained in law and are attorneys, those who are lay judges, nevertheless, are referred to as judges and have the same rights as judges who are trained as attorneys. These judges are often part-time judges serving in courts of limited jurisdiction.[5] State constitutions determine whether state judges are elected or appointed. Some judges serve a term with the possibility for either reelection or reappointment.

Despite the quote from Dershowitz that introduced this section, the judge is the most powerful actor in the courtroom, and he or she must perform many functions. In many criminal matters and in civil matters, the judge may hear the case before him without a jury. In these instances, the judge must make determinations about the credibility of the evidence as well as the truthfulness or reliability of the witnesses. The proceedings are somewhat different when there is a jury. Primary to the role, the judge is expected to be impartial; to act without bias toward either side; to ensure that the rights of all are upheld; to ensure that defense attorneys and prosecutors follow rules of procedure; to instruct the jury on its duty; and to be the interpreter of the law or, to better illustrate the importance of the position, to interpret the constitutionality of the circumstances that are raised. The rulings become the law of the land. Of course, the more serious act in any case is when the judge passes sentence on the defendant. Sentences can range from fines to years in prison or even the death penalty.

Federal judges are nominated by the president of the United States and confirmed by the Senate. Prior to Senate confirmation hearings, the nominee is subject to a background check by the FBI. The candidate is also subject to additional review by the Senate Judiciary Committee. Once the recommendation is passed on to the full Senate, only a simple majority, or 51 percent, of the Senate is required for the confirmation. There can be one small snag to what is otherwise a somewhat uncomplicated process, and that is a "filibuster."[6] In this case, to bring the filibuster to an end, "cloture"[7] is invoked and sixty votes are required.

Five Basic Steps to a Career as a Judge

Step 1: Get an education.

Generally, the minimum requirement is a bachelor's degree. Among the skills for success in this occupation include analysis, logical thinking, speech, and research. Skills for competent performance on the judicial bench can be acquired through the college curriculum, and more specifically courses that include public speaking, government, English, philosophy, and history.

Step 2: Become a lawyer.

A majority of federal, state, and municipal judges are required to have the degree of Juris Doctor (JD). In addition, anyone seeking to become a judge must pass the bar exam given by a specific state and acquire experience working in the legal system. Many attorneys are permitted to practice law in more than one state by passing the bar exam in each specific state.

Step 3: Apply your knowledge.

All those aspiring to become a judge should determine which court they desire to work in, although appointment procedures will be different depending on the type and location of the court. When an opening in the chosen court is available, apply for a judgeship.

Step 4: Gain political support

An important part of this process is gaining political support. Individuals interested in becoming judges should be aware that this occupation is very competitive, and potential judges must be able to make a favorable impression on those who hold the power to place them in their desired positions. You will have to convince the nominating/appointing persons that you are worthy of the position.

Step 5: Get appointed or elected.

Members of the Judicial Nominating Commission are in charge of appointing state judges. In order to become a judge of a different sort, however, partisan or nonpartisan, elections are held by the state.[8]

The U.S. Supreme Court

U.S. Supreme Court justices are nominated by the president, generally have prior court experience, and require approval by the Senate. Senate hearings for U.S. Supreme Court positions often have political overtones that expose and explore the judge's background, question previous judicial decisions, and query personal conduct. Judge Clarence Thomas[9] is an example. He was accused of sexual harassment two days before the Senate vote. Other federal court nominations are much less rigorous. Once confirmed by the Senate, federal judges serve for life. However, federal judges may be impeached for misconduct. Supreme Court Justice Abe Fortas[10] is the only example of a U.S. Supreme Court Justice being impeached,[11] and this serves to illustrate the rarity of impeachment. The salary for a federal court judge now exceeds $200,000[12] and may not be reduced during their time in office.

One of the more unique aspects of the Supreme Court is that anyone can become a justice. Curiously, when it comes to the U.S. Supreme Court, the nominee also does not have to be a lawyer. As a matter of fact, there are no education requirements at all for the position. The primary requirement is a nomination by the president followed by Senate confirmation (see Article 2, Section 2, Clause 2 of the U.S. Constitution). There are no education or experience requirements. There is no bar examination to be passed. However, should someone wish to pursue this career path, they would have to exhibit very special qualities and convince some powerful and influential people that they are right for the job.

Federal Judges

Article III courts are those that make up the judicial branch of the federal government:

- U.S. District Courts
- U.S. Court of International Trade
- U.S. Court of Appeals Circuit Courts
- The Supreme Court of the United States

The federal judiciary also includes Article I judges, who preside over courts or tribunals (a panel of judges) of limited power and jurisdiction, often connected to government departments and agencies. These courts are different from those of the judicial branch. For example, judges who sit on the U.S. Court of Claims do require nomination by the president and Senate approval (like Article III judges do); however, they only serve a fixed term of fifteen years. Another example are judges for U.S. Bankruptcy Courts. Appellate judges of the U.S. Court of Appeals Circuit Court make these appointments. They provide jurisdiction over a particular bankruptcy court's territory. And some judges are hired. Article I judges (administrative law judges) serve the hiring agency, such as the Social Security Administration's Office of Disability Adjudication and Review.

State Judges

The process for becoming a state judge is determined by each state constitution, and the qualifications vary. There are states in which the judge is appointed through a committee. Other states have elected judges. Some states require an appointment by the governor and approval by the Senate. The length of time in office varies from serving for life to serving for an elected term. In each case the process for determining a judgeship is set forth in the state's constitution.

Circuit Judges

In many western and southern states, because of the distance between cities and lower populations, there are not enough cases to warrant the establishment of a full-time judge. Judges are then asked to ride a circuit, which means a judge travels from one city to another on a regular scheduled calendar. These judges preside over a general jurisdiction, which means they may preside over any type of case, from traffic tickets to murder trials.

Municipal Court Judges

Municipal court judges are appointed by the local chief governing authority, such as a mayor, and approved by the local council. These are generally appointed for an annual term and require reappointment each year. The positions are very political and usually controlled by the local party in control.

DEFENSE ATTORNEYS

The defense attorney is an integral actor in the criminal justice process. The purpose of the defense attorney, whether public defender or private attorney, is to ensure that the defendant's rights are not violated, that is to say, that the defendant gets a fair hearing before the court. Representation by a defense attorney is a constitutional right and has been upheld by the U.S. Supreme Court.[13]

Arrest, being charged with a crime, and criminal prosecution are not guarantees that someone is guilty. The defense attorney helps to ensure that someone is not convicted for crimes of which they are innocent. Unfortunately, and despite constitutional guarantees, innocent persons are at times found guilty and in some cases have even been executed. In other cases, there have been travesties of the judicial process, such as the infamous prosecution and harm done to the Scottsboro Boys.[14] Zealous work on the part of defense attorneys has helped to rectify some of the wrongdoing. A lesser-known case was detailed in John Grisham's book *An Innocent Man*.[15] In this case, like others, a life was destroyed in spite of exoneration. The work of the defense attorney is arduous and fraught with the possibility of miscarriages of justice. However, everyone is entitled to be represented by competent defense counsel.

PROSECUTORS/DISTRICT ATTORNEYS

The prosecutor, also referred to as the district or state's attorney, is the second-most powerful actor in the courtroom. The prosecutor decides which cases to try for criminal offenses, determines the appropriateness of the plea bargain, and decides the degree to which the defendant will be prosecuted. In addition, the prosecutor will also make recommendations for the sentence. Prosecutors are most aware that their position is a political position that can allow them to advance to public office. New Jersey Governor Chris Christie made his reputation as a tough federal prosecutor who fought public corruption, and that became his platform when running for office. Chris Christie is an excellent example of advancement from attorney to federal prosecutor to chief of his federal office to governor of his state.

OTHER ROLES FOR ATTORNEYS

Other roles for attorneys in the court include the defense of the accused and convicted. Legal Aid, the American Civil Liberties Union, and the Innocence Project are three of the better-known efforts through which attorneys may voluntarily pursue support for indigents accused of crimes, subjected to violations of their rights, represented by incompetent counsel, or convicted, that is, the challenge to discover whether the defendant was accorded due process. More recently, every state has developed what have become known as Innocence Projects.

There has long been supposition that many persons are imprisoned for crimes they have not committed. The problem has always been how to prove it when there have not been issues of due-process violations. The advent of DNA[16] has proven itself to be invaluable in these efforts. Innocence Projects join attorneys and investigators to reexamine evidence, and in some cases, to search for evidence either not available or that has become lost over time. Many of these cases are one, two, or more decades old. Innocence Projects seeks to have its clients exonerated, that is, to prove that they did not commit the crimes for which they were convicted.

These do not, as the saying goes, turn someone loose on a constitutional technicality. There have been by-products of DNA analysis, such as affirming the guilt of someone or of discovering the person who actually committed the crime. Again, these are often the result of DNA analysis.

Innocence Projects teams are often comprised of a lead attorney, graduate students, and others. They reexamine cases and help search for evidence. Law school students practice their craft by filing motions, and other interested parties concerned in the pursuit of justice are engaged in the process of discovery.

SHERIFFS

The sheriff's position was discussed in Chapter 4. Since ancient times the sheriff has had numerous assignments, including court security. The sheriff provides officers to ensure courthouse security (including the protection of judges, prosecutors, and others) and to transport offenders and suspected offenders between the jail and the courtroom.

CORONERS

The prosecutor's office oversees many functions critical to criminal justice. The coroner is one such position, whose salary ranges between $48,000 and $72,000 per year.[17] The office of coroner is somewhat unique in its function inasmuch as there is close cooperation between the coroner and the prosecutor as they prepare a case for trial. The coroner will advise the prosecutor what is evidence for presentation in a trial and what is not. In the media, the coroner has been portrayed as a medical doctor who performs autopsies to discover cause of death (death that is unattended by a doctor, and to ascertain whether it is a homicide, suicide, or accident), and whether or not malfeasance has occurred. In reality, the coroner may or may not be a medical doctor, depending upon the specific state's requirements. Of course, if they do not possess a medical degree, then they will not be performing an autopsy. However, they will lead the investigation that prepares evidence for the prosecutor and then, if needed, testify in court.

FORENSIC SCIENTISTS

With a median salary of $58,610,[18] the forensic scientist is a newcomer to the criminal justice field, but it has seen increased popularity and emphasis in the academic field, often with its own curriculum. The courses are interesting and include exposing students to the more graphic side of crime scenes, as well as taking them through the process of crime scene analysis. One colleague, Professor Joe Paglino (see his profile in Appendix 1), a retired detective for the Monmouth County, New Jersey, prosecutor's office, creates an actual crime scene somewhere on campus for his students to examine and evaluate as their final examination.

The forensic scientist is the latest member of the criminal justice profession. These scientists are usually members of the prosecutor's office with advanced degrees in forensics, chemistry, and biology. They examine evidence for accuracy and help to develop the prosecution's strategy for presenting their case in court.

PROBATION

Probation versus Parole

Probation and parole officers are discussed in other sections of the book. However, they are worthy of mention here because of the special functions they perform for the courts. The terms *probation* and *parole* are often used interchangeably, although their functions are distinctly different. Parole is often under the jurisdiction of some larger state division, such as the Department of Corrections or perhaps a parole board. Probation is usually under the jurisdiction of a county court, and probation officers report to the judge. Parole officers are generally sworn law enforcement officers, whereas probation officers are not.

Probation Officers

The probation officer is the eyes, ears, and legs of the court. The functions of the probation officer include investigation, service provider, counselor, and enforcement. The investigative duties of the probation officer involve preparing the various reports required by the court, which include bail reports; retention reports; court scheduling in the absence of a court clerk; reports verifying information, such as prior records, defendant's personal finances, and possible mental health issues; and much more. Another report is the presentence investigation report, which details many facets of a defendant's background to help the judge in the complicated decision-making process of determining the appropriate sentence.

The enforcement duties of probation officers are not unlike those of a parole officer, except that they also report to a judge, ensure that the orders of the judge are carried out, and make recommendations to a judge for the management of the offender. The work of a probation officer tends to be more diverse than that of a parole officer, and it is more geographically specific.

Job Tasks in Probation Work

- Investigation
- Presentence investigation reports

- Case documentation
- Violation reports
- Child custody and visitation reports
- Counseling
- Initial interviews with offenders
- Individual supervision of offenders
- Family counseling
- Personal counseling
- Financial planning
- Service referral and coordination
- Job training
- Educational opportunities
- Employment assistance
- Transportation
- Shelter and subsistence
- Treatment programs
- Special programs
- Enforcement of court orders
- Probation violation
- Probation revocation recommendations[19]

OTHER JUDICIARY STAFF

The work of the judiciary requires a diverse staff. We have already discussed those at the uppermost level (judges and attorneys) and considered that they generally require law degrees. Others, such as bailiffs, clerks, and reporters, are referred to as "officers of the court." Textbooks often downplay these positions or provide very little information about them. However, the job seeker should not ignore these positions, as they pay a decent salary and may be a stepping-stone to other positions in the judiciary or the criminal justice system.

Bailiffs

The bailiff, with a median salary of $42,360,[20] might go unnoticed in the courtroom except for when he announces that the judge is entering or leaving the courtroom—a very formal moment usually accented by the announcement, "All rise!" The bailiff's responsibilities are actually much greater, however, and include keeping track of attorneys, witnesses, and prosecutors to keep the court working on schedule. Depending upon the court, there may be other duties, as well, such as informing the defendant's attorney of the outcome of a case.

Court Reporters

Court reporters, with a median salary of $48,160,[21] are also referred to as court stenographers. Court reporters may be hired as needed on a case-by-case basis or they may be salaried employees. They require special training as stenographers and for operating the machine upon which all court language is recorded. The court reporter also has to pass a state proficiency test. The court reporter must be very accurate, because their report becomes the official record of the court proceedings. In addition, during court proceedings it is quite common for the court reporter to read back to the judge what has transpired in order for the judge to make a ruling. There has been an effort to replace this position with more sophisticated recording equipment, but this suggestion has had its drawbacks: First, it makes recall more difficult and time-consuming. In addition, recording equipment will pick up all the noises of a courtroom, potentially making some of the more important parts of the recording unintelligible.

Court Clerks

The court clerk, with a median salary of $37,340,[22] maintains the calendar for the court, and in court it may be referred to as "calling the calendar." The court clerk performs duties critical to the court's functions, including administering the oath, maintaining the files of the court, and keeping the evidence secure. This position may be a stepping-stone for someone preparing to become an attorney, or the position may be occupied by an attorney who is preparing for a position in the prosecutor's office. In some jurisdictions, the court clerk may prepare writs and other court documents as directed by the court.

SUMMARY

In many respects the court responds to criminal justice matters much like a case manager. Where does this case belong? Who should provide supervision? What resources are available? What resources are needed? The questions could go on and on. The court and its actors must be prepared to interact with police, probation, corrections, community corrections, and private nonprofit agencies.

There are new functions for the courts that require specialized training for those judges and staff assigned to them. This is the largest growth area with the most expansion in the judicial process. They include the special or problem-solving courts, such as drug court, domestic violence court, gun court, and reentry court. There are other special courts, which provide unique circumstances for judges, inasmuch as the judge, as in the first case, sees the case through from beginning to end, maintaining jurisdiction and oversight. Or, as in the second case, the court may pick up the offenders as they are about to reenter the community and ensure that reentry is a smooth transition in which the needs of the criminal justice client are met with appropriate resources.

Many more of these special courts have emerged around the country, following the documented success of drug court. This is not to suggest that these other courts will be as successful as drug court (there has been insufficient research to state that they actually are successful as of yet), but the model holds the potential for greater success. In these cases, the judge is no longer the generalist of the court, but becomes an authority in the special circumstances of victims and offenders as well as the more effective means of management to prevent future recurrences of the crime, while maintaining the welfare of the victim, the offender, and society.

Program staff of the court, depending upon funding sources, may operate in independent units or may report to the probation department with work assigned to probation officers.

Working for the court, in any capacity, is distinctly different from employment in the other areas of the criminal justice system (law enforcement and corrections).

6

The Federal Government

INTRODUCTION

The federal government is the most diverse and complex set of criminal justice agencies to understand. Some agencies are relatively small, while others have been extensively developed. Each agency has its own set of requirements because of the establishing legislation for the agency. Some operate exclusively in the United States (such as the FBI), while others work exclusively beyond the continental boundaries of the United States (such as the CIA).

The U.S. Bureau of Labor informs us that the federal government is the largest employer in the nation with more than two million law enforcement and civilian employees, including about 95,000 who are authorized to carry firearms. These employees occupy more than four hundred different positions.

Employees of state and local branches of law enforcement may work their entire careers in one state or one community. However, federal officers know from the moment of the application that they are not constrained by location and may have sudden relocation not only to other states or areas under U.S. protection but also to foreign countries. Approximately half of the federal workforce is located in the District of Columbia, New York, California, Texas, and Florida. These locales are the major sites of U.S. offices, border protection, import/export security, and other sensitive assignments related to U.S security.

The work of federal law enforcement is distinctly different from state and local police departments. The majority of local police work happens on the beat and while responding to motor vehicle violations. The federal law enforcement officer is more likely to respond to white collar or corporate crime and violence, counterfeiting, drug smuggling, drug production and distribution, postal fraud, environmental threats, and protective services for the president and other high-ranking government officials, including when traveling abroad. A simple breakdown of officers is to describe them as either investigative or uniformed. Park police[1] and game wardens are two, and there are others, in the uniformed service. The investigative force is extensive and includes the better-known agencies of the FBI, CIA, DEA, EPA, ATF, and the Secret Service. Some of the lesser-known would include the Postal Service and the Department of Agriculture. It is not uncommon for there to be overlap of services between the departments, cooperative ventures, and at times competition between the agencies because of events or investigations that enter into the responsibilities of more than one of the federal agencies. The list of agencies above helps to indicate the vast diversity of employment in the federal service.

THE FEDERAL GOVERNMENT EMPLOYMENT SEARCH

The federal government is somewhat unique when it comes to postings for positions. In all likelihood, the federal government probably receives a greater number of job applicants than any state or local personnel office. The website for job openings is www.usajobs.gov, or the Federal Jobs Digest at www.jobfed.com. *Note: Jobs are usually posted for one week only.* This means that if you are interested in a specific job(s), you must make weekly visits to the website for updates. The large volume of applicants has led the federal government to use private agencies to screen potential applicants for them. With this in mind, it is even more critical that your application process is meticulous. You should:

1. *Adhere to all dates.* If you are late submitting the application, it will probably be discarded. Be careful to send in the application by the

due date, as well as any supporting documents, or if given a time frame, then send the documents within the allowable time frame.

2. *Do not leave blank spaces on your application.* Blank spaces tell the reviewer that something is missing or that you may be hiding something. Blank spaces are a job killer. Blank spaces may result in the immediate rejection of your application.

3. *Double-check that your application is complete.* Go over the application line by line. Review the job posting. Highlight on the posting the application requirements. Check each requirement to ensure that you have successfully answered/provided for each requirement and each document.

4. *Review your KSAs.* Federal employment is very specific about matching the right person with the right position. *KSAs* mean *Knowledge, Skills*, and *Abilities*. To put it another way, the KSAs should be represented on your application through the answers to the following questions:

- What do you know?
- What have you been trained to do? and
- Can you apply this knowledge to real-life situations?

KSAs are critical in your résumé. If they are not incorporated correctly, your résumé will very likely be rejected.

Knowledge, Skills, and Abilities (KSAs) are the requirements needed to perform a job that are demonstrated through qualifying experience, education, or training.

Each vacancy announcement will list the KSAs required in terms of "specialized experience," or "selective factor" requirements. In determining whether you qualify for a certain position, reviewers will evaluate your education and experience against the KSAs for each position. Because each position is different, the requirements for each will be different.

When you apply for federal positions, it is important for you to show that you meet the "specialized experience" and "selective factor" requirements for the position in your application package.

You can do this by either including the information in your basic application or by addressing these requirements separately from your application. Go to the following website for KSA information: www.csrees.usda.gov/about/jobs_faq.html.[2]

If you choose to address your KSAs separately, you should keep your responses brief and to the point. You need to relate your responses to the requirements of the job for which you are applying, and you should give examples that clearly demonstrate how your knowledge, skills, and abilities meet the requirements of the specific position. If you choose to rely on your basic application rather than write separate responses to the KSAs, you should be sure your application covers all the KSAs so the reviewers don't have to read between the lines to connect your basic application to the KSAs. As the applicant, you are responsible for showing how your education and experience meet the requirements for the posted position.

If you are unsure of how to write a KSA, you have the option of going to the above-mentioned website. A second option is to visit www.writeKSA.com. This website will help you write your KSAs for a fee of about $30. There are several other websites that provide sample KSAs. One website is www.reference.com/motif/business/free-ksa-samples.

5. *Make sure your résumé accurately answers the three most important questions.* These include: What do you know? What have you been trained to do? Can you apply it?
6. *Highlight your skills.* The reviewers of your application will be looking for those specialized skills, talents, and aptitudes that match you with the needs of the job.
7. *Do not assume that your résumé for one federal job is appropriate for all federal jobs.* Different jobs will list specific KSAs for that job. Make your résumé reflect the ways in which you possess the required KSAs. Prioritize them according to the position posted. In some cases it may be best to create a section on your résumé that addresses the KSAs specific to the job posting.

Citizenship

You must be a U.S. citizen or become a naturalized citizen to qualify for federal employment. On very rare occasions, waivers are available to legal aliens for hard-to-fill positions when no qualified U.S. citizens are available; however, the applicant must also qualify according to U.S. Labor and Immigration rules.

Education Requirements

The education requirement for careers in federal agencies varies from agency to agency. Some agencies, such as the FBI, are very specific if you consider the diversity of academic study that is acceptable: accounting, electrical engineering, information technology, or computer science; fluency in a foreign language; or a degree from an accredited law school. Consider these other requirements for the FBI: two or three years of professional work experience; one year of law enforcement experience may be substituted for an advanced degree; and the successful completion of the FBI training academy, with eighteen weeks of training located at the U.S. Marine Corps base in Quantico, Virginia.

Age Requirements

Many federal criminal justice positions have a maximum age at which employment must be initiated due to federal law enforcement pension requirements. However, in certain situations, a waiver may be granted that extends that requirement.

Some federal agency age requirements include:

- The administrative office of the U.S. courts: maximum age 37; positions include probation officers, pretrial services officer, statisticians, and investigators.
- U.S. Marshal's service: minimum age 21 and maximum age 36.
- Federal air marshal: maximum age 40.
- Federal Bureau of Investigation agent: maximum age 34.
- Immigration and customs enforcement agent: minimum age 21 and maximum age 35.

- Immigration and Naturalization Service (border patrol) agent: minimum age 21 and maximum age 34.
- Bureau of Alcohol, Tobacco, and Firearms agent: minimum age 21 and maximum age 35.
- Drug Enforcement Administration agent: minimum age 21 and maximum age 36.
- U.S. parks police officer: minimum age 21 and maximum age 37; mandatory retirement at age 57.[3]
- U.S. fish and game warden[4]: minimum age 21 and maximum age 37.
- U.S. Secret Service agent[5]: minimum age 21 and maximum age 37.
- Treasury enforcement agent: maximum age is the date immediately preceding an individual's 37th birthday (see résumé James F .Kenny, PhD, provided in Appendix 1).[6]

SALARIES

Federal salaries are commonly more generous than those found in state government. Salaries are affected by the type of job, length of service, and promotions. Salaries are based on performance and by testing. For example, federal agent salaries begin in excess of $60,000 a year. The U.S. Bureau of Labor Statistics reports that national median pay in 2005 for police officers and deputy sheriffs is $47,560.[7]

BACKGROUND CHECKS

Applicants for federal employment will undergo rigorous background checks in an effort to eliminate anyone who may be detrimental to the work of the hiring agency. These are investigations into the personal conduct and character of the applicant. The background check will minimally include criminal history, references, previous employment history, credit checks, and checks of social networking sites.

Qualified applicants must also complete an employment panel interview prior to final selection. Normally, interviews are held within the general area (about 250 miles round trip) from where the applicant resides.

Applicants must pay travel expenses to and from the interview site and to their first employment location.

THE FEDERAL BUREAU OF PRISONS (BOP)

(See Bob Hood's profile provided in Appendix 1.)

The Federal Bureau of Prisons (BOP) prides itself on its professionalism. Retired warden Robert Verdyn, who rose from the ranks of correctional officer to warden, has no tolerance for his officers being called "guards" because of their training and performance. He once remarked that being a "warden" was "the best job in world." The BOP opened its first training academy for correctional officers in 1930 in New York, and it is among the earliest of prison systems to open an academy.

The BOP requires that an employee must be hired in the agency prior to their 37th birthday, but for certain job titles this may be waived to age 40:

> The Attorney General has determined that the initial appointment of employees into Federal Bureau of Prisons law enforcement positions must be prior to their 37th birthday, with the following exceptions: Physician Assistant, Medical Officer, Dental Officer, Registered Nurse, Nurse Practitioner, and Chaplains of some faith traditions. Psychologists may be waived up to the date immediately preceding their 40th birthday.[8]

The Federal Bureau of Prisons has a central office located in Washington, D.C., and is operated through six regional offices throughout the United States. The BOP operates 185 prisons and camps, 14 privately managed facilities, and 5 community corrections management facilities that house more than 215,000 federal prisoners.[9] A visit to their website will provide a broad perspective of the number of prisons and types of correctional services.

ORIENTATION TRAINING

All persons appointed to the Federal Bureau of Prisons must successfully complete in-service training as a condition of employment, including

200 hours of formal training within the first year of employment. This includes orientation to the physical plant, familiarization with policies and procedures, and techniques for supervising and communicating with inmates in their daily activities.

Several examples of positions in the BOP include the following:

- Chaplain
- Clinical psychologist
- Corrections officer
- Dentist
- Medical doctor
- Nurse practitioner
- Physician's assistant
- Registered nurse
- Social worker
- Administrative staff
- Warden

Orientation training includes:

- 80 hours of institutional familiarization at the facility.
- 120 hours of specialized training at the Federal Law Enforcement Training Center (FLETC), which serves as the BOP residential training center located at Glynco, Georgia,[10] normally within the first sixty days after appointment and as scheduled by the Employee Services Department. This training includes four components: firearms, self-defense, written academic test on policies and procedures, and the physical abilities test (PAT).

The physical abilities test consists of:

- Dummy drag: Drag a 75-pound dummy 3 minutes continuously for a minimum of 694 feet.
- Climb and grasp: Climb rungs of a ladder and retrieve an item; ideal requirement 7 seconds.
- Obstacle course: Ideal requirement 58 seconds.

- Run and cuff: Run one-fourth mile and apply handcuffs; ideal requirement 2 minutes, 35 seconds.
- Stair climb: Climb up and down 108 steps with a 20-pound weight belt; ideal requirement 45 seconds.[11]

All applicants must meet the physical requirements for positions for which they are being considered. This examination will be conducted without cost to the applicant, usually by a federal medical officer, and will also include a urinalysis test for drug detection. Applicants should not wait to get to the academy to get themselves into shape. Successful applicants will be in good physical condition prior to reporting for training. The academy schedule is so rigorous that the applicant will not have time to diet and exercise outside the required program.

The Bureau of Prisons, in conjunction with the U.S. Public Health Service (PHS), offers well-qualified students an excellent employment opportunity through the Senior Commissioned Officer Student Training and Extern Program (COSTEP). Through Senior COSTEP, students in select health-related fields of study are commissioned as ensigns in PHS during the final year of academic study toward a qualifying degree or residency. Students receive full salary and benefits in exchange for an employment commitment at the sponsoring agency after graduation. For more information, call (202) 353-4110.

COSTEP is a work-study partnership between students, educational institutions, and various federal agencies. It offers students valuable work experience directly related to their field of study and provides formal periods of work and study while they are attending school. After completion of academic and work requirements, students may be eligible for permanent employment.

The Student Temporary Employment Program (STEP) provides temporary employment opportunities that can last for as long as the individual is a student. Employment does not need to be related to the student's academic field. These positions are located in the central office, in Washington, D.C. For more information, call (202) 307-3177.

The Summer Temporary Employment Program creates training and work opportunities in a wide variety of positions for individuals who can work only during summer months. The work ranges from office support, trades, and labor occupations, to positions in professional fields. These begin about mid-May and end on September 30. Applications are typically accepted from December through April 15. For more information, call (202) 307-3177.

Over the past thirty years, the bureau has trained more than four hundred doctoral-level psychologists, and each of the ten psychology pre-doctoral internship programs continues this commitment to training by providing eligible clinical and counseling graduate students with a well-rounded, high-quality experience. Each program strives to prepare interns for entry-level service as a practicing clinical or counseling psychologist. While individual training sites employ different training models to achieve this objective, all training sites have several common features.

VOLUNTEER, INTERNSHIPS, EXTERNSHIPS, WORK-STUDY, AND SUMMER EMPLOYMENT PROGRAMS

To become a volunteer, you should contact the Federal Bureau of Prisons facility closest to you. Volunteers should apply six months in advance of their anticipated start date. This will allow for an appropriate background check to be completed. All inquiries should be referred to the attention of the institution volunteer coordinator (IVC). A complete listing of IVCs may be found in the appendix of the *Community Volunteer Handbook* (see www.bop.gov/jobs/volunteer_handbook.pdf).

Each federal training site may provide interns with special training opportunities. These opportunities will be specific to that site. Some examples of training offered include: forensic assessment, substance abuse treatment, or behavioral medicine. Some training provides experiences with special treatment populations, including geriatric, female, HIV-positive, or violent offenders.

Internship opportunities exist in many of the legal branches in the Office of General Counsel including: labor law, commercial law, real estate and environmental law, litigation, discrimination complaints and ethics, legislative and correctional issues, and the legal administrative branch (FOIA). Among the experiences provided are opportunities to handle projects that broaden legal experience and knowledge. Interns are taught to conduct legal research and to draft legal memoranda, opinions, and correspondence. Eligibility for employment includes completion of a first semester of law school. There are summer and full-year internships during which the student may volunteer.

The U.S. Department of Justice uses an online application process. Candidates may complete and submit an application electronically through the Office of Attorney Recruitment and Management's website at www.usdoj.gov/oarm.

SUMMARY

Federal employment opportunities are perhaps the greatest in scope of any employment agency. Similar to other governmental employment, the process of finding a job that interests you, waiting for an opening, the application process (among the more rigorous of all applications), waiting for acceptance, going through training, to finally be given an assignment is a very long progression. You will need patience and endurance to work it through from beginning to end. There are those who will become discouraged. We suggest that you look at the length of the process as opportunity. Once you have decided to pursue this as a career path, there are many courses of preparatory action. In addition to what we have already detailed, such as interview preparation, you can do more. The first step would be to familiarize yourself with the specific agency of interest, learn its history and scope of operation, and familiarize yourself with some incidents (cases) associated with it. Make a list of what requirements you already match and which you may fall short of. Develop a plan that will allow you to address each shortcoming—and set attainable goals. Review the KSAs and firm up any area that falls short or in which you are not strong. For that matter, review your abilities in each area and seek to improve them all. Personal growth must always be an ongoing process. Your strengths and abilities will determine the outcomes in your job search and your career advancement.

7

Getting the Job, Entering the Field, and Career Advancement

INTRODUCTION

This chapter will provide the tools you need to prepare to search for, pursue, and attain employment and advancement in the criminal justice system. Hopefully by now you have read about the different fields in criminal justice and are not too badly confused. Optimistically, you have begun to narrow the area(s) in which you might be interested. With any luck, you are not feeling overwhelmed with the diversity of positions and you have begun to understand the difference between dramatized versions of jobs and the real work that is done in the profession. There are strategies and tools you can develop that will make your employment search more efficient and productive. While efficiency will make the process smoother, we all realize that in the end, getting the job is what matters. This may seem ambitious for one chapter. However, your preparation for the employment position also sets the stage for your advancement in the criminal justice system. This is true whether you continue your career within the starting agency or shift your career as opportunity presents itself into other criminal justice agencies, or perhaps even outside the criminal justice field.

FINDING JOB OPENINGS

Finding job openings may be as important as actually attaining employment. You can only apply for the jobs that you know about. Part of the answer is to expand the areas in which you search for employment opportunities. In addition to any that are mentioned in this chapter, you should ask others who have jobs to which you aspire how they found their jobs, or where they looked. In either case you may find places to look that you previously did not explore.

In Chapter 2, "Exploring Careers in Criminal Justice," the value of visiting potential worksites, websites, professors, internships, and volunteer opportunities were discussed in some depth. This chapter will begin with more ideas for locating job openings, as well as discuss the importance of tools such as a cover letter and résumé, the practice of networking, identifying appropriate references, completing applications, preparing for and sitting for an interview, taking entrance exams, preparing for academy training, some points on personal presentation, how to conduct yourself during the first days on the job, and after all this, what to do should you find that the job you have been hired for is *not* for you. The last point may come as a shock, but it happens. As you go through the process of the search, exposure, interviews, training, and reporting to the job, things occur that may warn you that this is not a job you want. If this happens, it is not the end of the world! It is simply a wake-up call and an opportunity to move on—to find more satisfying employment and life satisfaction elsewhere.

Jobs are posted everywhere: on bulletin boards, on websites, in human resources and personnel departments, in newspapers, through friends and colleagues, and via search agencies (or headhunters[1]). Some jobs are posted quietly, that is, they are not advertised because the agency does not want to be overwhelmed with those they may consider to be non-candidates—they want someone special. You must be tenacious in your search. You can go to some sources every day, such as Indeed.com, and find new postings. Other sources only come out periodically or are not posted at all. Some agencies or companies do not like to post for jobs and instead prefer to search by word of mouth. If you have made the rounds of career fairs, built your network (which we will discuss later), and taken advantage of every occasion to make yourself known, then you may be one of those who will be reached out to by an agency, one of your colleagues, or someone else who is aware of your credentials and your ability to fill the slot. The answer to this is to prepare, update, and continue your personal development, and *network, network, network*.

What follows is more specific information about what you should do when you find an appealing job opening.

READING THE JOB POSTING

Read the posting carefully. Use a highlighter to make the important points in the posting stand out. You want to make sure that you understand exactly what the hiring agent is looking for and that you possess the qualifications for the job. Read the job specifications and qualifications thoroughly, and understand and adhere to deadlines and specific requests. Oftentimes, there are do's and don'ts listed in the postings. Obviously, you must be able to fulfill the do's. However, when a posting tells you not to do something, *DON'T DO IT!* For example, the posting may state that you should *not* include transcripts or references because they will be requested later. Do not think that including them will help you when you are specifically instructed not to do so. Dates and deadlines are critical. You *must* adhere to them. If your application is late, it may not even be looked at. If the posting says "Until a choice is made," then you need to submit your materials as soon as possible. In some cases, the postmarked date on the application may count toward your score; that is, the earlier the submission the better. In some cases, the date on the application may even qualify you for a move up on the list because your application was received before another. A note of caution, however: Speed can actually become detrimental if you sacrifice quality. Make sure your supporting documents are well-prepared.

THE COVER LETTER

(See the sample letters provided in Appendix 2.)

You should include a cover letter with your application. The letter should be professional in appearance and in content. At the top of the letter, you should include the title of the position for which you are applying and the position number if listed. A specific area may have posted for several positions, and you want to make sure that your application materials reach the appropriate reviewer. Your letter is an opportunity to specifically state why you are applying and to briefly cover any special skills, experiences, or events in your life that make you stand out or that you want to emphasize because they enhance your presentation. These are generally events that are not included on your résumé. The letter is your opportunity to state why you are the best candidate for the job, *not* to rehash your application or résumé. The points you emphasize may become interview talking points later. If you have never written a cover letter, see a counselor for guidance and review of the letter.

Main Features of a Cover Letter

- Name
- Address
- Phone number
- E-mail address. (Take a look at your e-mail address. It should be professional. If it is cutesy or includes terms meant to denote some aspect of your personality, such as "dark master" or another appellation, then set up a new e-mail name and address for yourself.)
- Date
- The name of person to whom the application is being sent
- Their title
- Company name
- Company address
- Posted position title and position number
- Dear _____, [salutation]
- Paragraph 1: Description of why you are writing. Explain why you are interested in the position.
- Paragraph 2: Description of your qualifications. Provide solid experiences and examples of strong qualities that make you a viable candidate.
- Paragraph 3: Addendums to your application package: résumé, references, the fact that transcripts (if required) will follow, and a request for an interview.

- Sincerely,
- Your name
- Sign your letter in black or blue ink. (Blue ink is often requested by some agencies because it indicates that this letter is not a copy of other letters that you have sent.)
- Enclosures
- The résumé
- References (if requested); otherwise say "upon request"

HOW IMPORTANT IS YOUR RÉSUMÉ?

If a job interview is not predicated on a civil service test score, then your résumé may become the vehicle that will either get you the interview or result in rejection. Rejection, of course, may be the result of failing to meet the qualifications. How you develop your résumé to meet those qualifications will be determined by your status, which is whether you are right out of college, looking for advancement, hoping to change professions, in the middle of your career, or influenced by some other factor.

The bottom line is that your résumé should qualify you and in some way make you stand out. Résumés that arrive in response to a job offer are usually put in a pile and then scanned later. A common practice by agencies is to hire an independent contractor to do a job search or résumé review. Therefore, it is important that your résumé be accurate and present the information in such a way as to catch the eye of the reviewer for further assessment. The content you provide is your opportunity to have your résumé receive more than a cursory glance. Your résumé, by itself, will not earn you a job, but it may open the door for future consideration. Your résumé must get you an interview where you can sell yourself.

On a very basic level, your résumé reassures the employer that you meet the most basic requirements for the position. It must also advise the employer what you bring to the table and convince them that you are an individual who possesses the professional standards and skills for the job. The appearance of your résumé can be the initial argument that you do possess the professional qualities and skills necessary for the position. Think of your résumé as an advertisement that must get the employer's attention.

Résumé Tips

(See Appendix 4 for additional help in putting together a solid résumé.)

- Make it professional.
- Use good paper.
- Don't clutter the résumé with details in small fonts.
- Carefully consider any use of highlights, such as bolds and italics. Too many of these are distracting. Each emphasized item must make a point.
- Whenever possible emphasize on the résumé those personal abilities that correspond to the employer's stated needs. Place experience first, education second. (If you have an excellent cumulative grade-point average, list it. If you graduated cum laude or summa or magna cum laude, list it.)
- The exception to putting your experience first is if you are a recent graduate. In this case, list your education first because often the recruiter must verify that you meet the educational requirements.
- Consider not listing your cumulative grade-point average if it is under 3.0.
- Specifically match your talents and abilities to the employer's stated needs.
- Cover the basic requirements of the position (education, experience, etc.).
- Specify your awards and accolades.
- List any certificates you have earned.
- List your education, experience, and other evidence of your talent (such as awards) in reverse chronological order.
- List your membership in and service to professional organizations. (Caution: We now live in a world in which political correctness has become overemphasized. While there are those who might flaunt their ethnicity or other cultural traits by listing any associated organizations, this is not wise to include on a résumé.)
- List any volunteer experience and community service work.
- Do not list references unless specifically required to do so.
- State the job you seek as an objective.

- Be honest.
- Do not list your political affiliation.

Once the résumé is completed, always carry copies with you. Note: Carry *copies*—more than one—because you never know who you will meet or how many copies of your résumé will be needed to jump-start your career.

JOB KILLERS

Hopefully, you are reading this sooner rather than later. We live in an electronic age that exposes all of us to inquiry. Many employers now Google job applicants and research them on Facebook, YouTube, LinkedIn, and other social and professional websites for personal background information. Potential employers may even ask for the passwords to your accounts. Give them the password, but be aware of what they might find. The pictures you post (the one with you sprawled out on a couch with a liquor bottle in your hand will not be seen as complimentary), the stories you write (wild times at 3:00 a.m. on a weekday will not be seen as indicative of someone who is prepared to work), and the information you provide (that new tattoo depicting gang symbols) on each of these sites says something about you. True story: One young man completed a DEA interview in which the interviewer asked whether he had ever experimented with drugs. The applicant emphatically replied, "No!" The interviewer then pulled out a picture of a social media posting of the applicant and his friend with what they described as the "world's biggest blunt"—which they had just rolled themselves. The interviewer asked for an explanation, and the applicant was turned down for the job. The applicant committed at least two major sins here: He lied, and he was seen with an undesirable substance on a social media post.

One careless slip may be enough for a potential employer to make a judgment that immediately removes you from the pool of candidates. Once you post something, it is out there forever. These are photos and statements that ultimately characterize who you are as a person, and once they are posted, they cannot be withdrawn.

NETWORKING

This may be the most valuable tool you possess throughout your career.

Networking Defined

Networking is the ability to meet people who may have knowledge, advice, or contacts that contribute to your career search, advance your career, or help to prepare you for life after your career.

Networking Tools

These include your résumé, your list of contacts, your personal presentation, your speech, and how you dress.

The A, B, and C of Networking

A. To help you select a career
B. To help you advance your career
C. To prepare you for what comes after your career

Networks are lines of communication that can develop into important and dependable colleagues and potentially lifelong friends. Colleagues developed through networking are invaluable sources of support, encouragement, advice, guidance, and information that improve the quality of our professional lives. Similarly, as we network, we join other networks that become interconnected. Notice the impact that the professional networking site LinkedIn has already made on the lives of people. Look to see how expansive LinkedIn and Facebook have become.

Former president Lyndon B. Johnson once attended a funeral of someone related to a senator with whom he only had a passing acquaintance. That senator later gave a vote to legislation that was important to President Johnson. This illustrates an important point about networking: Take advantage of opportunities to be available for your fellow man, whether they are friend or colleague. You never know when you will need them or when they will be there for you.

Networking begins before you ever land your first job interview. By the time you are reading this, you will have already considered at least one career and probably several others. Now it is time to get serious.

Who do you know that you can speak with? You may have already started down this path with a relative, perhaps a friend of the family, or you may have heard a presentation that caught your attention. Now you can begin to learn more about your choice(s). You will do some readings in course assignments. Read some more and start writing down questions you can ask those you know and others whom you may encounter. You want to be prepared for anyone you meet. Similarly, always review the list of "My Ten Points." You are waging a campaign for your career. You don't know when you will meet that person who may be your entrée into the field of your choice or perhaps even a career change that you have not considered. Career preparation and networking are daily activities.

In all likelihood, if you network, it may lead to that first job interview. Many jobs never make it to a posting, whether classified or even within offices. These jobs often exist only in the minds of the hiring authority. The authority knows what is wanted and may not seek a rush of applicants.

Getting the job, advancement, changing your career path, preparing for life in retirement, and much more can be enhanced by networking. Personal preparation is an ongoing effort. Whether you are just starting out, looking for advancement, preparing for a job that will open up, or perhaps seeking to make changes in your position, there are deliberate and calculated actions you can take. Think of this as a battle plan, a strategy that is designed to promote you, or to achieve what you want.

An Eleven-Step Networking Strategy for Career Development

The following is a step-by-step strategy that will help you plan and negotiate your career from finding the first job to settling into a comfortable and satisfying retirement.

1. **Design a personal strategy.** This is preparation. This is your opportunity to chart your career. This is about what you want to accomplish and what tools you possess to achieve that first position.

Ask yourself, What is my ideal job? Next, assume that you are successful, then ask yourself, Where do I want to be in five years? This should be followed by: In ten years? In twenty? When do I want to retire? What will it take for me to retire? At this stage of the game, it may be a bit of a stretch to think about what you want to do in retirement, but this strategy will set the stage for that time. You do not have to answer all of these questions at this time, but some answers will begin the process and help you find the correct path for the future. You cannot know where your planning and experiences will lead you, or to put it another way, what doors they may open. One door opening may mean an entire shift of plans for the future; those shifts may be the difference between success and failure or perhaps between just getting by and being satisfied in your professional life.

Caution: As you draft your plan, the future may seem intimidating. Our role models and heroes may seem larger than life. Refer to Appendix 1 for a list of profiles of prominent people who have served in the field of criminal justice. Select those who most closely relate to your personal aspirations. Read their profiles. Some started out in entry-level positions, and had they remained there, they would have had careers served in anonymity. Those we have profiled were selected because they broke out—they had a plan and they reached for new heights, even unexpected heights. This is not a matter of whether you can see yourself in their shoes, but whether you can implement your own plans. Think big, large, grand—what do you have to lose except success if you do not plan and instead leave your future to chance? You can and should place each idea you have into your plan. This is grist for the mill. This is material for evaluation now and in the future for what is good for you.

Put this plan into writing. If you have a home office or a workspace that permits a display, put your plan on the wall; keep it in your face. The plan is a combination of where you want to be, what you want to do, and what you hope to accomplish. This plan is a work in action. The plan will undergo change with new experiences, accomplishments, and setbacks. Do not call setbacks "unfortunate"; we suggest you look at them differently—as opportunities, or learning experiences. Did you ever notice that even when times are bad, some people just seem to keep moving forward or manage to recover that much more quickly? Those people are not sitting back and waiting for opportunity to come to them; they are already prepared and even now are preparing for the next prospect, the next change, no matter how unexpected. Hint: Look up *paradigm shift*, an important and often misunderstood idea. Paradigm shifts are always the things to come, the unexpected. Preparation for the future is ongoing.

2. **List all of the positions in which you are interested.** Look at your list and determine which items have qualifications you already meet. Remember, your career starts by getting your foot in the door. Prioritize your list. You can advance this step by recognizing that you are interested in positions for which you do not possess qualifications. Now, you can decide whether to get those qualifications. Or, if they are beyond your reach (and part of this decision-making process is to consider whether the pursuit of those credentials will be a future goal), determine whether they may be more attainable in the future.

3. **Review your credentials for each position.** Highlight those positions that meet your credentials. Which other positions are you interested in? Highlight them with a different color. There are at least three benefits to be gained by this step. The first is obvious. Those for which you already qualify will be your first process in the job market. Second, you will know which other positions interest you and you can identify which qualifications you lack. Third, remember we mentioned above that some people are always preparing for change. You just entered that world. You may choose to pursue missing credentials for these other positions. Keep moving forward. That which stops moving goes nowhere.

4. **List anyone and everyone you can think of who has a relationship to each position, and relist them if there is any overlap.** Utilize your friends and others to provide you with contacts. From time to time update your list to include new contacts and their information. Anytime you meet someone new, ask for a card, then write on the card some notes about the circumstances of the meeting and especially if that person asked you to contact them for something. Don't dismiss such a statement. This person may have seen something in you that you have not considered. Volunteering is a valuable way to meet new people and to demonstrate personal skills. This kind of work can add to the diversity of your contacts. Here is a

list of potential contacts with whom to start building your network. Remember, you may add others to this list. As you encounter them, they may say something that catches your attention. Your task is to enter the names of any contacts alongside each category listed below.

Family members
Friends
Former employers
School guidance counselors
Business owners
Local politicians
Neighbors
Professors
Former coworkers
College career placement office workers
Fellow college alumni

When it comes to networking, always be prepared. You never know when someone will just pop up, such as a fellow shopper in a supermarket or perhaps while you are relaxing on a beach. Chance opportunities do happen, and the value for you will lie in your readiness and acceptance of the moment.

5. **Prioritize who is closest to the positions of primary importance.** Start with your A list, those closest to jobs for which you are already qualified. Contacting someone you don't know for the first time may seem awkward or be difficult for you. Perhaps someone you know can be your first point of contact, and then become your entrée to those you have never met before.

6. **Review your résumé and make copies.** You must keep your résumé up-to-date. There are different types of résumés, and there is a skill to writing a winning résumé. Remember, this is one of the important tools that will help you get your foot in the door. If you have any doubts about your résumé or your ability to produce a good one, then it may be worth your while to hire a professional service to review your résumé for you. ResumeEdge.com is one site that will do this for a fee.

7. **Review your list of "My Ten Points."** This was discussed in Chapter 3. Review these points periodically so that the responses come naturally and remain applicable to your most recent experiences. These are the points you want to make to potential employers, and they are safe responses to tricky questions. Remember, you don't want to be caught flat-footed during an interview with a question that confuses you or leaves you stammering for an answer.

8. **Make an appointment to visit each of your contacts personally.** (Be on time for any scheduled meetings!) You should make an appointment and be professional even if the person is a close friend or colleague. You want to be considered a professional, so you should begin to act like one. Bring a résumé with you, along with your file of credentials and a notebook. Perhaps you will be asked for a résumé or during the interview there will be an opening for you to say, "I brought my résumé and other documents with me if you would care to review them." Your ability to produce a document upon request shows that you are prepared and proactive about your job search. There may also be questions about something you have not thought of. Perhaps the contact would like to see other supporting documentation. Make a note of what they request and specify when you will provide the documentation. This should occur within forty-eight hours or sooner after your meeting. Don't let someone move in front of you with their résumé and other information because you delayed getting the requested information to the interviewer—keep the process going if the ball is in your court.

Here is some guidance for that initial meeting with a contact. First, be goal-directed and demonstrate that you know what you want. This could be one of your ten points; that is, you will make a specific statement about your goals. And keep your questions to the point. Your statement may begin with, "I am looking for a job in..." Your questions should include something like, "Is there someone you can refer me to?" Never forget to ask, "May I use your name as a reference?" Do not assume that it is acceptable to do this; your contact will appreciate the courtesy. You are establishing a relationship with that contact because they have already established their value in a field, so be sure to ask if they have any advice for you. People like to talk about themselves, and you are meeting them because they are experts. That question will give them the opportunity to respond from their level of expertise.

Many jobs never make it to a posting, whether classified or even within offices. These jobs often exist only in the minds of the hiring authority. The authority knows what is wanted and does not seek a rush of applicants. If you manage to catch the attention of a hiring authority and you are prepared (with résumé and credentials in hand), you may become the successful applicant for the unposted position.

You should come away from each meeting with more than what that person can offer. In other words, you are learning about conducting a job search, beginning to anticipate what might happen during an interview, and discovering how you will respond to a job posting. You should assess the results for what will be said about you. That is, you do not want to ask someone for a reference unless you are sure of what they will say. For example, you do not want a letter to begin with, "[Your name] was in my Intro course and my experience with him was only for those fifteen weeks. I can tell you he received excellent grades, but the time period was too brief to provide much other information of substance." Such remarks will not help you get your foot in the door! You want someone to be able to say specific things, such as that you were on time, you work well with others, you can ask intelligent questions, etc. You want your contact to be able to provide specific examples of your work ethic and qualifications.

Whether it is the person just starting out on a career search, or even a seasoned veteran, there is an error that many people make. After you have made a contact, *be sure to follow up!* It is just good manners, and it suggests to the contact that you are serious about your job search. In addition, people like to feel appreciated. While you may follow up in any number of ways, perhaps the most simple is to draft a short thank-you note expressing your appreciation for the help and advice if it was given. This may provide you with a little edge—you are reminding them that you met, and a card is not imposing. Finally, even if the contact does not result in a job, send a thank-you note or make a personal call anyway to let them know that they were helpful.

9. **Maintain a network file**. The computer, flash drive, or another portable electronic device is a good place to maintain and back up your network file. The important points for the file include name, title, address, phone number, and agency. Make notes about how and where you met, colleagues you have in common, and discussions you have had.

You can never say everything about yourself in one conversation. In fact, one initial conversation may only allow for generalities. Most conversations do not allow you to present yourself with all of your best attributes in an organized fashion. But your résumé can do that for you. It is never too soon to prepare one, and after it has been prepared, you should continually update it with your new accomplishments. (See sample résumés in Appendix 4.) Always carry a résumé with you, and be sure to protect it in an 8½ by 11-inch envelope.

You will probably begin to realize after a short while that your contacts have relationships with one another; after all, your contacts have their own lists of contacts that help them to excel in their careers. It is a small world, so act as you want to be treated and do not burn bridges. Your grace and respect for others will help you overcome many obstacles, and you will not have a bad reputation circulating among your contacts.

Networking is a two-way street. The contacts in your network also likely want to advance their careers. Through the network, you and they may share some common goals. When you find an opportunity that applies to someone in your network, go ahead and share it. The information may be regarding a job opening that does not interest you, or an article about something that you know someone else is interested in. For example, someone in the network may be looking for a particular item, perhaps a book or a documentary, and you happen to know of it. Send the information to them. Your generosity will be remembered. Keep in touch with those in your network. Even a brief e-mail to say hello can work wonders.

10. **Don't burn bridges.** A career is a long time. Along the way, you will encounter many people—both good and bad. They are liable to show up when you least expect them, perhaps as your newly appointed supervisor, or perhaps you have eclipsed them and they are now your subordinate. In either case, you do not need either a hostile boss or a hostile subordinate. Try to leave every encounter, job, and advancement, on the best possible terms. (See the section titled "Finding Out the Job Is Not for You, or How Do You Move On?" at the end of this chapter for more detailed information.)

11. **Maintain the network throughout your career.** Your network is like the old TV game show on which you were able to call a lifeline. Your contacts are there to provide career guidance, help you prepare for new positions, help you explore new options, be of assistance during tough times, and more. They are invaluable.

Networking Safety, or What Not to Do

You will meet many new people, both in person and on the Internet, as you go about building your network. Unfortunately, not everything about networking is positive. Things can happen outside the network that can hurt you. Similarly, there are things that you may do yourself outside an official capacity that can hurt you. We live in a world where our lives have become ever more transparent. Social networks by design and intention are meant to spread to others information about you—and that includes both good and bad information. You should take caution when providing addresses, phone numbers, and especially personal information, such as Social Security numbers. Social networking has made it too easy and too attractive to reveal a great many details about ourselves. Ask yourself, how much do you want someone to know about you? Is there information that you have revealed that you now see as embarrassing? Has someone else posted something about you that a) you would rather not have be shared, or b) you know is untrue? Pictures tell stories, and the viewer will make judgments. You cannot later say that something was unintended. If it is out there, you can't bring it back. Sometimes it is about perceptions. You may think something is within acceptable limits, but others have their own perceptions. For example, perhaps an opportunity opens up for someone, but as those in the hiring positions discussed that person, someone remarks, "Oh, he's a drinker." The potential hiree was not known for having a drinking problem, but the person making the comment remembers that every time he has seen the applicant at a function, he has had a drink in his hand. Such a perception is almost impossible to recover from, just as things that go out into cyberspace can never be withdrawn. As our mothers used to say: If you don't have something good to say, then say nothing! This is sage advice.

A former director was out to dinner with friends and made some unfavorable comments about his agency. He did not realize that one of his superiors was nearby and overheard the comments—he lost his job the next day. Let us add to the advice just given: Think before you speak!

The Last Word about Networking—It Works!

You should work to keep your network in place throughout your career. The network is a tool that, when used to your benefit, will assist you in your job search and with exploring career options. If you want a career, dress the part, speak like a professional, and be prepared with a résumé.

PREPARE, PREPARE, PREPARE

Stephen Covey's[2] *Seven Habits of Highly Successful People* is a powerful book that can help you prepare for a career and then become successful in that career. While each chapter provides good commonsense ideas, one of his foremost proposals is that as you develop and move forward, you must "Sharpen the Saw." There are so many ways you can use this advice. For example, keep your contacts up-to-date with new developments in your life that are important to your career. There are any number of ways you can improve yourself and make yourself more attractive to your employer—and to future employers. One of the better tools is to improve yourself as a writer. While there is a notion that this skill is honed in college, that is not always the truth. We become better writers as we practice our writing in different contexts. Those contexts include:

- Your résumé
- Letters (especially your skills in writing different types of letters)
- Reports

- Case notes
- Papers and articles

This is not a complete list of types of required writing, but it is a list of types of writing that you need to know about and in which you should hone your skills. The last item is one that students and others often find the most challenging, and for some it is very intimidating. When we write and/or publish our work, we expose our ability for many others to see, be critical of, and challenge. You must take risks, but there are ways to minimize those risks.

Write and allow others to read and be critical of what you write prior to submitting it. Give it to someone whom you trust and let them be frank with you about what you have written. Many colleges have writing labs that can help you. You can also help yourself. There are general guides to writing, and there are some that are more specific. For example, and assuming that you are seeking a career in criminal justice, you may wish to pick up a copy of William A. Johnson et al., *The Criminal Justice Student Writer's Manual.*[3] This is a well-thought-out guide to most of the problems encountered by those who attempt to write in this field and has specifics for different types of writing in the criminal justice profession.

There are many places you can seek publication for your work to get you started. These include letters and short articles to magazines and newspapers. The more challenging assignments will come as you hone your writing and research skills. These would include articles to peer-reviewed journals, but these provide greater status, and potentially greater exposure to those in the field. In addition, they look great on your résumé. The point should be obvious: Do not neglect your writing skills.

CAREER EXAMPLES

George wants to work in community corrections. He has joined and has been attending the monthly meetings of a professional association. In one month's newsletter, there is a listing for a position at a halfway house. He goes on the Internet to review the organization. He mentions the job to one of the members he has gotten to know, and that person knows a director in the organization whom he says he will call. The director is delighted to have a reference from someone he knows. George gets an interview and shows up well-prepared with his résumé and other documents. George gets the job.

Bill wants to be a corrections officer. He knows a family friend who is a corrections officer. The family friend explains that the work is tough and the hiring process is arduous, but he should not be discouraged. The friend suggests that Bill follow the steps carefully and call him for advice as he needs it. The friend arranges for a visit to a correctional institution. Bill is enthusiastic and starts the process. He follows up with the friend periodically, who advises him what will be coming up in the process, and Bill keeps his interest high. Bill is now making a career in corrections.

Margaret is unhappy with her current career choice and feels trapped because she has been with the same agency for ten years and is vested in their pension plan. She goes to Human Resources and speaks to a counselor, who reviews her résumé and experiences. Margaret learns that she can transfer from her present position to another one; however, she will have to qualify for the new position by taking a civil service test. Margaret has not taken any tests for a long time. The counselor suggests that she obtain a prep book, which will allow her to see the kinds of questions on the civil service exam and to take practice tests. The counselor also advises her that the more often she takes the tests, the better she will score. Margaret finds several positions that interest her, reviews the specifications for those jobs, and watches for test opportunities. Margaret has now taken several tests and has scored well enough to rank high on the lists and receive calls for interviews.

Sam is having dinner with friends and mentions that he would like to become a police officer. One of his friends knows a police officer and arranges for them to meet. The officer invites Sam to the station house and shows him around. He tells Sam that he will have to take the civil service test for law enforcement. In the meantime, he might qualify as a special officer, but he would have to go through training. As a special officer, Sam is able to demonstrate his commitment to the process. After taking the civil service test and completing police academy training, Sam is enthusiastically welcomed to a position on the police force.

In each of these instances, there are some key points to notice: 1) Be involved; 2) take action; 3) be prepared; 4) present yourself well; and 5) get the job! While these are fictitious examples, they are drawn from the authors' experiences with their students. These are examples of how to use the tool of networking.

PRACTICAL SUGGESTIONS

Many techniques, tools, and processes for networking have been discussed. However, there is much more to learn. While there are only a limited number of hours in a day, nevertheless, you must work to stay in touch with your network. There are times when you can do this casually, like over lunch or dinner, or perhaps during a game of tennis or a round of golf. An e-mail saying hello might be sufficient. Take the time to show an interest in the affairs of others; ask how they are.

Relationships should never be one-sided. There will be times when one of your contacts may serve the needs of another of your contacts. A network is a chain of relationships with reciprocity. LinkedIn offers the opportunity to cite other members' skills. You don't have to wait for someone to cite you; instead, take a moment and cite them for their abilities. Business cards are a great tool for helping people remember who you are; give them freely, but avoid handing them out indiscriminately or pushing someone to just "take one."

THE APPLICATION

As you progress in your job search, we recommend that you visit the Linke-dIn website, www.linkedin.com/job/law-enforcement-jobs/?trk=jserp_related_searches, for various listings of criminal justice jobs. Applications have rules for completion, which you must follow precisely. If they require applications to be typed, then type! We further recommend that when you visit the LinkedIn website that you download several applications, some for jobs you might currently be interested in and some that are not as immediately attractive. There are three purposes for this suggestion. First, we want you to see different types of applications and the various ways in which similar questions can be asked. Second, each of these downloaded applications can provide you with the opportunity to practice filling them out. We finally suggest that you save your practice applications for when you fill out a real application. Your practice answers can save you time and, more likely than not, help you to prevent making errors when you complete a real application.

Some agencies allow you start an application process (such as submitting a résumé) on their website, to which you may return later. Note: Be aware of information about sending your application over the Internet. This is particularly important if it specifies that the application process is complete once you send it. You must *be sure* that you have included *all* appropriate and *required* information *before* you send it. Always check the application twice before hitting Send. One suggestion is for you to download the application and fill it in away from the site. Then, once it is completed, go to the site and fill it out in one sitting. Always reread it thoroughly before submitting. This means to correct misspellings, incorrect grammar, and anything else that does not read well.

PRIOR ENCOUNTERS WITH THE POLICE

Arrests, criminal charges, and convictions all may have consequences along the road to criminal justice employment. They do not necessarily mean a dead end, but if handled inappropriately, they can result in immediate rejection from the employment process. In all likelihood there will be a box on the application form that requires you to check it if you have ever been arrested, charged with a crime, or convicted of one. *Be aware* that this does not ask for a conviction alone, but whether you have ever been arrested and/or charged. Failure to check the box and answer any questions relevant to these matters is considered a falsification of application. Generally, there will be a space to elaborate on the circumstances of your encounter with the police. And when you are selected for an interview, you will have the opportunity to explain the specifics of the encounter. You should be candid when you provide your explanation, neither downplaying nor embellishing. Do not make excuses, but if there are legitimate mitigating factors, then you may need to include them.

YOUR REFERENCES

You will have to determine whether to submit references with your application. Some jobs do not wish to have the references included; others do; some want letters of reference to accompany the application; and some application processes do not tell you that they want them or that they will request them later. Some application processes generate an automatic request for references as soon as you submit the application. Oftentimes, these applications also permit you to go back in and check the status of your application, and to see what letters, transcripts, or other documents have been received by the hiring authority.

Choose your references carefully. Each reference provided should know you and be able to speak not only to your qualifications, but to your character, as well. (Review the section on networking in this chapter for additional information about references.) While a reference does not need to be a lifelong best friend, they should be more than a recent or casual acquaintance. Think of what your reference can and is willing to say about you. Review the questions below to help in this assessment:

- Can they describe you in work circumstances?
- Can they describe you under stress?
- Can they attest to your knowledge and ability to deliver?
- Can they describe you developmentally?
- What do they know about your future aspirations?
- What can they say about your family or family background?
- Are they familiar with anecdotal incidents from your life?
- Can they speak to your successes?
- What do they know about the job to which you are applying and your suitability for the work?

These questions may help guide you in your selection of references.

You should also know the job for which you applying, including the title of the position. However, you should also be aware of the type of work you will be asked to perform. For example, if the job requires you to drive and you have an expired or suspended driver's license, you are setting yourself up for a problem during the interview process. Interview questions may revolve around the expected work. Most job descriptions will include sample descriptions of the work expected, and there may be other types of required work at the same location. Contact the work site and when possible make a visit. Have a list of questions prepared ahead of time that address the types of work performed there.

Quality preparation will be an asset when you request that someone write a reference for you. You may wish to provide them with some specific examples of work that is described in the posting and ask them to assess your ability to perform that type of task. Your reference can then address this specifically in the letter they will write for you.

THE EXAM

Many criminal justice positions require entrance or civil service examinations. You have a choice. You can go into the examination cold or you can prepare for the examination. If your career is important to you, then we strongly urge you to prepare. There are a variety of ways you can do this.

- Read books, websites, and other material about the agency and the job.
- Enroll in a test prep course.
- Obtain books specially written for the type of job you will be tested on. (Some prep manuals are listed for you in Appendix 8.)

THE INTERVIEW

(See Appendix 3.)

Presentation is everything. The interview begins as the door opens. Presentation refers to your appearance, your walk, your talk, your greeting, and how you have prepared yourself for the interview. Do you know who will be doing the interview? Do you understand the expected work performed in the position? What do you know about the agency? Who is the supervisor? Who are the clients? What is the mission statement? What is the salary? How does someone advance in the position or the company? What are the benefits? These are some of the questions you should be able to answer *before* you appear for the interview. Those answers you don't know you should be prepared to ask during the interview. At some point, the interviewer probably will ask you if you have any questions. Being prepared is impressive!

Know where you are going, plan the route, and arrive on time. Plan your travel to arrive early. Bring copies of all documents that you have sent ahead of time. In the event of multiple interviewers, someone may not have been presented with copies of your application, and it will demonstrate your preparedness if you can simply hand them out if that appears appropriate.

Bring additional information, such as copies of certificates, licenses, or awards that are relevant to the position.

Visit the hiring agency's website. Get answers to the questions listed in the beginning of this section. Make a note of any answers you cannot obtain from the website. These may become *your* questions during the interview.

A special note about waiting for an interview: Don't just sit there and do nothing. Bring a book, perhaps a book about the career work you intend to do or something else that is stimulating. This may be an excellent entrée into an interview. That is, the interviewer may see the book you are reading and ask what you think about it. Once more, this is something you should be prepared for. Prepare a response about the book. By the way, *before* you go in for the interview, be sure to use the restroom—do it early rather than later—and don't keep the interviewer waiting. You do not know how long the interview will be, and you do not want to be uncomfortable or to have to ask to leave the interview to use the restroom. Again, you should be prepared.

Big Note: Turn off your cell phone! The interview is more important than your call. Answering the cell phone during an interview is rude.

THE TRAINING ACADEMY

(You may wish to review Chapter 4, "Careers in Corrections," for more detailed information about academy training.)

The training academy may take place in any of several environments. There may be an academy that serves a region or one that serves a state. Perhaps it will be at the county college, but if the agency is very large, then the academy may be sponsored by the hiring agency. The academy training cycle may last from a few weeks to a few months. The recruit will receive a variety of training that is likely but not exclusively to include classroom instruction, firearms on a range, self-defense, first aid, excessive force, emergency response, and material that is specific to a job or a state. The training academy is only the beginning of your preparation for the job. Many recruits are clearly aware that when it comes to the job, there is the textbook and then there is on-the-job training. Oftentimes, academy training will end with a period of time spent doing on-the-job training with a seasoned officer/employee.

PREPARING FOR THE TRAINING ACADEMY

The training academy will be a test of your ability to learn and of your physical endurance. Get in shape mentally and physically before attending the academy. Chapter 3, "Careers in Law Enforcement," has already discussed how your participation in physical education classes and sports during college can help prepare you for the physical component of your academy training. If you have been away from school for a while, you may wish to set up a training regimen for yourself, which should minimally include conditioning, endurance, and strength training. You should also prepare yourself academically. Get into the habit of reading and writing. Take some time each day, preferably at the same time, to read. After reading—write! You don't have to read the great books of philosophy (although they may be of use to you). Read novels, as well as some general texts or other books about your intended career. Then write about what you read.

Depending upon which agency you will be working for, you may be able to access their curriculum and expectations online. You can always contact the agency and ask to speak to the academy director or an aide for advice about the makeup of the academy training program.

FIRST DAYS ON THE JOB

You have worked hard, and now you have arrived! Now is the time to apply what you have learned. The classroom and the textbook present an ideal, and there will be vast differences between the ideal and the real, or the pragmatic. There will be many who will be willing to give advice and guidance, and there will be others who will help you reluctantly, if at all. As you report to work each day, there will be new assignments and with them come new challenges. Presuming that you have a supervisor who is a skilled and seasoned professional, you will be allowed to take your time and feel your way into the job. Unfortunately, criminal justice is one of those fields that present changes and challenges on a day-to-day basis, sometimes even from minute to minute. Criminal justice events occur that require immediate decisions and oftentimes action to which you must bring into play all those things you have learned in so many settings from the classroom to the academy. Sometimes there is no textbook answer or established policy to guide you. You may need to make a decision on the spot and simply hope for the best. However, the better trained you are, the better you will respond to all circumstances.

No one can predict how events will play out, and they may not turn out like they are glamorized on TV. During your first days on the job, you may be assigned to a senior person in uniform, or perhaps a senior staffer. If not, then you will have to make an assessment of those around you and determine who is best qualified to answer your questions. What is important is that *you do not let questions and concerns go unanswered! Get answers!* Those answers may eventually protect your job—and even your life.

FINDING OUT THE JOB IS
NOT FOR YOU, OR HOW DO YOU MOVE ON?

There are at least two perspectives to this scenario. The first is when the supervisor recognizes a problem. After hiring someone, employers generally do whatever is possible to help the new hire fit in and learn the job. Unfortunately, despite the best efforts, there are those circumstances in which the employee does not work out. One of the more difficult tasks for a supervisor to undertake is to tell people that they need to move on. The job might have been hurting them, or they were either hurting someone else, or they potentially could harm someone else.

The second case is when you discover that the job is not right for you. There are so many things that can happen on the job that provide signals that something is wrong—such as becoming stressed out, unhappy about reporting for work, or argumentative; not seeing eye to eye with your coworkers, not accomplishing your given tasks successfully, and more. When you take a moment of soul-searching and are honest with yourself, you will know that for whatever reason, the job is not what you anticipated it to be. Perhaps once this decision is reached, however, you will wonder how to manage losing a paycheck. The paycheck, however, while important, is not the primary reason to hang on to a job; your happiness and well-being are the most important, and if you hang around too long, then you or someone else may actually get hurt. When job situations deteriorate and you hang around too long, you risk damaging your reputation, as well as any hope of getting a good reference for future employment. This can damage future job opportunities.

The Letter of Resignation

When you reach the decision to leave, do not immediately submit a letter of resignation and stop reporting to work! You have several different options before you take this step.

Schedule a visit with your supervisor or, if your agency has an employee assistance program, go speak with a counselor. Remember, early on this book discussed that in the work world, it is important to place the right employee into the right position.

How you make a decision to leave a position (or move on to a promotion) is important. You have probably heard the expression "Don't burn your bridges," or "The people you passed on the way up you will see on the way down." The point is that life presents us with a wide variety of opportunities—and the occasional curveball. There are two important points of order:

First, leave every position gracefully.
Second, treat people as you would wish to be treated.

Leave Every Position Gracefully

A professional acts like one. You will meet those you leave behind again, perhaps as colleagues who also have moved on, as subordinates who are now your supervisors, in agencies that you wish to return to, or in some other setting.

There are many ways you can make a graceful exit. Express kind words to your fellow employees, such as "It's been great working with you. Please stay in touch. Here is my contact information." The same advice applies to supervisors: "You have been a terrific boss, and I learned a great deal. I have really appreciated the opportunity to explore my potential here, and it has prepared me for new opportunities. Please call me if any questions come up about the projects I was working on." Of course, the most considerate thing you can do as you depart from a job is to finish any open assignments, or at least leave them in good condition for someone to pick up. *Never* leave a position without giving adequate notice.

Generally, a letter of resignation is suggested. Take the time to write it well and to include some of the remarks listed above. You always want to do whatever you can to leave on the best terms possible.

Remember that your boss can give you a reference to another agency, or know of someone hiring, or have other positions for you to explore. Your supervisor will probably appreciate your candor that the job is not working out. Too often, an unhappy employee develops into a problem employee, and this circumstance may be paving the way for the employer to terminate the employee. This is a mark that no one wants on their record.

Career Advancement

This topic is much too involved for this book. Nevertheless, it seems appropriate to provide a few suggestions, in addition to the related material in Chapters 2 and 3. Advancement is about more than getting to the next position. Do what is important for you to achieve your next step. Always keep in mind the *big picture*, your plan for five years, ten years, twenty years down the road, and retirement. Take care of your whole person, including your physical, educational, and financial health.

Staying in shape physically will help you keep a career from being derailed by illness. Join a gym if you have time, or at the very least stay active. Your fitness will also contribute to a more satisfying and healthy retirement.

Education can be an ongoing journey. It can help with your current career, help you to change careers, and help to set yourself up for a new and perhaps entirely different career when you retire.

Financial health is current, ongoing, and essential for the future. Getting the job you want is not a signal to rush out of the starting blocks and start spending or wildly running up credit cards. Any failure to maintain good financial status can affect you all along the continuum of life. If you dig a financial hole now, you will have to dig yourself out later, and this will affect how you plan and prepare for the future. At the very least, as you start out in your career, attend a seminar or take a course in personal financial management. There are rumors that Social Security and other pensions that have been relied upon in the past may not be around, and individuals will have to assume more responsibility for their financial futures. Unfortunately, for many, even if there is still an available pension and Social Security, they may not be sufficient to ensure a secure and fruitful retirement. There are many ways to build a nest egg to supplement those incomes, but to do so requires your planning and action as soon as possible.

THE AWKWARD DEPARTURE

There may come a time, for any number of reasons, when a departure may be awkward or unpleasant, such as when the agency you are leaving is already shorthanded. Perhaps you are aware of supervisors in your agency who do not respond kindly to those who are either seeking new jobs or are being considered for new positions. You have little choice in these situations. First, do not advise supervisors, or even fellow employees, about your plans. Second, advise potential employers that you are experiencing a hostile work environment. Unfortunately, this may hamper your effort to get a new position, but it is still better than to have someone call to check on your work record and receive a negative response. Hopefully, you have references who will stand by you and defend your personal and work record. Third, follow all other suggestions, such as giving appropriate notice and writing an appropriate letter of resignation.

SUMMARY

Hopefully this chapter has set you up to prepare for your career in the criminal justice profession. In similar fashion, if you are meticulous in these preparations and follow through on them, they will also help you set yourself up for a future, that time when you earn your promotion, receive other career opportunities, and retire from the world of work.

8

Criminal Justice Ethics

"Being ethical is when no one else is looking."

—Jay Albanese

INTRODUCTION, OR THE
SLIPPERY SLOPE OF CRIMINAL JUSTICE

The quote listed above is the subtitle to a book by Jay Albanese.[1] In this simple statement, he manages to sum up what confounds those who examine the actions of those in the criminal justice profession who violate ethical standards. A vast amount of the responsibility of each component of the criminal justice system occurs out of sight from the general public (and can be a great source of temptation). For example, prisons operate behind tall walls protected by armed guards who allow neither admittance nor exit from the prison. Police do not invite civilians to accompany them on investigations, to crime scenes, or to arrests or other circumstances. Non-police personnel are excluded from most law enforcement circumstances. No one is allowed access to the evidence files of prosecutors except as they offer up evidence to the defense as required by law. Criminal justice operations exclude the outsider from observations of its practices. Many courtroom activities take place outside the courtroom and are never recorded by the court stenographer. Those conversations occur in chambers, in private offices, and in other places. In those settings, determinations are made about the applicability of constitutional law, the plea bargain, the admissibility of witnesses, and even what the witness will or will not testify about.

Preparation for your career should include both basic and specific awareness of what is meant by ethics for various components of the criminal justice system. Associations, including the American Correctional Association (ACA), the American Parole and Probation Association (APPA), and the International Association of Chiefs of Police (IACP), have each developed ethical standards for their members. You will find these codes of ethics listed in Appendix 16, "Codes of Ethics."

Nevertheless, we become aware of unethical conduct because someone somehow recorded it, unknown documents are discovered, a witness comes forward, a "sting" is conducted by an investigating unit, a message is posted on Facebook or on a video on YouTube, or something else occurs that thrusts the act into the forefront of public knowledge. When this occurs, an advocate, an investigator, or perhaps even the media grasps hold of the problem and does not let it go. Then, like a dog with a bone, interested parties scrutinize and analyze the incident until more and more people are aware of it and the increased attention leads to some form of resolution. The consequences are that names such as Rodney King or Mark Fuhrman become, at least for a short while, household names or that some special commission or governmental investigation occurs. In other cases, such as that of Serpico or the New Jersey State Police (for racial profiling), entire agencies become suspect of wrongdoing and more serious action is taken. The formation of the Knapp Commission is an example in the first instance, or the agency like the New Jersey State Police, is placed under Federal Consent Decree[2] in the second instance. The agencies and the professions are connected by the tarnished reputations, and public confidence is eroded.

Ethical issues affect everyone, and no area of the criminal justice profession is immune from them. They are broad in their types of occurrence and impact on individuals and their public perceptions of professionalism, and they affect the general confidence of society in the ability of each area to perform its touted functions. The uniqueness of ethical conduct in the criminal justice profession goes beyond good and bad or moral and immoral—it is directed by the state and U.S. constitutions, codes of conduct, and rigid construction of policy and procedures. Criminal justice professionals have considerable power, which at one extreme includes decisions of life and death (such as in police shootings and executions) and at another extreme includes turning a blind eye, or acknowledging that someone had to be held accountable for a crime, even if it was the wrong person—an innocent person.

There are several purposes for including an ethics chapter in this book. They include:

- Helping the future professional toward the development of being an ethical person who will contribute to the field.
- Helping the future professional develop critical and analytical skills—to go beyond the status quo.
- Helping the future professional begin to understand the pressures that will be placed upon them.
- Helping the future professional begin to understand the types of ethical dilemmas that occur in practice and that conflict with training, policy, and justice.
- Helping the future professional become more open to the exercise of moral and ethical judgment at the toughest times, such as when no one is looking.

Our actions are influenced by various sources of information, such as social events, media, personal interactions, colleagues, and training. At different times, something happens that reminds us just how precarious is the balance between ethical and unethical conduct. There is a job to be done, and sometimes even the best of people fail to maintain ethical standards. The famous Stanford prison experiment was conducted by Dr. Philip Zimbardo.[3] He used graduate students to assume the role of guards and others to be the prisoners. His students ultimately became aggressive, abusive guards, and the experiment had to be terminated. The student prisoners accepted the posture of the convict and became subservient to the prison conditions. His findings proved that the role frequently determines the actions of the player.

Abu Ghraib, a military prison for prisoners of war, became a painful real-life example of the Zimbardo experiment, with more serious consequences for the guards. The prisoners endured a variety of abuses, such as being forced to be naked and then have physical contact with one another. One of the more damning pieces of evidence came in the widely publicized photo of PFC Lynndie England standing with her rifle on her hip, a cigarette hanging out of her mouth, and one foot placed on a prostrate naked prisoner. Perhaps, as we often hear, she was only following orders. Perhaps her actions felt like a patriotic thing to do at the time. In all likelihood, however, she received encouragement from the wrong sources—and her conduct resulted in a prison sentence. These abusive acts violated standards for the treatment of prisoners of war, as well as violated their cultural and religious traditions, mandates, and practices.

After the egregious events of Abu Ghraib, Zimbardo wrote again about the abuses that occur when power is not regulated, calling it "The Lucifer Effect."[4] We could postulate that at least some of those who engaged in the abusive behavior believed that they were doing their duty, or at the very least were being loyal to their country and what it stands for. Nevertheless, what they did was wrong. In this case, they were soldiers in military uniform who represented the United States.

Every individual is responsible for maintaining a balance between their personal beliefs and their actions. We often refer to this as "being objective." The criminal justice professional is surrounded daily by events and persons that represent the worst that can occur. Maintaining objectivity is difficult in the face of so much input that encompasses illegal and immoral behavior.

The simple explanation for being ethical on and off the job is to know the difference between right and wrong and be able to make the correct decision (sometimes in the face of considerable pressure). Professional posturing suggests that criminal justice professionals are trying to do what is correct, such as attempting to safeguard society. However, the personal dilemma comes when the answers are not so clear cut. One way to view this is to ask the questions, does the end justify the means? and, does my decision transcend the single event?

Perhaps we can all agree that achieving safety as a consequence of taking action is a desired goal. However, our society is governed by a constitution as the foundation for democracy, and the end result must be judged by the process that achieved a particular conclusion. This discussion is not about the legality or the illegality of what someone does. Specifically, if someone steals, that is a crime and unethical. However, if someone decides that the only way to safeguard society is to deny someone else a basic right, then that is also unethical and illegal, even if the motivation is correct. Unfortunately, we have many examples both in fact and in fiction where the denial of rights has resulted in unlawful conviction, detention, and even execution. Thus, the process must be considered as it affects outcomes, and persons in responsible positions must adhere to the law and the policies and procedures that dictate their actions.

A slippery slope develops when the first unethical indiscretion occurs, is not responded to, and then advances as the actions progress to more egregious forms of misconduct. This is especially destructive when the actions result in a desirable outcome and justifies the process in the mind of the agent, thus encouraging future acts of unethical conduct as the means of ensuring that the job be successfully completed.

TYPES OF UNETHICAL CONDUCT

Those who work in the criminal justice profession possess positions of considerable power, some much more than others. Often unethical conduct is a matter of circumstance. Some examples include setting quotas for tickets, racial profiling, stealing during an investigation, sexual harassment and other sexual misconduct, substance abuse (both on and off the job), sleeping while on duty, creating a hostile work environment, favoritism, accepting gifts or discounts because of one's uniform, and many more. Some of these acts are illegal, and the consequences in such cases are more severe.

THE CONSEQUENCES OF UNETHICAL CONDUCT

The consequences of unethical conduct are many. Individual consequences range from reprimands to criminal charges. In some cases, the conduct may be far-reaching and may result in dismissals, demotions, transfers, and changes to policy and procedure. In other cases, the misconduct breaches constitutional guarantees. In such cases, the severity is greater and can include a Federal Consent Decree.

Overall, acts of unethical conduct erode confidence in governmental operations. Public service is one reason for the existence of the components of the criminal justice system. Law enforcement, the judiciary, and corrections officers and employees appear less as providers of public service when illegal acts and unethical conduct become known. Criminal justice professionals may have forgotten who their client is and for whom they perform their services when they operate outside the limits of the law or when their behavior is guided by selfish motivations.

A FEW PRINCIPLES THAT GUIDE
CORRECT AND ETHICAL DECISION-MAKING

Equality in the eyes of the law is a fundamental principle. An individual's position in the criminal justice profession is not to be used to single out persons or groups.

- Law must be the determinate of our behavior. Criminal justice personnel are the instruments of the law, and they must operate within the boundaries of the law and the written policies that specify their limits of behavior.
- As agents of the law, criminal justice professionals may not take advantage of either situations or people.

All too often, criminal justice professionals find themselves on a slippery slope of correct action because of very simple events. They may question, *What harm is it if I accept a doughnut, a free meal, a bottle of Scotch, or an envelope of cash?* The doughnut may seem to be a small offering, but what are the implications of an envelope of cash? If the professional accepts such gifts, is he or she then obligated to provide special favors? What will be expected? Is he or she now obligated to operate or to allow others to operate outside the boundaries of the law? In many respects, the criminal justice professional must be held to a higher standard. They are public servants who are expected to adhere to ethical dictates, not only on the job but also in their private lives.

Members of sworn law enforcement service are never "off the job." They maintain their authority even when off-duty. They still possess their badge and their weapon. Likewise, civilian members of the criminal justice profession represent their agencies at all times. The criminal justice professional needs to be mindful that when they say something detrimental about their agency or their fellow employees while "off the job," someone else may hear the comments or see them acting inappropriately.

WHY DO VIOLATIONS OF ETHICAL CONDUCT OCCUR?

There are many reasons to account for violations of ethical conduct. Each area of the criminal justice profession engages in training and oversight to ensure ethical conduct among its employees. The police and corrections officers are overseen by internal affairs units, and the courts are armed with administrative units to review the work of judges, prosecutors, and defense attorneys.

First among the reasons for unethical conduct would be inadequate training. Training academies usually have their curriculums approved by an agency or board that certifies the course content. In some cases, however, the content may be taught inappropriately or important points may be deemphasized. In other cases, the on-the-job training may actually undo the academy training. In some cases an individual(s) may just "go rogue," that is, for whatever reason, knowingly and willfully decide to violate policy and standard operating procedures.

No one likes everything that they have to do while on the job. However, rules, morals, and laws must govern our behavior and dictate appropriate standards with others. Power is never an acceptable reason to exceed these standards.

RESOLVING THE ETHICAL CONTROVERSY

The criminal justice career will have many intersections from the point of hiring, to attending the academy, to continuing education, to training and retraining exercises, and to memorandums that serve as reminders of what is expected, i.e., what is appropriate conduct. Administrators control each of these occasions in order to help maintain ethical conduct. At the same time, administrators, supervisors, and managers at each level must also be role models for the expected behavior. Constant vigilance, review, and oversight are essential to maintaining ethical conduct. There are many associations connected to the criminal justice profession that seek to promote ethical conduct and good practices. Many are listed here, and others in Appendix 12.

CORRECTIONS

The American Correctional Association (ACA) developed its code of ethics in 1975. Since that time, it has promoted ethical conduct in the corrections field and has established various training programs that provide professionals with certifications. In addition, the ACA has established a certification process for correctional facilities. The process to become certified is quite involved. Correctional institutions will spend months preparing for the inspection process that leads to certification by the ACA. Accreditation is voluntary. (See the ACA Code of Ethics in Appendix 16.)

There are many private nonprofit agencies that seek to promote professionalism and excellence in the field. They include:

- The International Community Corrections Association (ICCA): www.iccalive.org
- The International Corrections and Prison Association (ICPA): www.icpa.ca
- The Correctional Education Association (CEA): www.ceanational.org

PAROLE

Information about the American Probation and Parole Association (APPA) may be found at www.appa-net.org.

POLICING

There are four primary law enforcement membership associations:

- The National Sheriff's Association (NSA): www.sheriffs.org
- The National Organization of Black Law Enforcement Executives (NOBLE): www.noblenational.org
- The International Association of Chiefs of Police (IACP): www.theiacp.org
- The Police Executive Research Forum (PERF): www.policeforum.org

The Commission on Accreditation for Law Enforcement Agencies, Inc. (CALEA, www.calea.org), was formed in 1979. Some of the functions carried out by CALEA include maintaining a body of standards that has been devised by members of law enforcement to address a number of topics, including racial profiling. Accreditation by CALEA is voluntary. The CALEA Standards can be found in Appendix 16 of this book.

THE COURT AND THE PURSUIT OF JUSTICE

The court is an arena of highly charged personal, political, constitutional, and emotional decision-making. The extraordinary talent of Alan Dershowitz (also a Yale University Professor of Law, emeritus) is well-chronicled. His understanding of the ethical complexities of adhering to the law in the pursuit of justice is quite clear in what he describes as:

Rules of the Justice Game
- Rule I: Almost all defendants are, in fact, guilty.
- Rule II: All criminal defense lawyers, prosecutors, and judges understand and believe Rule I.
- Rule III: It is easier to convict guilty defendants by violating the constitution than by complying with it, and in some cases it is impossible to convict guilty defendants without violating the constitution.
- Rule IV: Almost all police lie about whether they violated the constitution in order to convict guilty defendants.

- Rule V. All prosecutors, judges, and defense attorneys are aware of Rule IV.
- Rule VI: Many prosecutors implicitly encourage police to lie about whether they violated the constitution in order to convict guilty defendants.
- Rule VII: All judges are aware of Rule VI.
- Rule VIII: Most trial judges pretend to believe police officers they know are lying.
- Rule IX: All appellate judges are aware of Rule VIII, yet many pretend to believe the trial judges who pretend to believe the lying police officers.
- Rule X: Most judges disbelieve defendants about whether their constitutional rights have been violated, even if they are telling the truth.
- Rule XI: Most judges and prosecutors would not knowingly convict a defendant whom they believe to be innocent of the crime charged for a closely related crime.
- Rule XII: Rule XI does not apply to members of organized crime, drug dealers, career criminals, or potential informers.
- Rule XIII: Nobody really wants Justice.[5]

These bold, tongue-in-cheek statements of Dershowitz help to indicate the difficulty for practitioners (judges, prosecutors, defense attorneys, law enforcement officers, and corrections personnel) to be instruments of justice, especially if these are truly the beliefs held by criminal justice practitioners.

The American Bar Association developed the Model Code of Judicial Conduct as a guide for judges. This code is intended to help steer judges in the right direction given the unique circumstances of their position. Judges must exhibit impartiality in their determinations of constitutional fairness. Pollock[6] points out the five canons of the code:

1. Impropriety and the appearance of impropriety
2. Impartiality and diligence
3. Personal affairs
4. Extrajudicial activities
5. Political activity

YOU: THE ETHICAL CRIMINAL JUSTICE PROFESSIONAL

You are important to the image of criminal justice as a profession and to the image that others hold of you, your colleagues, and the profession. The ethical person will earn the self-respect of his colleagues and help to maintain a culture that includes mutual respect.

You have examined your options, pursued the job, and earned the opportunity to be an employee in the field of criminal justice. Now you will have, on a daily basis, the prospect of deciding how you should conduct yourself and treat others. This is not a matter of political affiliation. This is a matter of right conduct that rises to a level above that necessary for the ordinary citizen. You are a public servant. Read the available codes of ethics that govern your job—then apply them. If you do not choose wisely and instead violate those codes, then you run the risk of suffering consequences for those actions. You don't want or need to ruin your career. Take the time to review some of the strange and inappropriate behaviors committed by criminal justice staff. Type "criminal justice misconduct" into the Google search bar to find examples of unethical and illegal misconduct committed by members of the criminal justice profession. You will find as many examples as you should need to explain to you what it is and what will happen as a consequence of inappropriate behavior.

9

Life after the Career or "I Can't Live on That!"

INTRODUCTION

You haven't even started your criminal justice career yet, so why should you begin to consider your retirement? The response is quite simple. There are many who enter the field of criminal justice, but because it seems so far away, retirement receives too little attention. Of course, by the time retirement is considered, too often at a mid-career point or later, much valuable time has elapsed, and planning now must be rushed and may not produce adequate results.

The career employee, at the beginning of their career, can begin to address the retirement issue by addressing four questions. The answers to these questions will not produce the final answers, but they will get you started. That is, as you plan, and as life events unfold, your needs and priorities will change. You cannot anticipate all of the life experiences that will add meaning and satisfaction to your career. In all likelihood, you will have unexpected encounters that may change your perspective through the years. Those experiences very well may alter your plans and cause you to shift course in your goal setting. But still, the following specific questions should be considered:

1. How should I retire?
2. When should I retire?

3. How should I prepare to retire?
4. To work or not to work during retirement—that is the question.

As you read through this chapter, start to jot down notes that address these key questions. Hopefully as the chapter comes to a close, you will have a preliminary outline that will guide you and from which you will be able to assess your personal growth and the fulfillment of your retirement planning.

THE FAILURE TO PLAN

I sat in my first retirement seminar when I reached the twenty-fifth year of my career. I had believed I had started early enough and had done enough to financially prepare myself for retirement. Nevertheless, I took notes throughout the morning session and nodded my head knowingly as point after point suggested that I had done okay. Things were looking up, even though those notes indicated that I had a great deal to look into before I signed the papers for my retirement.

However, the afternoon session began with a new speaker, a financial advisor who began with a startling opening remark: "For many of you in this room, I hope that you will run out of money in the first six months of your retirement." He paused and I looked at him in disbelief. Others looked on in shock. How could he say that to these hardworking folks who, after twenty or more years of effort, suddenly had their retirement right front of them? I could see panic in the eyes of several people in the room.

He clarified his remark by saying that even with their pension and probably with Social Security, there would still be insufficient income to maintain their current lifestyles and financial obligations. He emphasized that many of them would not be able to live as they had dreamed of living during retirement. He went on to suggest that the sooner they returned to the workforce, the better it would be to obtain employment that could provide the difference in income they needed, and even to supplement their income if things got tougher. This was sound advice. He also mentioned that the cost of living would increase, and that cost-of-living adjustments, or COLAs,[1] would not keep pace with inflation. The comments that many made in this seminar indicated that they had believed that as long as they maintained an equivalent income in retirement through their pension and Social Security, they would be fine. They had not taken into consideration that living would become more expensive in retirement, and that inflation would reduce the value of their available retirement income.

His message never left my head. A short time ago, I listened to an employee I have known for over twenty years commenting that she would walk out the door the day she reached her twenty-fifth year. She reasoned that her paycheck would be coming in for the rest of her life. It only took one clarifying question to realize that she had no clue what she would be receiving in her retirement. She did not understand that her "retirement paycheck" would only be a fraction of her current paycheck. When she realized her error, she exclaimed, "But I can't live on that!" She had committed the unpardonable sin of never attending a preretirement seminar, never consulting with a financial advisor, and never paying attention to the statements that she had received advising her of what she would receive once she was in the retirement system. Also, and most unfortunately, she had done nothing else to financially prepare for her future, and now she sees herself having to work for many more years. In one moment of revelation, her plans for retirement evaporated. The good news was that she had not yet submitted for retirement, which would have caused her to live considerably less well than she had when working. She could now maintain her employment and make the preparations she should have made earlier for a future date that now would not come soon.

WHAT TO HAVE AFTER RETIREMENT

In retirement you will likely want to live as well, if not better, than you have during the working years of your career. You will want to make sure that your benefits will last throughout your retirement. You will want to ensure that you have provided yourself with enough discretionary income to last throughout your retirement. You will also want to make sure that your retirement years are productive. I, for example, look forward to playing regular rounds of golf—and I know I will spend more on golf than I ever spent during my working life.

Preparation for life after your criminal justice career can and should begin even before your career is initiated, and then it is continued throughout your career. The financial world is changing, and how we perceive retirement will probably undergo an even more radical shift given the current economic woes of the nation and the changes being made by corporations and public retirement systems. Those currently in the field have already seen changes that have forced them to reconsider their retirement plans.

There was a time when Social Security was seen as the vehicle that would carry people through their so-called golden years. This was eventually followed by the combination of a pension and Social Security, and finally this was supplemented by Medicare. The point is that as individuals, we have little control over how employers and the government manage our retirement options. However, individuals with guidance and planning can prepare adequately for their futures. The likelihood is that Social Security has a terminal lifespan and may disappear from the retirement landscape in another decade. Pensions and medical benefits associated with retirement have already begun to shift and decrease; for example, rather than employer-sponsored pensions, the change is moving toward employee-managed 401K plans. Corrections officers in New Jersey, as another example, recently saw their pension decrease from 65 percent to 60 percent at twenty-five years. Also in New Jersey, there will be no COLAs (cost-of-living adjustments) for thirty more years. That means that while inflation rises, there will be no supplementary increase in pensions.

If you are looking for a career, have just begun your career, or are in the middle of your career, visit your state or federal pensions and benefits website to get an overview of how they are structured and why they are structured as you see them. How you apply them to your plans will change during your life experience. Let's use the State of New Jersey's pension allocations as an example for those in law enforcement and those who are civilians. Law enforcement personnel are entitled to the 60 percent pension option and medical benefits upon retirement after twenty-five years. There are important choices here to be made. If the employee remains on duty after twenty-five years, the pension will increase 1 percent per year, up to a maximum of 65 percent. If you start your career in law enforcement later in life, however, you must take into account the mandatory retirement age of sixty-five. Also, the rules of retirement may change over time. You need to be aware of these rules so that you can plan accordingly.

The changes that have taken place in the past twenty years have placed even greater responsibility on the individual to prepare for his/her own retirement, and that trend will likely continue.

The fact is that if you have chosen criminal justice as a career, you will probably reach eligibility for retirement at a relatively young age. Most state and federal jobs in criminal justice require only between twenty to twenty-five years of service (now thirty years in New Jersey), and that the individual be approximately fifty-five years of age (now sixty years of age in New Jersey) or older to qualify for retirement and a pension. Many law enforcement positions require twenty years of eligibility for retirement, and age does not matter. However, what is an "adequate" pension now at retirement may be much "less than adequate" twenty years from now as inflation eats away at it and COLAs do not keep up. Of course, the cost of medical care is also increasing.

The amount of the retirement benefit varies between civilian and law enforcement positions. At mid-career you may be asking yourself, should I work until I am older or should I seek out another career or some other source of income? Your personal response will more likely be dictated by what you have done up to that point. Your agency's human resources department can help you with your decision. Many agencies now conduct retirement seminars on a regular basis that are geared toward employees at different points in their careers, such as mid-career seminars. These seminars can advise you on your retirement benefits and your available options. However—and take this as a warning—during your career and at these seminars, there may be little or no notice, or perhaps there is too little emphasis placed on other available options, to help you prepare for retirement. Your responsibility will be to discover those options and then to plan for their implementation. During your career orientation, you should ask the human resources representative whether there are any other benefits available that have not been discussed during the session. Sometimes benefits, such as deferred compensation plans or a 401K plan, are overlooked. Many other employees who have taken advantage of these benefits can provide you with their personal story of their value.

You can compare various options to your current level of income and job benefits. For example, you can begin to recognize what may no longer be available at retirement, make some determinations about how and/or where to spend your retirement, and finally calculate your cost of retirement. Here is a major caution in those calculations, however: Never neglect or underestimate potential medical costs. As we age, the cost of our health care and medications will increase, and these often represent our greatest continuous cost in retirement. Surgeries, when needed, also have prohibitive costs if they must be paid for privately. Managed care will more rigorously examine what it defines as "elective surgeries" and "necessary" medications and thus make them more difficult to obtain or be paid for by insurance. You owe it to yourself to protect your quality of life if you wish to maintain it upon retirement.

Life consultants advise us that at the time of retirement, we will need at least 70 percent of our existing salary to ensure that we will not run out of money during retirement. Young adults, because of their youth, do not typically consider the problems that affect the aging population. Let us provide you with one more consideration that almost never gets discussed until someone is at the end of their career: Have you ever thought about the cost of long-term residential health care? Age takes its toll on all of us, and you may experience a disability that someday will negatively affect your quality of life. The cost of long-term care (without insurance) will quickly eat through any savings that you have accumulated. There is insurance for this, and the sooner in life that insurance is purchased, the less expensive it will be. The question for you is, how much insurance will you need, what type is appropriate, and when should you purchase it?

Mid-career is usually too late to begin retirement planning. Half of your career is already over. Half of your time to prepare for retirement has been lost. Half of your time for savings to grow is gone. Your retirement planning will be much more effective if you begin your first day on the job and manage your preparations throughout your career.

WHAT BENEFITS DOES THE JOB OFFER?

Obviously, your first responsibility upon obtaining employment is to ensure that you have set up your employee benefits in a fashion that will enable you to be provided for while you are working. These benefits generally include life insurance, medical benefits, and benefits to provide for your family. Then, there are other benefits.

Unfortunately, benefits for your future may be only casually mentioned, glossed over, or completely neglected. These benefits may be discussed as if they, at this time, are of minimal importance to you. This may be because retirement does seem so far away and there seems to be plenty of time for you to plan. In reality, these benefits may be as valuable or even more valuable than your pension. One example would include a deferred compensation plan, or an employer-matching option.

DEFERRED COMPENSATION

Deferred compensation plans allow employees to take part of their salary as pre-tax dollars and invest it tax-deferred. Pre-tax dollars refers to money that is not taxed, and by investing this way it may place the employee in a lower tax bracket. The benefit is that not only is the dollar amount invested greater, because it is pre-tax dollars, but the money grows tax-free until retirement or the assets are subject to distribution. A common comment I hear is that people think they cannot afford to make that contribution. My counterargument is that you can't afford to *not* make that contribution! Think of it this way: Out of every three dollars that you place into a deferred compensation plan, you will have lost one to taxes. Generally, an employee may not remove dollars from such a plan without paying a penalty. However, there are exceptions for its use, and in some cases, that use is also not a taxable event. Such a plan implies a promise by the employer that upon retirement or other distribution of the funds, the employer will provide those funds. This should not be a problem in public employment.

For you to think that you have plenty of time or that you cannot afford to participate in this program is a mistake. In reality, you cannot afford to delay your preparation. Consider this: What if something happens, a layoff or a personal injury, which forces you to discontinue your career in criminal justice? There could be layoffs or perhaps you experience a catastrophic illness. What will you do then? What are you prepared to do? Planning and action helps to put in order the means to survive the unforeseen.

A financial sacrifice today will provide for your future security. The funds that are put into a deferred compensation program are a down payment on a secure future.

PREPARATION FOR THE UNDERGRADUATE

Your academic preparation and career exploration are addressed as you advance in your undergraduate curriculums. Even as an undergraduate, you can begin to prepare for contingencies during your employment and for retirement. Preparation should be both personal and financial. Ask yourself what else you like or enjoy. You can take classes for a minor, for a future career, or that enhance career flexibility. You can also take a course in personal finance.

There are several practical and valuable benefits to this approach, and both are related to your future job satisfaction. First, if you ever have to leave criminal justice, then you have something to fall back on. Second, you may be able to utilize the minor area during your career to transition into a new position. Third, you may use this other skill development for personal satisfaction during your career and then segue it into a new career path upon retirement.

Careers seldom consist of remaining in one position for the duration of employment. Many of us have greater aspirations as we begin our careers; that is, we have already begun to think about where we want to go and when we want to achieve our goals. Selection for promotions or new ventures may depend not only on job performance, but also on how you have prepared yourself before you start on a job.

There is the possibility that your other preparation, that not directly associated with your primary choice of career, may provide you with satisfaction while you are in your career by doing something else, perhaps something unrelated. For example, many criminal justice professionals do consulting work or teach part-time for colleges and universities. These are personal choices, but there are other choices you may pursue, perhaps something non-professional, something unrelated to your choice of vocation.

Examples of undergraduate minors or graduate degrees that have great applicability include social work, psychology, law, counseling, or business. The last example may help you to obtain an administrative position. Criminal justice students frequently seek employment in law enforcement. However, the stress of the law enforcement positions may become an impetus to pursue other interests when the career comes to an end. This is not to suggest that you need to look outside of law enforcement, but rather you could look at other areas of criminal justice. The lure is to stay connected to the criminal justice profession, because this is what is familiar and comfortable, but to work in a different capacity, such as civilian administration.

Whether you will or will not work in your retirement is a personal decision that can be affected by many things when you have reached the point in your life to retire or to change careers. Among the influencing factors can be the satisfaction or dissatisfaction you have had in your career, your health (which should never be neglected), what you can physically do, your family status (whether you have a spouse or children), and much more. Let us consider a few potential options, while remaining aware that there are many more than we can explore in the pages to come.

THE PRACTITIONER TURNED ACADEMIC

Many who have enjoyed long and distinguished careers in the criminal justice field as either law enforcement personnel or as civilians have prepared themselves for a second career as academics. Many former practitioners have gone on to successful careers in teaching, writing textbooks, or chairing academic departments (see the profiles of Robert Louden and Raymond Rainville found in Appendix 1). The difference between what each of these has chosen to do is the level of academic attainment, the ability to achieve subject matter expertise, and how to combine that with their personal ability.

The study of criminal justice encompasses two rather broad areas in the academic community: criminal justice theory and law enforcement. Preparation for a career in academia requires two considerations. The first would be to decide the subject matter, followed by enrolling for an advanced degree.

THE PRACTITIONER TURNED
CONSULTANT, EXPERT WITNESS, OR ADVISOR

The better-educated and more successful career employees will find a variety of exciting post-career (and sometimes mid-career) opportunities. The opportunities to be a consultant, an expert witness, or an advisor will depend upon how you have managed your career. Obtaining an advanced degree will provide more impressive credentials. Steady advancement in a career validates your expertise. Writing for publication about your interests, experiences, or research additionally authenticates your expertise, especially if those publications are in peer-reviewed journals. And finally, but not exclusively, speaking about your experiences at organizational meetings and other social venues, and more importantly conferences, provides social exposure and peer recognition.

The ability to be a consultant, expert witness, or an advisor will be marked by the manner in which you have performed during your career, any accolades you may have received, and other triumphs that mark you as a standout or simply as someone with expertise in desired areas. If you desire such an opportunity, then it would be wise for you to approach every presentation (in person and in writing) as an opportunity to demonstrate your potential.

SUMMARY

In the beginning of this chapter, the following four questions were presented for your consideration:

1. How should I retire?
2. When should I retire?
3. How should I prepare to retire?
4. To work or not to work during retirement—that is the question.

Hopefully, you have not only begun to think about these questions, but you have begun to put in writing what you will do to address them, as was suggested in the introduction. Consider your future as a blank slate upon which you will etch your life narrative. That ongoing chronicle will be the substance from which you may periodically review where you have been. A line in the book *Jonathan Livingston Seagull* (Bach 1970)[2] helps to illustrate the importance of this approach. A young seagull approaches an old seagull and asks about where he is going and how he will get there. The wise old gull admonishes him that he should "look with your understanding to know where you have been and then you will know the way to fly."

Self-examination of what has been is critical to future preparation. Where have you been? How did you get from place to place? What is the result of happenstance or preparation? A critical and honest analysis may be scary or even daunting, but it is essential, for without it you will not have a measure of your fulfillment and the contentment that comes with knowing that you did your best.

Stephen Covey (2004)[3], the author of *The Seven Habits of Highly Successful People*, offers many tidbits of advice such as "sharpen the saw," which essentially is the suggestion to keep up your preparation, your education and in that fashion you will be more prepared for what comes next. However, he has another expression that should not be neglected. He says to "seek first to understand, and then to be understood." If my understanding is correct, Covey is attempting to help us with our communication processes with other people. After we speak with students who are trying to sort out their career beginnings, or professionals who are looking to create fulfillment in their retirement, we often find that they have not tried to first understand themselves, their own successes, or how to translate those into a satisfying retirement. Readers, there is one primary message that this book has attempted to emphasize, and that is for you to prepare. It is now in your hands, and it is your responsibility.

We wish you well for a successful career.

List of Appendices

1. Directory of Profiles in Criminal Justice
2. Interest, Inquiry, and Cover Letters
3. A Guide to Interview Questions
4. Sample Résumé and CV
5. The Career Fair Plan
6. The Benefits and Downsides of Online Courses
7. Document Portfolio Checklist
8. Civil Service Examinations
9. U.S. Federal Law Enforcement Agencies and Websites
10. Important Websites
11. Criminal Justice Jobs
12. Private and Nonprofit Agencies and Professional Organizations
13. Vermont Police Academy Basic Training and Physical Fitness Training
14. Paying for College
15. Criminal Justice and Trade Publications
16. Codes of Ethics

Appendix 1

Directory of Profiles in Criminal Justice

1. **Len Black**, correctional manager, State Use Industries
2. **Heath "Hank" J. Brightman**, EdD, professor and director, Applied Research and Analysis, War Gaming Department, U.S. Naval War College
3. **Mary-Ann Conte**, BA, MSW, juvenile corrections social worker
4. **Ania Dobrzanska**, MS, CCM, state policy advisor, Bureau of Justice Assistance (BJA)
5. **Robert Hood**, MEd, warden, ADX; correctional/criminal justice consultant
6. **James F. Kenny**, PhD, federal agent, professor, Fairleigh Dickinson University
7. **Roger Lichtman**, correctional architect
8. **Robert Louden**, NYPD lieutenant; hostage negotiator; director of criminal justice, Georgian Court University
9. **Bohdan Orichowsky**, juvenile parole officer
10. **Joseph Paglino**, detective, Monmouth County Prosecutors Office; professor
11. **Raymond Rainville**, PhD, Department of Criminal Justice, St. Peters University; New Jersey Probation Services
12. **Ralph Rojas**, officer, Port Authority Police Department; assistant professor of justice studies
13. **Brian L. Royster**, EdD, New Jersey state police officer; professor
14. **Darcella A. Patterson Sessomes**, PhD, DSW, LCSW

15. **William Ussery**, police officer, professor, clinical psychologist
16. **Len Ward**, parole officer, professor

INTRODUCTION

These profiles in criminal justice cannot contain all the potential profiles that have been and will be collected to supplement this book. The following profiles are meant to be a small sample of those who have had successful careers in criminal justice. These are their stories, their paths through a career. The personal stories are intended to be inspiring as well as provide some guidance as you plan your own career. If there is a lesson to be learned from these profiles, it is that a career may start a certain way, but events, planning, education, and training can and will take you on paths you could not foresee. We believe that is part of the adventure, the sense of achievement and satisfaction that comes from a career. Each person tells about their career in criminal justice in their own way. We asked for this so the reader would have an opportunity to see them in their careers through each person's perspective on their own experience.

1. **Len Black**, correctional manager, State Use Industries

   I came into the world of criminal justice (CJ) by accident. I had never given it a thought. I met a gentleman who ran an organization in the Department of Corrections, and he suggested I get some business background and contact him afterward about joining his organization.

   It happens that I did leave the field of social work and got some experience in the newspaper business. After about a year, I contacted the gentleman to see if there was still an opportunity available. There was, and he brought me in as an assistant buyer. The organization was the Bureau of State Use Industries within the NJ Department of Corrections. This organization operates the manufacturing shops in the state's correctional institutions.

   Over the next few years, I worked my way up in the organization to become a buyer and eventually the assistant chief, chief, and director. During that time I earned a certified public manager credential and obtained my master's in public administration from Rutgers University.

During my career, we opened new industries, moved into the services arena, and provided inmates with unique work opportunities. The most important thing I learned, and it's still applicable today, is that you need to play well in the sandbox. Nothing in any organization gets done without the help and support of others. If you alienate people, you won't go far (in my opinion).

It also helped that we changed our organizational structure to support the implementation of Enterprise Resource Planning software. With the assistance of a consultant, we changed our organizational structure and developed individual business units and a strategic plan with measurable results. You might ask, What does all this have to do with CJ? Well, it's all about life and managing within an organization. If you don't set measurable goals, you'll never achieve them. How can that help your stakeholders or customers? Whether it is in criminal justice or in rocket science, the core requirements for success remain the same.

During the course of my career, I became active in many related professional organizations. First and foremost was the American Correctional Association (ACA) and the New Jersey chapter of the American Correctional Association. Directly related to my job was another professional organization affiliated with the ACA, the National Correctional Industries Association (NCIA). I eventually became the president of the NCIA and would later serve as board chairman and the recipient of their highest honor, the Rodli Award. I also was a member of the Association of Government Accountants and the Trenton/Princeton/Monmouth chapter of the American Production and Inventory Control Society (APICS). As you probably have determined, I feel very strongly that membership and participation in professional organizations can be and is very beneficial.

The decision to retire from my career with the State of New Jersey was not difficult. What I didn't do well was to plan what I was going to do when I reached Florida. Fortunately, due to many of the friendships and associations I'd made over the last thirty years or so, I had many opportunities. I decided to start my own consulting firm and provide consulting services to both government and businesses.

An opportunity arose that I could not refuse, and that was the chance to work with my wife, who is an instructional designer. So I am reinventing myself and I'm applying things I've learned over my career to my new job as a senior consultant for Learn2perform. I will be involved in strategic workforce planning, workforce analytics, and workforce planning. I recently obtained my certification of strategic workforce planning through the Human Capital Institute.

I wanted to touch on some other areas. First, get all the supervisory experience and education that you can. As a matter of fact, get all the education you can, period—especially if it's free. Even if it's not free, get it! Second, join professional organizations. Take the time to make friends within these organizations and use them as a resource. Their experience can be very valuable to you.

2. **Heath "Hank" J. Brightman**, EdD, professor and director, Applied Research & Analysis, War Gaming Department, U.S. Naval War College

"The first river you paddle runs through the rest of your life. It bubbles up in pools and eddies to remind you who you are."[1] As I look back over my twenty-five years of experience in the criminal justice arena, no one quotation more aptly describes where I have been and where I am traveling in my professional career. This "bubbling up" began with my earliest opportunities as a law enforcement ranger and as a chief park ranger with the National Park Service, where I worked on a variety of environmental issues, predominately focused on illegal hazardous waste disposal activities and natural resource management improprieties.

Later, as the criminal research specialist for the Newark field office of the U.S. Secret Service and as the department chair and an associate professor of criminal justice at Saint Peter's University, my understanding of white-collar criminal investigation—particularly environmental fraud and money laundering, deepened into the darker, murkier pools and depths of exploring public corruption. Ultimately, this awareness of corruption control strategies and cultural challenges to ethical decision-making has become the cornerstone of my post-9/11 research for the U.S. Navy, the organization for whom I have worked in both a military and civilian capacity for the past eleven years.

If the criminal justice arena represents the overall environment, and white-collar criminal investigation, fraud, and corruption control depicts the river, tributaries, and inlets of my career thus far, education is definitely the paddle that has afforded me the opportunity to successfully navigate these waters.

Although now more than two decades into my career, I still find myself seeking out new opportunities for learning within the social sciences. I hold a doctorate, three master's degrees, and a bachelor's degree in fields as diverse as natural resource management, education, criminal justice administration, mental health counseling, and organizational leadership.

Even when equipped with the proper paddle, it would be nearly impossible to negotiate the turbulent waters of white-collar criminal investigation and corruption control without a boat crew equally adept at identifying these obstacles. Garnering the ability to read these challenging navigational charts is greatly aided by professional organizations such as the Association of Certified Fraud Examiners and the International Association of Law Enforcement Intelligence Analysts.

The river of criminal justice research and practice runs wide and deep, and is best traversed by those who hone their coxswain's skills though discipline, repetition, and teamwork. Lifelong learning, intellectual curiosity, and a commitment to serving others are critical to keeping the boat afloat, even in times of the most formidable turbidity.

3. **Mary-Ann Conte**, BA, MSW, juvenile corrections social worker

This is my job as a social worker. I often wonder how I ended up working with incarcerated youth, but my journey has led me to the most stressful, yet rewarding job. When I graduated with my bachelor's degree, I was working as a cocktail waitress in Atlantic City, unsure as to what direction I wanted my life to go.

I began to travel around the world. I wanted to learn about other cultures, religions, beliefs, and history. My adventures took me to countries like Thailand, Spain, Belgium, Italy, Morocco, and the nations of Africa. I returned to college to pursue my master's degree with a different attitude. I wanted to change the world. I had a renewed sense of vigor, and I truly believed that if I could change one child's life, it would all be worthwhile. It was a struggle. I noticed that I was a rare breed in my classrooms. Many students only worked part-time, but I had bills to pay, food and gas to purchase, etc., so I had to work full-time. There were no other options.

During my graduate coursework, I had to intern at two different locations. My first internship placement was at a hospice. I really enjoyed counseling families during their greatest time of need. I also counseled children at a bereavement camp. I became close with the families that were assigned to me. I would visit them and seek solutions to their questions. Eventually, however, my clients began to die, and this took a toll on my psyche. I had become so close to the families and shared so many laughs that it was literally depressing me at the funerals. I felt that I had lost a friend, and I did not think I could handle a job with so much death and despair.

My second year of internship involved a placement in a middle school. I was being supervised by a child study team, and I really thought that working in a school system would be enjoyable. I learned about IEPs and self-contained classrooms. I facilitated a life-skills group with special needs children. Special needs children needed a lot of attention, and I looked forward to spending time with them every day. I realized then, however, that I did not want to work in a school system. I wanted to work with more challenging clients.

I noticed in the Help Wanted section of the newspaper that the Juvenile Justice Commission was hiring social workers. I sent my résumé and eventually interviewed for a job working with incarcerated youth at a community home in Trenton, New Jersey. I was hired and dove in with both feet, soon realizing that this was the job I'd been searching for. I eventually transferred to Camden to another program for boys, but I wanted to work with females. A position opened up for a social worker at the female community program.

I had heard that working with the female population could be quite challenging. I was a little nervous initially, but I soon realized that the females just needed a lot more attention. I have been working with this population for about five years now, and I would have to say that it has been the most rewarding time of my life. Females have specific issues such as children, molestation, gang initiations, and a lot more problems that I had never imagined until now. It has been a learning process, not only for me, but for them as well.

A female social worker is much different from a male social worker. On one hand, I have experienced many typical female issues, so I can relate to them. On the other hand, I am still being educated by them because today's society is very different from when I was a juvenile. Building trust is the most important piece of advice I can give to future correctional social workers. One must *always* tell the truth, even though those listening may not want to hear it. It is imperative that you never "sugarcoat" anything.

The females whom I have counseled have committed crimes as serious as vehicular manslaughter to minor crimes of a violation of probation. Symptoms of PTSD have increased, as well as molestation. This is the struggle that social workers face every day. You hope and pray that you can give them enough knowledge to succeed.

The females who come from the inner cities have witnessed crimes that no one should ever see in their lifetime. Neighbors getting shot, domestic violence, drug dealers—these are all part of their daily lives. Most of them have become numb to violence. They see it as "normal." Not until they enter the program and receive counseling from a psychologist do they realize they have symptoms of PTSD.

There are those select few who give birth to children while they are incarcerated. The families have to take care of the child while the juvenile completes her sentence. Unfortunately, these young mothers miss out on such milestones as "first steps" and "first words." Building a bond with one's child is very important during the first year, but this cannot happen if the mother is incarcerated. This creates a difficult problem for the child, the mother, and the family. My job is to make sure that the family visits regularly with the child and/or arrange transportation with other agencies to assist with this process.

4. **Ania Dobrzanska**, MS, CCM, state policy advisor, Bureau of Justice Assistance (BJA)

Ania Dobrzanska is a Bureau of Justice Assistance (BJA) state policy advisor and the Second Chance Act of 2007 program lead. Formerly, an adjunct faculty member at the University of Maryland

University College (UMUC), she taught Juvenile Delinquency. Prior to joining BJA, she was with the Moss Group, Inc., a private Washington, D.C., criminal justice consulting firm, where she assisted with implementation of the Prison Rape Elimination Act (PREA). Prior to that she worked as a grant manager at the American Correctional Association (ACA). Dobrzanska holds a BA in psychology and administration of justice from Rutgers University and an MS in justice, law, and society from American University.

She is a certified corrections manager (CCM) and has been involved in several capital cases as an expert consultant on social history and personal culpability. Dobrzanska has published several articles in *Corrections Today* on issues of professionalism in corrections and leadership. She is the co-author of a chapter on the history of prisons in *Prisons: Today and Tomorrow*, and the co-author of an article on the adjustment of life-sentence prisoners published in *Corrections Compendium*. Dobrzanska is a published writer of fiction and a playwright. Her award-winning (2005 Tacenda Literary Award for Best Short Story) short story, "Dances with Dragons: Memories of the Hole," appears in *The Crying Wall*, a book she co-edited. This story, along with a co-authored play, *Settling Scores*, which was originally published in a literary magazine, are reprinted in an anthology entitled *Lethal Rejection: Stories on Crime and Punishment* (Carolina Academic Press, 2009). She served as a co-editor and a contributor of the fourth edition of *Life Without Parole: Living in Prison Today*. Dobrzanska received a Commander-in-Chief's Coin of Excellence from Military Order or World Wars for putting together a youth leadership conference for at-risk youth in 2005. Dobrzanska is a recipient of the 2006 Notable Alumni Award conferred by American University's Department of Justice, Law, and Society.

5. **Robert Hood**, MEd, warden, ADX; correctional/criminal justice consultant

Bob Hood is a nationally recognized correctional professional with over thirty-six years in local, state, and federal criminal justice experience. He retired from the Federal Bureau of Prisons (BOP) as the warden of the nation's most secure institution—the U.S. Administrative "Supermax" Penitentiary in Colorado. He was responsible for the most violent, disruptive, and escape-prone inmates in federal custody.

Mr. Hood's career started as a correctional educator (teacher) after completing an internship within the New Jersey prison system. He found working with student offenders rewarding on many levels. Since almost 97 percent of his students would eventually be released to the community, it was satisfying to assist with their individual reentry needs.

Career advancement required additional academic and work experiences. He received a MEd in special education with a concentration in criminal justice studies. At work, he volunteered for many activities and signed up for training whenever available.

Advancement within the field of corrections required mobility. After working for the New Jersey prison system, he relocated to Texas to teach within the prison school district. Eventually he moved again to join the Federal Bureau of Prisons (BOP)—again as a correctional educator. As relocations occurred, he taught criminal justice studies at local colleges and universities.

During Mr. Hood's tenure with the BOP, he was the warden of three major correctional institutions, the chief of Internal Affairs, and the assistant director of the Federal Law Enforcement Training Center.

Security magazine identified Mr. Hood as one of the "Top 25 Most Influential People in the Security Industry," and CBS aired a *60 Minutes* special on his ability to effectively manage the most secured prison in America.

Although now retired from the federal prison system, Mr. Hood continues to consult on correctional matters. He serves on advisory boards to several companies and criminal justice colleges.

Mr. Hood is an active member of the American Correctional Association, the North American Association of Wardens and Superintendents, and the International Association of Corrections and Prisons. He sees great value in membership to professional organizations and consistently attends their annual conferences.

As Mr. Hood reflects back on his career, the most important aspect he recalls is working with other people. Once he prepared for a career in corrections, work became more than a job—it was a rewarding lifestyle.

6. **James F. Kenny, PhD; federal agent; professor, Fairleigh Dickinson University**

After graduating from college (with history and political science majors) in 1978, I decided to continue my graduate education (with an MA in social studies and political science and a PhD in criminal justice) part-time at night while working full-time during the day.

I began my professional career in insurance management and as a Congressional aide. In early 1981 I accepted a position as a U.S. treasury officer, and later assumed several management positions (as a supervisory U.S. treasury officer, a training group manager, the chief of review, the chief of advisory, the district director's representative, and the district quality officer).

While my official posts of duty were located in New Jersey, the Agency sent me to complete short-term assignments in Washington D.C., Texas, Massachusetts, Rhode Island, New York, Pennsylvania, and Connecticut.

My career at the treasury department prepared me for a successful career in academia. My law enforcement experience provided real-life illustrations for teaching criminal justice courses. Being trained as a federal instructor and encouraged to develop programs in workplace violence and threat assessment provided skill sets for future classroom and professional training.

In addition to working full-time with the government, I began to teach college courses (Criminal Justice, Criminology, White-Collar Crime, Western Civilization) part-time and conduct professional seminars/webinars on school/workplace violence, threat assessment/reduction, and bullying in schools (high/middle/elementary), other federal agencies, the New Jersey Department of Education, and private companies and associations. One of my most challenging assignments was working with the Virginia Tech faculty, students, administrators, and community after their shooting tragedy.

Since 1999 I have taught criminal justice courses at FDU. I have attained the rank of full professor and received the Distinguished Faculty and Outstanding Teacher Awards. In addition, I serve as both the graduate and internship coordinator for the Criminal Justice Department. I started and chaired the threat assessment team at FDU for ten years.

7. **Roger Lichtman**, correctional architect

As a young architect, I knew I wanted to work on large projects with a social impact. In other words, I did not want to design homes or shopping centers for wealthy people, but rather I wanted to provide the tools to improve a social infrastructure. This basically left two avenues for my pursuit: health care and criminal justice. Early in my career, I was presented with the opportunity to develop justice projects exclusively, and I have since been working with clients to envision their dreams in jails, courthouses, juvenile facilities, and prisons. I have never looked back. I have over thirty years' experience with criminal justice architecture, and I have experienced all aspects of criminal justice design. This includes architectural programming, needs assessment, studies, site selection analysis, master planning, security design, construction administration and documentation for new construction and for renovation/rehabilitation projects.

I have had the opportunity to work all over the United States on a variety of justice projects. Additionally, our firm was hired by the commonwealth of the Northern Mariana Islands to develop a comprehensive criminal justice master plan that included a jail, a juvenile facility, and an immigration facility, as well as renovation to the holding facilities on the more remote islands. The project lasted over six years.

Today's criminal justice student would be advised to keep an open mind to new opportunities. One of the more successful avenues to accomplish this is through membership in professional organizations. In that manner one can work with colleagues for the betterment of the field. It also presents an opportunity to present a sounding board for new ideas.

8. **Robert Louden**, NYPD lieutenant; hostage negotiator; director of criminal justice, Georgian Court University

On June 20, 1966, an almost college graduate—with one course left in a bachelor's degree in business, which was completed the following summer—entered the NYPD Police Academy as a rookie cop, a probationary patrolman. He did not know or care that nationwide only approximately 3 percent of policemen and -women had completed college. On July 1, 1966, he and his approximately

1,000 classmates hit the streets. Entry-level NYC-mandated training would occur irregularly until February 1967. Their mission was to assist the department—the city—in countering urban unrest, riots that were plentiful throughout the country that summer. Eight-, ten-, and twelve-hour tours of duty in the inner city were not uncommon. Sometime after completion of my BBA from Baruch College/ City University of New York (CUNY) in 1967, I was contacted by the Police Academy and encouraged to apply to law school or graduate school. I declined the law school suggestion, but I began the applicant process for graduate school, including preparation for the Graduate Record Examination (GRE). A few years earlier in 1964, the CUNY had created a new college, John Jay College of Criminal Justice, which I entered in the fall of 1969 in pursuit of an MA in Criminal Justice. Thanks in large part to the U.S. government, based on recommendations contained in the 1967 *Challenge of Crime in a Free Society*, cops such as I were able to attend college or graduate school with our tuition paid by the Law Enforcement Education Program (LEEP) of the Law Enforcement Assistance Administration (LEAA). I finally earned my degree in 1977, the maximum time allowed by school policy. In the interim I was detailed to a headquarters staff position (house mouse), largely because I had a college degree; I was promoted to sergeant (1971) and moved back to patrol duty, this time in Greenwich Village; and subsequently transferred to the Detective Bureau and charged with monitoring confidential investigation funds, including informant payments, because I had earned a business degree.

I remained in the NYPD Detective Bureau through two more promotions, to lieutenant (1980), and then to commander of the detective squad (1983), for another ten years, eventually retiring in 1987.

Although I may not be able to directly link my relative success in policing and later in academia, I still value and endorse college education for police officers for a variety of reasons, including the ability to acquire new knowledge, skills, and abilities that can be applied not only on the job, but also in the other real worlds that one inhabits. I also found that following the classroom-related routines of reading, writing, and engaging in critical thinking helped me to prepare for and pass the civil service promotion examinations. Good police departments and good colleges are, as they should be, value-based institutions. The potential synergy between the two provides for a better society.

In some ways I look at the collegiate experience as having made a trip through Oz! Through it, we can enhance what is already in our heads, unlock parts of our personalities, and strengthen our resolve to do the best we can.

9. **Bohdan Orichowsky**, juvenile parole officer

Bohdan Orichowsky is an excellent example of someone who has worked in various capacities in and around the criminal justice field before settling into his present position. He has worked in the criminal justice profession for more than twenty-three years. Bo began his employment in the adult mental health field and moved on to after-school programs for disturbed youth. He worked as a social worker in juvenile residential services for the first eight years and has served as a parole officer for the previous fifteen years—a capacity in which he believes he better serves troubled youth. Bo served four years in the United States Marine Corps and holds a BA in psychology and an MA in counseling.

I have been working in the criminal justice field for over twenty-two years, the first eight years as a social worker, and the rest as a juvenile parole officer. Prior to working for the state, I served four years in the Marine Corps, got out and completed my bachelor's degree in psychology and a master's degree in counseling.

I had been employed in the adult mental health field, having worked with community programs and community outreach, supervised independent living programs, and developed an after-school program for emotionally disturbed children in Camden County.

After several years of working in this field, I became disenchanted with my career choice and decided to try another career. After a few unrewarding jobs, I decided to return to the field of social work, and through a friend, I was referred to a position with the State of New Jersey.

I started my career as a social worker in the adult prison system, first working in the general population and shortly thereafter in the administrative segregation unit (the lockdown unit). After about two years, massive layoffs occurred, and I was told that if I wanted to continue working for the state, I would have to transfer to the juvenile division, where I was assigned to what is referred to as a "special needs" program. The program is an off-grounds residential program for incarcerated juveniles deemed to have psychological issues, thus requiring more specialized treatment than is offered in the juvenile jail.

One of my responsibilities was case planning—setting up after-care services for the juveniles prior to their release back home, specifically setting up mental health and counseling services, and when applicable, assisting in enrolling them back in school, as a majority of those returning to school were classified as "special education students."

Later in my career as a social worker, the state created the Juvenile Justice Commission, which in part included juvenile parole. I took an interest in parole, in that I found that juvenile parole was much more involved in dealing with the young men than adult parole was. For example, when juveniles are released, they are seen on a weekly basis for at least two to three months or longer before being considered for less contact. I also found that the case planning I was doing as a social worker was also being utilized in Parole, and that parole officers were more involved in making sure that the juveniles were participating in mandated counseling services. I believed that I could do more good in working with the young men in the community rather than in the program. The young men all had great ideals that they claimed they wanted to achieve once they were released, but I knew all too well that without a strong presence to guide and encourage them on the outside, their enthusiasm would quickly lose out to the lure of the streets that had gotten them into trouble in the first place.

I was accepted for the Juvenile Parole Officer Program and I successfully completed the training program. After completing a probationary period as a parole officer, I was assigned to work in various counties, and I usually worked alone in some of the major cities in New Jersey.

I came to Parole without any high expectations of having all of my parolees be successful. My experience had taught me that not all of the juveniles whom I had dealt with were determined to do well in life. There were those who did strive to do better. Some were able to turn their lives around. A few examples include one who became a truck driver, another who became a certified underwater welder, and others who went into vo-tech schools, the business field, and even college.

My attitude toward the parolees is that I will work toward ensuring that their conditions of parole are met and help all who are under my supervision, but I also accept the fact that not all are willing to comply with their parole, nor do they want the help that is being offered to them. For those who want the help and improve the quality of their lives, I do all that I can to assist them in working toward their goals.

10. **Joseph Paglino**, detective, Monmouth County Prosecutors Office; professor

Joseph R. Paglino was born and raised in Brooklyn, New York. After obtaining his bachelor of science degree in criminal justice from Saint John's University, New York, Joseph obtained the position of confidential investigator for the Office of the Chief Medical Examiner in New York City. As part of this assignment, Joseph was tasked with the investigation of homicide crime scenes in all five boroughs of New York.

Joseph subsequently advanced in the field of law enforcement in securing the position of detective for the Brooklyn District Attorney's Office in Brooklyn, New York. While there, he was assigned to the Major Offense/Career Criminal Unit, the Transit Crime Bureau, the Auto Crime Unit, the Supreme Court Bureau, and the Night Fugitive Strike Force.

Upon relocating to New Jersey, Joseph achieved the position of detective with the Monmouth County Prosecutors Office in Freehold, New Jersey, where he is currently employed. Joseph has served in the White Collar Crime Unit, the Child Abuse/Sex Crimes Unit, and the Bureau of Technical and Forensic Services. In that capacity, Joseph has personally investigated a multitude of homicide, suicide, and suspicious death scenes, as well as kidnappings, robberies, and burglaries, and participated in undercover "sting" operations involving stolen property and Internet crimes against children, which earned him the President's Award for outstanding police service in 1992 and 2001.

His professional affiliations include the International Association for Identification, the Fingerprint Society (United Kingdom), and the American Translator's Association.

An instructor, Joseph has taught courses in fingerprints, photography, crime scene investigation, and Spanish at police academies, colleges, and universities. He is also an adjunct professor of psychology and criminal justice at local universities. Scholastically, Joseph is the recipient of a master's degree in forensic psychology and is currently pursuing a PhD in criminal justice.

Additionally, Joseph is a published author, collaborating with his partner, Mauro Corvasce, in the works *Modus Operandi*, a writer's guide to how criminals work, and *Murder One*, a writer's guide to homicide, both published by Writer's Digest Books.

Joseph has appeared in numerous media outlets, such as television and in print. Additionally, he has worked as an advisor to the Discovery Channel in the production of a mystery CD-ROM.

11. **Raymond Rainville**, Department of Criminal Justice, Saint Peters University; New Jersey Probation Services

Moving to New Jersey as a thirteen-year-old, I entered into an exciting cosmopolitan environment. After finishing high school, I moved on to college with the desire to be a high school history teacher. When I graduated from Monmouth University in 1966, I discovered, much to my dismay, that there was actually no real need for history teachers. So I did what many young people in Monmouth County do: I hopped on a bus to New York and found a job in the commercial credit industry. In early 1968, I was summoned to jury duty. One day during the lunch hour, I accompanied a college friend (who was unhappy in his employment) to the county personnel department. The county personnel director asked if I wanted to fill out an application. I asked what jobs he had open and he asked whether I had a degree and in what area. After I told him my degree was in history, he asked if I wanted to be a probation officer. I said no, that I didn't want to chase kids around. He said that I would actually be a counselor to kids with problems. After the interview, I finally agreed and entered into my life's journey of probation services.

During my seven years with the Monmouth County Probation Department, I did everything: adult and juvenile, supervision and investigation and family services. I soon became the department's training officer and the representative to several county social agencies. As the department grew bigger and began to diversify, I specialized in handing juvenile cases, which had been my original goal. Later I was given the opportunity to organize the Volunteers in Probation program.

With my training background, I was offered a position with the Administrative Office of the Courts, Probation Division, as the assistant chief of probation training. When my boss was temporarily reassigned to be the head of a probation department, I became the acting chief of probation training, soon-to-be chief of probation training. During my time in training, I reorganized the program and built a truly comprehensive training unit. Since I was working with professionals in the field, I decided to further my education and was accepted to the doctoral program at Fordham University. During this period I served as chief probation officer of Union County, New Jersey, a large urban-suburban probation department. During my tenure at Union, the department won three national awards for new and progressive programs (the first job bank for offenders in New Jersey, specialized caseloads for alcoholics and substance abusers, and the Union County Volunteers in Probation program).

I then returned to the Administrative Office of the Courts with the goal of using my new field experience to revive the training program. I then was approached to take over as the director of the state's child support enforcement program. I first declined, because I wanted to work on the training program; I reluctantly agreed to cover the position for six months. Six months began a span of twenty years in child support enforcement. After receiving my doctorate in sociology/criminal justice, I began to teach at the university level, which led to my next career in teaching criminal justice.

After retiring in 2001, I decided to put my education and experience to work. I have taught at the College of New Jersey and Brookdale Community College, and I finally joined the faculty at Saint Peter's University. In 2008 I became the chair of the Criminal Justice Department.

12. **Ralph Rojas**, officer, Port Authority Police Department; assistant professor of justice studies

Ralph Rojas Jr. is currently the assistant professor of justice studies at Southern New Hampshire University. Professor Rojas holds an MPA (master's in public administration in administration of justice) and an MS (in criminology) from Long Island University (NY) and an AB (sociology) degree from Fordham University (NY). He is presently writing his dissertation on police drug abuse at the University of Baltimore (Maryland).

Professor Rojas has over thirty years of criminal justice experience—including teaching, administrative, managerial, and consulting roles in higher education and posts in law enforcement, corrections, prosecution, and criminal courts. He has also held several educational positions in teaching, course development, program modification, and program development in the fields of police, corrections, and forensic science at colleges and universities in New Jersey, New Mexico, and Colorado.

Professor Rojas retired after a distinguished twenty-year career with the Port Authority of New York and the New Jersey Police Department. Earlier, he worked for the New York State Department of Correctional Services and the Brooklyn District Attorney's Office in New York City.

Professor Rojas is a member of the Academy of Criminal Justice Sciences (ACJS), where he is a certified criminal justice program reviewer; the American Society of Criminology (ASC); the New Jersey Association of Chiefs of Police (NJACOP); the New Jersey Association of Criminal Justice Educators (NJACJE), where he was a past president; the New Jersey Association of Forensic Scientists (NJAFS); the founder and past president of the Colorado Association of Criminal Justice Educators (CACJE); the founder and president of the New Hampshire Association of Criminal Justice Educators, the Northeastern Association of Criminal Justice Sciences (NEACJS), where he has held numerous executive board positions, including as the delegate for New Jersey and presently the second vice president; and the Southwest Association of Criminal Justice (SWACJ), where he was the October 2008 Denver Annual Conference site coordinator.

13. **Brian L. Royster**, EdD, New Jersey State police officer; professor

In the beginning of 1985, I was uncertain about my future. During this time frame, I had already joined the U.S. Army Reserves, but I didn't want to be a full-time soldier. I had no idea what I wanted to do in life. By happenstance, a friend walked in and I noticed that he had lost a significant amount of weight. He was a former Newark special police officer. I inquired about his sudden svelte appearance. He told me he was in the New Jersey State Police Academy. At the time, I was not aware of this agency. He said a test was being given and suggested that I take it. My expectation of passing the test was not high, because I had never taken my education very seriously. I subsequently passed with a score of 61 out of 100. I later learned that I was actually accepted under an affirmative action policy, which made me feel like a "special case." Back then I didn't realize the importance of this policy, but I vowed never to feel like that again.

I entered the NJSP Academy in the fall of 1985 and graduated twenty-six weeks later, in January 1986. The academy was rewarding because it gave me the mental and physical discipline that I needed at that time in my life.

My first assignment was working at Hope Station in Warren County. It was an eye-opener for me because I had never been in that part of the state before. As my career progressed, I ultimately became a detective after serving seven and a half years in the state police uniform. My duties changed; a detective must take numerous investigative courses before being allowed to conduct investigations. Detective functions also require an analytical mind-set because you're always trying to figure out a criminal's next step.

Over the course of my career, I had the pleasure of being assigned to some of the most prestigious units. A few that stand out include: Central Security, EEO, AA, Electronic Surveillance, Solid Hazardous Waste, Organized Crime North, and Counterterrorism, but the one that was most rewarding was being a part of the FBI Joint Terrorism Task Force (JTTF).

The JTTF is comprised of officials from federal, state, county, and local agencies. The task force's function is to investigate cases involving potential acts of terrorism. Non-FBI members on the JTTF are sworn in as U.S. Deputy Marshals and are afforded powers to travel within the forty-eight contiguous United States and outside of the United States to effectuate arrests. Everyone on the JTTF is also required to have a top-secret national security clearance and CIA security clearance. My inclusion on the JTTF allowed me to assist in the tragic 9/11 investigation. This assignment was by far the most satisfying of my career, because I saw firsthand how agencies could put aside any internal conflicts and work collectively to solve the most heinous crime the United States has ever witnessed. It was also while on the JTTF that I received my first non-commissioned promotion to detective sergeant.

In retrospect, my entrance into the NJSP set the stage for my upward mobility. I realized, early in my career, that education would set me apart from my contemporaries. Beginning in 1987, I attended community college to further my education. I couldn't sit back and watch others advance and not be a part of the process myself. My insecurity from believing that I was a "special case" in being accepted into the NJSP was the impetus for me to seek out my advanced degrees.

During my twenty-five-year career, I have attained two associate degrees from Essex County College, a bachelor's degree from Montclair State University, a master's degree from Seton Hall University, a master's degree from New Jersey City University, a post-master's degree from Seton Hall University, and a doctoral degree from Seton Hall University. It took approximately twenty-two years of going to school on a part-time basis while working full-time in the NJSP, but it was worth it. In addition, I attended the FBI National Academy, which is considered the most prestigious training for law enforcement personnel. I firmly believe that education is important because it shows dedication, which should be a requirement for all future leaders.

My goal, after retiring from law enforcement, was to teach prospective police officers about the good and bad aspects of law enforcement and allow them to be more informed. When I subsequently retired in 2012, I obtained a full-time faculty position at Saint Peter's University. This position has afforded me the opportunity to join outside criminal justice educators' associations and network with my colleagues.

14. **Darcella A. Patterson Sessoms**, PhD, DSW, LCSW

The letters following Dr. Sessoms's name say a lot about the person and indicate a personal drive to achieve. However, they do not inform us of her journey from a humble beginning on the periphery of a criminal justice career to one of steady advancement to a position of distinction as the assistant commissioner of corrections for the State of New Jersey. Dr. Sessoms has successfully managed a career with community service as a volunteer, a worker for youth, and a citizen dedicated to contributing to social causes.

Darcella Anita Patterson Sessoms is a well-known leader in correctional social work education, policy, and professional practice. On September 7, 2004, she assumed the position of assistant director for the Office of Transitional Services (OTS) with the New Jersey Department of Corrections. On May 5, 2007, she was promoted to the position of director. After having served almost ten years in state government, on April 19, 2014, she was promoted to the rank of assistant commissioner.

Assistant Commissioner Sessoms manages the Division of Program and Community Services, which is responsible for the following prison system services: social work, education, religious services, victim services, volunteer services, residential community reentry programs (RCRP), the intensive supervision program (ISP), and county services.

Her career in social work spans over twenty years. During the past two decades, Darcella has worked in various arenas of social work policy and practice, which include but are not limited to domestic violence, HIV/AIDS, addiction, homelessness, juveniles, and incarceration. She is a licensed clinical social worker (LCSW) with the State of New Jersey and the commonwealth of Pennsylvania.

Dr. Sessoms is certified as a student in field instruction (SIFI) supervisor, and she is responsible for the oversight of the field placement experience for many social work students in the tristate area who are interested in a career in forensic social work with a specific concentration on reentry and corrections. Dr. Sessoms also serves as a part-time lecturer for Rutgers University, the Department of Social Work, where she currently teaches coursework on Diversity and Oppression. Additionally, she serves as a part-time lecturer for the University of Pennsylvania, where she teaches courses on American Racism and Social Change and has served as a teaching assistant for the course Criminal Justice Issues: Implications for Social Work.

Dr. Sessoms received both a bachelor of arts in sociology and a master's degree in social work from Rutgers University, New Brunswick campus. She received her doctorate from the University of Pennsylvania, School of Social Policy and Practice. Dr. Sessoms credits all of her success to her faith, her loving family, and the strong mentors in her life.

15. **William Ussery**, police officer; professor; clinical psychologist

I joined the force in 1969 during the Newark riots. A good friend asked, "Why would you join a police department? You are smarter than that." My response was a phrase from Ben Franklin: "It seems that everyone is talking about the weather, but no one is doing anything about it." I was raised in an autocratic household, flunked out of military school, and spent four years at USMC. These experiences confirmed that I could follow orders in a military environment, and I truly believed that I needed to contribute this background to a police career.

Finding a job was fairly easy; everyone was hiring. One department could not get my fingerprints because of my labor as a mason's helper. (They told me to use Jergen's lotion for a few weeks!) Another department had an entrance application that was so long and involved that my ADHD personality could not finish it. I was exempt from the NJSP at that time because I wore glasses. A mentor from the state police told me that I could get a job anywhere else, but *not* in my hometown. Well, the application was only two pages long and I didn't listen.

Highlights are difficult to recall. I was promoted to lieutenant after a relatively short time in Patrol, jumping over all of the sergeants. I credit this to almost completing my associate's degree in police science.

A specialty of mine was investigating fatal motor vehicle collisions. I also attended most if not all of the post-autopsies performed in our community. In fact, one highlight was a DWI conviction that had been corrupted by several breathalyzer readings and a blood test at the ER. Due to my contacts in the pathology unit at the hospital, a doctor described a chart that indicated that all of the readings (venular, as well as arteriol) had fallen within an acceptable variance. This case was also an MV collision that involved several fatalities.

My decision to take an early retirement was available due to military time served, and I saw opportunities to use my talents in other venues. I believed that being fifty-two years of age was more marketable than being fifty-five.

William J. Ussery, MA, LPC, has been a counselor since 1984, after receiving a MA in psychology from Fairleigh Dickinson University and his license in 1999. He has been employed by the COP2COP program at UMDNJ/UBHC since September 2000 as a mental health clinician II. His official title is mental health clinician II, and his duties include answering a helpline for law enforcement officers with mental health and substance abuse needs. These calls require assessments, referrals, peer counseling, and often a response to his specialty, critical incident stress debriefing.

Mr. Ussery has been trained in all levels of critical incident stress management (CISM), and he has been involved in crisis response since forming the Apollo team in 1984. Mr. Ussery was also certified to train peer counselors for CISM and QPR, a suicide prevention strategy. He has over twenty-five years' experience as a clinician, specializing in anxiety, trauma, and stress disorders. He was appointed an associate professor at the College of Saint Elizabeth, where he taught crisis intervention courses. Currently, he teaches crisis intervention to master's level students at Fairleigh Dickinson University.

16. **Len Ward**, parole officer; professor

Lenny Ward currently serves as the director of the Divisions of Parole and Community Programs for the New Jersey State Parole Board (NJSPB). As director, he oversees almost four hundred law enforcement officers and command staff within the Division of Parole, and he manages over $37 million in contracted services that provide direct support to the over 15,000 parolees under supervision in New Jersey.

Lenny came into state service in 1990, and he has served in multiple capacities within the Department of Law and Public Safety, the Department of Transportation, and the Department of Corrections.

Lenny graduated from Jersey City State College in 1973 with a BA, attended Brooklyn Law School, and received a master's degree in public administration from Fairleigh Dickinson University in 1997.

He is certified as an instructor by the New Jersey Police Training Commission, is certified by the U.S. Department of Justice in community-oriented policing, and is an adjunct professor at Fairleigh Dickinson University.

Appendix 2

Interest, Inquiry, and Cover Letters

Good communication is a sure key to success. Written communication provides the reviewer with the sense that you are a competent applicant and that you are serious about the position under consideration. Many young people are accustomed to communicating by e-mail. This can be a fatal mistake when applying for a position. Many people see e-mail as a temporary message; often e-mail is not copied or filed. Once read, most individuals have a tendency to ignore e-mails. A good written letter is usually read, filed, and attached to the appropriate file. A good practice is to use written correspondence for all of your letters.

Note: Your letter must be long enough to make your point. However, you must also keep your letter short enough to ensure that your recipient will read it. The letter should be no more than two pages long. Here are some steps to help you.

First, type your letter. This demonstrates a professional effort on your part.

Second, state at the beginning type of position you are seeking (in department or section of the agency you are interested). This will help ensure that your letter goes to the right person and that it will be assessed according to agency need. If you can, research who should be the recipient of your letter and address it to him or her with the correct title. State in the first paragraph that you are attaching or have included a résumé. (See Appendix 4 for sample résumés.)

Third, briefly but succinctly describe how you would make a contribution and emphasize a few of the stronger assets you bring to the position.

Fourth, state early on why you are interested in them and why they should be interested in you. Make a statement such as, "I have the experience relative to the needed tasks of the agency," or something softer when you don't have the experience, such as, "I am confident that I possess the competence to adapt to your workforce." Another approach would be, "I believe that I am an excellent match for this position because of my preparation and experience." You may reiterate the job requirements listed in the job posting, followed by your specific qualifications and examples of matching work that you have already performed and are performing. Address your talents (assets) with positive examples of applications in the past. This is the time to mention any internships, volunteer work, and other relevant experiences you have had. You should also mention if you had any opportunity to be innovative during these previous experiences. This is also the place to mention any academic assignments that you completed that have relevance to the job you are seeking.

Note: Your remarks should be specifically addressed to the agency of interest. That is, find out about the agency and its work so you can target its mission with your experience.

Fifth, in your final paragraph, request an interview to accomplish one of the following:

A. Explore a current job opening.
B. Explore your options if there is no current opening. This is the exploratory approach for you to get to know them and for them to get to know you.

The point is that you want to get your foot in the door. You want them to see your face and place your résumé in their hands. You want them to remember you.

Sixth, include all pertinent information that will enable them to get in touch with you—your full name, address, phone (and cell) number, e-mail address.

Note: Carefully review all correspondence and documents for accuracy. Correct misspellings, poor grammar, and incorrect punctuation. *DO NOT*

RELY ON SPELL CHECK. Write your signature clearly—it should not be a quick autograph.

Note: This is the time when you should be giving out your phone number, so consider the message on your phone. How would it sound to a professional calling in a response to an inquiry from you? Make sure your phone greeting is simple and polite.

You want to end the letter strong. Leave the reader with something memorable about you. Take a look at the "My Ten Points" that you developed and see if there is one strong statement that can sum up why they should hire you. Utilize what makes you stand out.

If you take the time to go online, you will find many helpful examples of letter styles (in addition to the format we include in this appendix) that will emphasize the type of writing to be done, the language you should use, and the format or construction of the letter that would be the most helpful.

Here are two sample letters you should consider for reference and style:

Letter 1: Letter of Interest Sample

Peter Smith

107 Sixth Street, Apt. 2B

Middletown, NJ 07001

Phone: 555-761-6111 e-mail: psmith123@gmail.com

May 21, 2015

Chief Ron Smith

Middle Village Police Department

123 Main Street

Middle Village, NJ 07777

Dear Chief Smith:

I am interested in law enforcement as a career, and I would like to inquire about any open positions at the Middle Village Police Department. Middle Village's training program for Police Special Officer II has been recommended to me by my criminal justice advisor as a place to start. I would be interested in learning more about your department's program and about any available opportunities. I have a bachelor's degree from Saint Peter's University in criminal justice. My concentration in that degree program included police administration and procedure, as well as courses in police culture, community policing, crime investigation, and constitutional law. I completed an internship with the Jersey City's Police Department, which allowed me to apply my course concepts to the police environment.

My résumé, which is enclosed, contains additional information on my experiences and skills. I will provide references upon request. I would appreciate the opportunity to discuss the special officers program with you, learn more about your department, and provide further information on my candidacy. I can be reached on my cell phone at 555-555-5555 or by e-mail at psmith123@gmail.com.

Yours truly,

Peter Smith

Letter 2: Sample Letter of Interest

John Q. Applicant
Street Address
City, State, Zip Code
E-mail
Phone Number

Date
Contact Person Name and Title
Company Name
Company Address
Position Posting Title and Number

Dear Mr./Ms. (or title):

I am applying for (Position Name) that was advertised or posted in the (Name of Newspaper) or listed at (Name of Website). I am enclosing for your review the completed application, my résumé, copies of certifications/special training, and a list of three references, as were requested in the posting.

My qualifications meet or exceed those listed in the posting, and I would like to emphasize a few of my personal strengths that make me a competitive candidate.

I have successfully completed training, internships, and other special events. My references are able to provide specific examples of the excellence I would bring to the agency. I have a history of outstanding performance in each position I have held and in each assignment that I have undertaken.

I have completed my (Highest Academic Degree) in criminal justice and have applied that training in my internships and previous employment. I can be reached during the day by e-mail or on my cell phone at (000-000-0000). Thank you for your consideration. I look forward to speaking with you to further explore the assets I would bring to your agency.

Sincerely,

(Your Name Handwritten Clearly)
(Your Name Typed)
[End the letter with a simple salutation, space for your written signature, followed by your typed name.]

Appendix 3

A Guide to Interview Questions

(See Chapter 3 for related information.)

A common suggestion to help people prepare for interviews is to tell them to *relax!*—a good commonsense viewpoint. However, as practical as that approach may sound, it must be coupled with preparation, and that means work—hard work.

A good place to begin your interview preparation is to research the agency to which you applied. If you have done this already, perhaps for a letter of inquiry, we suggest that you do it again. Who knows? Something may have changed. Learn as many specifics as possible. Some agencies have specializations or perform unique services. Your research will help you demonstrate your preparedness if the interviewer were to say to you, "We have a responsibility for . . . How do you see yourself fitting in with the other members of the team?" This, of course, is an opportunity for you to say something like, "I saw on your website . . ." You will have demonstrated that you can take initiative and plan ahead.

We have discussed the importance for you to develop an interview script and to utilize what we call "**My Ten Points**." This is the beginning of your preparation for the all-important job interview. Each *point* ideally is a response for many interviewers' questions. Your points will help you present to the interviewer such things as your intellectual (and at times physical) fitness for the job; the fact that you are you a team player; your basic skills, knowledge, and proficiencies for the job; your drive and ambition to be a good employee; and your values, which make you an exemplary employee. Interviewers do not automatically assume you want a job simply because you applied and came to the interview. At the end of this appendix is a chart for you to list out "My Ten Points." As you review this list from time to time, you may wish to refine it or even to change some items on it.

Here are some sample questions to help you develop your interview responses. These questions move from simple to more complex. Do not become complacent because the first questions seem easy or commonplace. Your demonstrated proficiency during an interview is only as good as the last question you answered satisfactorily. Your answers are your opportunity to mention something important that may not be presented in a résumé or cover letter.

A. "Tell me a little about yourself."

   The interviewer may be looking to help you relax, get the conversation started, and get you to provide some information about your background and training. Try not to be too casual, but keep your comments specific and focus on your accomplishments as they apply to the job.

B. "What do you see as your main strengths, and can you identify what may be your greatest weakness or two?"

   Identifying your strengths and weaknesses reflect on your self-awareness. You should be prepared to answer questions about your personal and professional development. Your answer to this question, like the other questions that will be asked, needs to help you stand out above the competition. Explaining what you perceive to be a weakness requires some serious thought. You cannot be cavalier about the answer. You need to convey to the interviewer that you are aware of your shortcomings and that you continually work to improve in those areas. Remember, no one is strong in all areas all of the time. The best answer is that while we rely on our strengths, we do not neglect our less-strong points and we seek assistance when it is needed.

C. "Why are you looking for employment in this agency?"

   This is a somewhat trickier question, and the interviewer may also be wondering why you are looking to leave your present job. Some subtexts in the questions are whether there is something wrong with you or your present position. Perhaps the interviewer is trying to determine if you stick with a job once you are employed, that is, whether you are loyal to your employer. You can begin your answer by describing what you did in your previous employment, emphasizing the highlights of the position(s), and segue that into something that describes the advantages of the position applied for and how this is could be an opportunity for you to build on what you have already accomplished. You may be able to show that you keep current with changes in the business, and help promote the idea that this agency is on the cutting edge of those changes. As you indicated in the earlier question, you have also continued to prepare yourself for change and this position represents a better fit for your career and personal goals.

D. "What makes you stand out from others who may be applying for this position?"

Caution: Don't fall into the trap of repeating something you have already said!

Your preparation for interviews should include a wide array of potential answers. (This is why you should prepare your "My Ten Points.") Your ability to be succinct may indicate your awareness about yourself and what drives you—what it is that make you passionate.

E. "Tell me about your relationships with your managers and fellow employees."

Hopefully, you have had good relationships with your managers and fellow employees. You should believe that your interviewer will be calling former employers for a reference. Be truthful when describing your experiences and whatever social skills you employed that made your relationships satisfactory and successful for the workplace.

F. "Where do you see yourself in five years?"

There are at least two perspectives to consider when answering this question. The first is that interviewers may be checking your level of ambition. Your review of the agency prior to coming to the interview should have helped you develop a vision of what you hope to achieve if hired here. As you answer this question, you may be describing how you intend to achieve those goals. This also may be an opportunity for you to ask questions now or at the end of the interview. Your conversation may begin with something like this: "I have described for you my goals and the means with which I hope to achieve them in this service. I would like to ask you for your opinion about those goals and my process for success."

The second perspective is that the interviewer may be seeking to discover your intentions about length of service at their agency. If you are not asked what your ten-year plan might be, you could respond with, "In ten years I see myself in _____ position." This shows you have an even bigger picture in mind for the job.

You should also be prepared for general questions. Again, the "My Ten Points" exercise will help. One example of a general question is, "How do you define success?"

YOUR PREPARATION FOR THE INTERVIEW

Take each of the sample questions above and prepare a response for them. Do not assume that this is a onetime effort. As you prepare for each interview and practice your answers, you may discover that your responses need refinement (especially since you will be applying for jobs with different functions). To be sure, each success you have, each new credential, and each of your work experiences will have the potential to alter your responses. Your answers may also be refined according to specific information you obtain about the agency.

You should practice to improve your interview technique. Among the things to consider are how to dress (see Appendix 5 for advice on this), voice inflection, the use of pauses, how to ask questions of the interviewer for clarification and about the job, hand gestures, body language, and more. Among the things you also need to learn about are the body language you bring to the interview and your use of verbal language.

One way to learn about yourself in an interview is simply to *practice*. In the best of worlds, seek the participation of a professional to conduct a practice interview. If no one is available or you are too uncomfortable to ask someone you don't know well, consult a friend. If this is necessary, then you have one example of why you need to practice! You need to be as comfortable as possible in the interview, so that you can focus on what is being asked of you.

If you wish to get a look at how you present yourself, set up your practice interview with a friend and prepare a script for the interview. Then record a video of the practice interview, and you and someone else who will speak honestly with you should review the video together. Look at how you are dressed, seated, and giving off body language. Listen to your responses. Take notes during the video. Practice making the needed changes and then, as Warner Wolf, the famous sports announcer, has said, "Let's go to the videotape." See if you succeeded and compare notes.

The setting for the practice interview should be simple—an office. The interviewer will sit behind a desk and you will sit in front of the desk. Try a variation on this with two chairs on opposite sides of a coffee table or two chairs on the same side of a coffee table, or after practicing with one person as the interviewer, have two or three persons interview you at the same time. When more than one person interviews you, your ability to focus is usually more challenged.

By the conclusion of the interview, you should also be able to ascertain whether you really want the job. Nevertheless, the interview may not answer all of your questions.

THE QUESTIONS YOU SHOULD ASK AT THE INTERVIEW

You will almost always be given the opportunity to ask questions at the end of your interview. Even if that opportunity is not put forward, you may suggest that you have a few questions if that is permissible. There are three kinds of questions to ask at this time.

The first questions will have to do with something that came up during the interview and for which you seek clarification. Form these questions carefully. This is not the time to challenge current practices in the organization.

The second questions are similar and have to do with your research about the agency. These will address your concerns about agency specifics that were apparent from the website, the job posting, or other sources of information. If you have written down the areas you are concerned with, you may wish to produce your notes for accuracy. Prepare your notes in a professional manner—typed.

The third questions are more common and address your personal and career needs. You should be able to address some of the following questions in your research about the agency, but if they are not readily available, then now is your chance to ask. Keep your list short. The following are only examples.

A. When might I expect to hear from you?
B. What is the starting salary?
C. What benefits are offered?
D. What hours/shifts would I be expected to work?
E. Who would be my supervisor?
F. Can you explain the possibilities for advancement in this agency?
G. Will I be working with a team, or will I have independent assignments?
H. Is there any training available for the position?

As was noted above, many of these questions, especially those related to salary, work hours, benefits, and training, may be listed on the websites, and you should attempt to have them answered before the interview.

MY TEN POINTS

(Do not neglect this!)

Point 1 –

Point 2 –

Point 3 –

Point 4 –

Point 5 –

Point 6 –

Point 7 –

Point 8 –

Point 9 –

Point 10 –

Getting an interview is not a guarantee of getting a job. Each interview you take part in is a learning experience and is practice for future interviews. These interview opportunities will help you to improve your skills in responding to employment questions and in making a good impression as you work toward landing the job that starts or advances your career.

Appendix 4

Sample Résumé and CV

(Applicants should reread the résumé section of Chapter 7 before starting to compile their résumé.)

The résumé is your door opener; it provides the recruiter with a glimpse of who you are and your qualifications for the position. Poorly written résumés will not get you an interview. Remember, the résumé should be short and to the point, written clearly, with attention paid to honesty and accuracy. There are many types of résumés. Two are provided here as examples: one for general applications, and the other for specific placement with a particular agency. A curriculum vita is a résumé usually intended for academic positions. It requires you to list all courses, including workshops and seminars you have taken and/or taught, and a complete list of your formal and nonformal publications.

Your résumé should be well-written, well-formatted, edited, and above all, professional. Here are some tips for a successful résumé:

1. Have it printed on good quality paper.
2. Place it in a large envelope—not folded.
3. When possible, print the recipient's name on the front of the envelope.
4. When possible, modify the résumé for the recipient or the intended job.
5. Include your basic information: name, address, phone numbers, and e-mail address.

6. List your objective at the top (customize whenever possible).
7. List your education, with highest level of education first.
8. Note any honors and awards that you have received (graduating summa cum laude, president of the student association, or having a paper published).
9. List work experience with most recent work first. List dates of employment and provide a short list of tasks for each job. Also list your internship in this section. If you have had the opportunity to travel as part of your education and it was related to criminal justice, list this under your work experience.
10. List any military experience, especially if you received any relevant training.
11. List any additional skills, including computer skills, foreign language skills, special licenses, or further training.
12. Ensure that all entries are consistent, especially the margins, dates, indentations, etc.
13. Review for word usage. Use a synonym guide or thesaurus to make your résumé more interesting.
14. Use a professional résumé preparer if you lack the computer skills to do the job yourself.
15. State "References provided upon request."
16. Evaluate your social networking sites for content that might be in poor taste.
17. Have your résumé reviewed for excessive length.

Here are some tips for what not to do:

1. *Do not* assume spell check or grammar check is correct.
2. *Do not* refer to social websites unless you are certain that you are represented there properly.
3. *Do not* use "cutsey" e-mail names—set up a new e-mail address.
4. *Do not* mislead, such as stating that you have competency in a foreign language when your experience is only limited to a few phrases.
5. *Do not* assume that you have thoroughly reviewed and edited your résumé. Have a friend or someone else also review it for spelling, grammar, duplications, inconsistencies, and awkward phrasing.

6. *Do not* try to impress using words that are not part of your regular vocabulary.
7. *Do not* include references unless they are specifically requested.
8. *Do not* use fancy fonts.
9. *Do not* clutter up your résumé with irrelevant information.

Amy Student

1609 Forest Avenue E-mail: amystudent12@gmail.com
Smalltown, NJ 07001   Telephone#: (555) 777-1234

OBJECTIVE: To obtain a full-time criminal justice position where I can contribute my knowledge, skills, and passion while still being a team player

EDUCATION: **Saint Peter's University**, Jersey City, NJ
Bachelor of Arts, criminal justice, anticipated graduation: May 2015
Current cumulative GPA: 3.923; criminal justice GPA: 4.0

J.F. Kennedy High School, Smalltown, NJ
Years attended: 2010–2012, graduated in June 2012
Lodi High School, Lodi, NJ
Years attended: 2008–2010

HONORS & AWARDS:
Dean's List, Saint Peter's University   Every Semester
Alpha Phi Sigma, National Criminal Justice Honor Society 2013–2015
     Vice-President 2015
Criminal Justice Students Association   2011–2015

WORK EXPERIENCE:
Site Coordinator, A.C.E Before/After School Program, Better Place, NJ   Oct. 2014–Present
- Worked first as a counselor from September 2012–October 2014 until achieving my current promoted position
- Co-manage a before/after school program with a total of 84 kids in grades K–5th
- Certified in CPR, EpiPen, and first aid.

GEM Criminal Justice Tutor, Saint Peter's University, Jersey City, NJ Fall 2013 & Fall 2014 semesters
- Worked with a college professor to lead my own interactive class discussion once a week
Sales Assistant, Buttercrust Bakery, Smalltown, NJ   May 2009–January 2015

- Certified Food Safety Manager by National Registry of Food Safety Professionals on August 9, 2013

EXTRACURRICULAR LEADERSHIP ACTIVITIES:
Gannon Debating Society
- President, Fall 2015–Spring 2016; Secretary, Fall 2014–Spring 2015
- Worked with partners in developing affirmative and negative cases for team-based National Educational Debate Association tournaments

Alpha Phi Sigma (Criminal Justice Honor Society)
- Vice President, Fall 2015–Spring 2016; Secretary, Fall 2014–Spring 2015

ADDITIONAL SKILLS:
- Bilingual speaker: Spanish and English

References are available upon request.

Brian Santos

1011 Broad Street, Middle Village NY 01001
(555) 333-0001 BrianSan@nt.edu

OBJECTIVE To obtain the position of patrolman with the Middle Village Police Department

EDUCATION Bachelor of Arts—Criminal Justice   Anticipated: December 2015
Saint Peter's University, Jersey City, NJ

INTERNSHIP Jersey City Police Department
Jersey City, NJ   August 2014 to January 2015
Academic internship (credit earning) with Jersey City Police Department.
   Duties include:
Assist officers in writing reports
Visit local middle and high schools for crime prevention program
Assist dispatcher with duties during assigned shift

EXPERIENCE All-Town Security, Inc.
Jersey City, NJ 07001   September 2014 to Present
Assigned to Newport Mall
Developed and implemented training for new security guards within the
   mall
Co-presented paper on topic of sexual assault awareness for company
   employees
Maintained foot patrol of the mall
Assisted department head with creation and implementation of crime prevention awareness campaign

A & B Lawn Service, Inc.   Summers 2013, 2014, 2015
Handled customer service and landscaping duties

LEADERSHIP & VOLUNTEER EXPERIENCE
Saint Peters University Criminal Justice Students Association 2012 to
   Present

Middle Village Volunteer Fire Department 2010 to 2013
Big Brothers/Big Sisters of East Jersey 2014 to Present

COMPUTER EXPERIENCE
Microsoft Word, Excel, Access, PowerPoint, Publisher, Adobe Photoshop

REFERENCES

Available upon request

CURRICULUM VITAE

Peter Smith, PhD
123 Broad Street
Middle Village, New Jersey 07701
Home: (555) 123-9999
E-mail address: psmith123@gmail.com

GOAL:
Seeking a full-time teaching position in the field of sociology/criminal justice, using a combination of my professional experience and graduate education for the benefit of students in an educational setting

SUMMARY:
Over ten years' experience within an institution of higher education, including eight years of teaching at the College of New Jersey, Department of Law and Justice; at Kean University, Department of Public Administration, Criminal Justice Program, and the Sociology Department; and at Brookdale Community College. Courses include: History and Philosophy of Corrections; Criminology; Community-Based Corrections; Probation and Parole; Juvenile Delinquency, Child Protection Agencies, and the Law; Comparative Criminal Justice; Judicial Process; Introduction to Criminal Justice; and others. Member of Alpha Phi Sigma, the Criminal Justice National Honor Society. Faculty Advisor of the Saint Peter's chapter of the National Honor Society. Faculty advisor to the Criminal Justice Students Association.

EDUCATION:
PhD Sociology. Fordham University, Bronx, New York
MA Counseling. Rider University, Trenton, New Jersey
BS Social Sciences. Monmouth University, West Long Branch, New Jersey

TEACHING EXPERIENCE:
2002–Present: Assistant, Kean College, Department of Criminal Justice
1994–2000: Adjunct Professor, The College of New Jersey, Department of Law and Justice

2001–2003: Adjunct Professor, Public National School of Public Administration and Criminal Justice, Department of Sociology
2001–2006: Adjunct Professor, Brookdale Community College, Department of Sociology
2002–Adjunct Professor: Saint John's University, Graduate School of Professional Studies, Department of Criminal Justice and Legal Studies

Other educational experiences include:
• Supervised student interns for Fordham University, Rutgers University, Monmouth University, The College of New Jersey, and other educational institutions
• Guest-lectured on the subjects of criminal justice and sociology at various colleges
• Chaired the staff development committee and the regional training programs committee of the National Child Support Enforcement Association
• Instructor for the New Jersey Bar Association, Institute of Legal Continuing Education
• Instructor for U.S. Department of Health and Human Services, Office of Child Support Enforcement

PROFESSIONAL EXPERIENCE:
April 1968 to September 1994
Senior Probation Officer, Monmouth County Probation Department, Freehold, New Jersey
Responsibilities included preparing pre-sentence reports and supervision of juvenile probationers; staff training officer; director of volunteers; field instructor for Monmouth College.

CONSULTING:
Served as a consultant, program developer, and seminar participant for the following organizations:
• U.S. Department of Health and Human Services
• U.S. Commission on Interstate Child Support Enforcement
• National Center for State Courts
• Institute of Court Management

- State of Illinois, Administrative Office of Courts
- Several other major private corporations

CONTINUING EDUCATION:
Participated in various seminars and workshops in the area of management, staff development, and social services, including Summer School of Alcohol Studies; Rutgers Youth Institute; AMA Training the Trainer Seminar; Personnel Administration; Criminal Justice Management; and Staffing Pattern Analogies for Child Support Programs.

PUBLISHED ARTICLES AND PRESENTATIONS:
- Child Support and Court Administration, "The Child Support Reporter," U.S. Government, Department of Health and Human Services, Administration for Families and Children, Office of Child Support Enforcement, 1999.
- Academy of Criminal Justice Sciences, 44th Conference, Las Vegas, NV 2004, Paper: "Immigrants and Crime Prevention," in *A Review of Traditional Patterns and Current Trends, Encyclopedia of Police Science, Third Edition,* 2006, "Politics and the Police."
- "Gateway Conference Strategies for Returning Offenders," Education and Employment Opportunities.
- Book review, "Who to Release? Parole, Fairness, and Criminal Justice," in the *International Criminal Justice Review*, September 2010.

PROFESSIONAL AFFILIATIONS:
- New Jersey Association of Criminal Justice Educators (2006–2007, vice president)
- Academy of Criminal Justice Sciences
- American Correctional Association, New Jersey Chapter
- American Parole and Probation Association
- Middle Atlantic States Conference on Corrections
- New Jersey Child Support Council (founding member, first president)
- Eastern Regional Child Support Association (ERICSA)

REFERENCES: Available upon request

Appendix 5

The Career Fair Plan

The career/job fair is a valuable resource for finding your entrance into the criminal justice profession. Look at it as opportunity for networking, career exploration, interview practice, and a job search. Career/job fairs are hosted by colleges, specific industries, and other agencies. You should prepare yourself appropriately for the career/job fair. This appendix is intended to help you with preparation to meet each contingency.

Agencies send representatives to these fairs to provide information, answer questions, collect résumés, and more. Some agencies don't advertise when they are recruiting, while others are always recruiting. Your task is to prepare for all opportunities when you attend. Some of the recommendations are rather simple, and you should look at them as a checklist—a checklist that you may wish to review after each career/job fair to ensure that all preparatory activity has been performed and determine what you may need to strengthen. After all, you may encounter something unique at some career/job fair that will benefit you at the next.

Each revision of your preparation will help to ensure that when you meet agency representatives, you will get their attention and improve the likelihood of a second interview. Be aware that how you present yourself and what you personally display will influence the representatives' perception of you and the chances of having your résumé receive serious consideration. You want to leave each fair with the feeling of satisfaction that comes from knowing you did your best to demonstrate your value to those companies you are interested in working for.

Here is your most important piece of advice for the career/job fair: *Be prepared!*

The following checklist will help you with this preparation for career/ job fairs.

1. Make a list of career/job fairs.

   Your list of career/job fairs needs to be updated regularly. The criminal justice or career services department at your college will likely have a listing of these fairs. Career/job fair listings can also be found in publications or on websites; for example, the New Jersey Association of Criminal Justice Educators lists fairs in its newsletter and on its website. Here is another suggestion: Utilize Google Career Fairs! You will discover more than you can imagine. This will be stated later, but for the record let's say it here, as well: After each fair, make notes to yourself about each employer/agency you visited and/or the name of each person who gave you an interview.

   Assuming you receive an interview or at least engage a representative in conversation, you may be asked whether you have any questions. This is the time to ask! Your preliminary review of agencies attending the fair should guide your preparation of questions. Write your questions down.

2. Obtain a list of employers/agencies/companies represented at the fair.

   Prioritize which companies represent the area(s) in which you would like to be employed. Review each by a) going to its website and learning as much as possible about the agency/company, or b) visit www.quintcareers.com/researching_companies.htm. We recommend that you visit this site to see the wealth of information it offers for your job search. This step is important because it will help you to skip agencies that are not relative to your vision for a career choice. Obtaining employment, especially for the career that you desire, takes work—*do not skip this step!* The career/job fair is not a sightseeing tour.

   Here are some additional valuable tips about career/job fair representation: First, career/job fairs are attended by companies, corporations, government agencies, private nonprofits, for-profit agencies, and individuals who have their own businesses. You should conclude from this list that you need a diverse preparation. See all of the tips listed below. Second, not all companies or organizations send representatives to every fair. If your needs are not met at the career/job fair, then it may be time to broaden your search, i.e., to the Internet and campus career services.

3. Preregister for the career/job fair whenever possible.

This is an often-ignored step, but it could be a fatal mistake if you choose not to follow through. Generally, you have to submit a résumé (see Appendix 4 for résumé guidance) to preregister. The point is that your résumé will then be screened by employers—and that means a decision about you may be made before you even get to the career/job fair. Of course, if your résumé has attracted the attention of an employer, the agency representative will already have your name on his list when you arrive, and you may get your first interview. If you are in your third year or early in your fourth year of college, your résumé may open the door to an invitation for an internship—some of which are paid.

Upon arrival at the career/job fair, check the listing of organizations and agencies to see if any new ones have been added. While you may not have prepared for them specifically, you will already have a general knowledge of what different organizations/agencies offer. Do not skip them; try to get their literature before seeing a representative so that you will have some familiarity with them when you do approach them. You can be honest with them. If you do not know something, do not be afraid to ask. Because they are late in registering, representatives will not have reviewed résumés ahead of time and you can feel free to offer your résumé.

4. Allow your résumé to open doors for you.

Review your résumé before each career/job fair. Consider having your résumé done professionally and printed on good quality paper. One of the more important things you can do is to have someone else review your résumé and proofread it for the mistakes you cannot see. Your résumé can help sell you. If it is sloppy, wrinkled, and contains bad grammar, poor punctuation, or worse yet, misspelled words, consider that you have already lost the job. Remember—spell check does not check for the right form of the word, only the correct spelling.

If you have read this book, then you know that we advocate being prepared for different types of careers. You will still have to find the one that best fits you. Some of you will have more than one interest in your choice of profession. Assuming you have more than one interest, prepare different résumés that list different objectives, and have sufficient copies for all of the employers you will see. This does not mean that you should hand out a copy of each résumé to every representative. Only distribute the form of your résumé to a prospective employer who has a specific opening that matches that résumé's objective—they will not want all that paper, only the résumé that fits. You have to get your foot in the door to find your niche or career path.

Caution: Some recruiters will not want to keep your résumé; they will simply scan the résumé to take it back to the office. Your résumé should therefore be crisp and clean, ready for a scanner.

5. Plan your attire, and dress professionally.

Everyone likes to think that they understand acceptable or attractive style, and that they have a personal style that is unique. You want to stand out as an applicant, but you do not want your attire to stand out for you; that is, your attire should not distract the representative's attention away from you. Some career/job fairs have recommended or required attire; find out if they do and dress accordingly. Get someone else's opinion about how you look, including your slacks, suit, colors, tie, shoes, etc. Nothing may be more important than the first impression you leave with the recruiter. *Never be underdressed!* Try to hit the middle of the road between that and overdressed, but when in doubt, be overdressed.

6. Prepare to meet representatives/interviewers.

The moment you approach a representative, their evaluation of you has already begun. Your initial preparatory task is your personal introduction. Representatives are impressed by students who can present themselves with self-assurance; "Good morning, my name is _____!" This can be followed by something like this: "I have read about your organization, and I was interested to learn that you _____." Or, "I noticed on your website that you have the ____ project. Could I hear more about it?" And, "I was curious about____." This is when you mention that "something else" that you would like to explore. Representatives are there to answer questions and show off who they are. Don't hesitate to ask the representative what they think are the highlights of working for their company.

In Chapter 7, we strongly suggested that you should prepare answers in the form of "My Ten Points." (See Appendix 3 for a guide to interview questions and the "My Ten Points" chart.) These answers should be broad in scope and thus acceptable both to a specific question and other more general questions. The point is that you should be prepared for any questions by the representative/ interviewer.

You should practice as many questions and answers as possible with someone else before going to the career/job fair. Do not give your list of questions and answers to them—let them come up with their own questions (in the role of an interviewer) and determine whether your answers adequately answer the questions. If this is an interview at a career/job fair, you will only be given a few minutes, more likely less than ten minutes, of a representative's time. Your preparation must ensure that you have said what is important quickly, concisely, and with confidence and enthusiasm. You have to be prepared. The consequence of failing to prepare is that your résumé may be set aside. Try to prepare yourself to ask a few questions at the end of the interview. These questions should be developed to show your interest in the organization. Your key objective for this interview is to do well enough to get a second interview, which is a better time to ask personal questions about salary, benefits, and advancement. (Never ask these questions during an initial interview unless the interviewer brings them up first.) This information may be available in the brochures provided by the representatives, and it is what they use to stimulate interest in their organization. A final concluding question might be, "Should I write a letter to schedule a second interview?"

If this is not an interview, you may only get one question that will require a broader answer. The key in this case is to make a statement, not a speech. The question will probably sound something like, "Why do you want to work for company X?" Your response should be a blend of expressing your interests and explaining how you would meet the company's needs. You will need to anticipate that the representative/interviewer will only have a few minutes with you, as there will be others wanting to see the representative.

Career/job fairs are known for the lines of students waiting to see a representative. This is actually an opportunity for you. Pay attention to the questions that are being asked by those in front of you, and more importantly, listen to the answers of the representative. Consider this an occasion for you to double up on your interest because you will be learning both from the questions asked and from the answers given.

You have to be ready, and you have to be good to make a lasting first impression. There are some physical things you can do to accomplish this. First, show enthusiasm; put a smile on your face. Second, make and keep good eye contact. Third, give the person a firm, not bone-crushing handshake. And fourth, practice good habits, such as no gum-chewing, no smelling of smoke, and no other things that could be remotely considered in poor taste.

7. Make the most of your time.

If a representative on your list has a long line of waiting students, don't just stand there. You can move on to someone else on your list first. You can also go visit someone not on your list who has no one waiting. This is an excellent chance to work on your informal conversation skills. You can assess how you ask questions and then take the next step after you get an answer. Consider this process as interview practice.

The career/job fair is not a social event, and you should take advantage of every opportunity to get your foot in a door. Students will talk among themselves as they stand around waiting. Be cautious of casual conversation. *Never* make disparaging remarks—about anyone or anything. You cannot be sure who might overhear you.

8. You may wish to bring a portfolio of your work with you.

The portfolio (see Appendix 7 regarding your document portfolio) should contain—in addition to copies of your résumé and perhaps a cover letter—copies of papers that you have written that received excellent grades and important remarks from professors, letters from internships, externships, and from volunteering or from specialized training. If you have received any training certificates, copies of them (never the original document) should be in the portfolio. Police departments or other agencies are impressed with students who have earned special skills. Let me provide you with an example. One of my former students had a certification as an underwater welder. I encouraged him to place that certification in his document portfolio. He mentioned it to a police department representative. That department was in need of a diver. Guess who got a job?

Some of this may be more than you will use at a fair. However, if it is an interview and you have attracted someone's attention, you will once more demonstrate your preparedness if you have the documentation to validate your preparation for entrance into a certain career field.

The portfolio is also an organizing tool—representatives like to see students who are prepared. Also, fairs provide students with advertising giveaways—pens, pencils, markers, stress balls, pads of notepaper, candy, and more. You want to have a place to put these things so you are not juggling them around when you pull out your résumé or other documents. Don't burden yourself with items you don't need.

9. Consider volunteering to help organize/set up the career/job fair.

This would be a unique time to meet representatives as you help them set up and guide them to their location. You will be the first to meet them, the first to offer your résumé, and then you can ask questions. This is not aggressive—this is proactive.

10. Network.

Network, network, network! Have we said this often enough? Review Chapter 7! Unfortunately, or perhaps fortunately, it is not always *what* you know, but *who* you know. Get a business card from everyone you meet. Make notes on the card or on a notepad about each interview or discussion with a representative. Be specific in your notes: List what was important and what was not. Most representatives will tell you what the organization is looking for. This is critical and should be placed in your notes to be included in the follow-up letter.

11. After the career/job fair, follow up with every recruiter or interviewer.

Send letters out immediately. Tell the company representative or HR person how excited you are, how interested you are, and what you would bring to the organization. Clearly state your qualifications in the letter (see Appendix 2 regarding writing letters) and the fact that you would like a second interview. Include another résumé. Promise that you will make a follow-up call and then do so. Thank the recruiter for attending the fair, for providing information, and for generating excitement about their organization. Send the letter to the address listed on the recruiter's card.

Good luck in your career search!

Appendix 6

The Benefits and Downsides of Online Courses

Colleges and universities are including more online courses in their curriculum. Your personal needs and your choice of college may determine how few or how many online courses you will have to take. For example, if you choose a non-traditional college, you will take more or potentially all of your courses online. More traditional colleges offer fewer online courses, but there is a recent trend to increase online courses in the curriculum. Traditional colleges are also developing hybrid versions of courses. Part of the hybrid course is taught online, and the other part is taught in the physical classroom. Professors are encouraged, and in some cases mandated, to produce online courses or to convert current classroom courses to online courses.

One key to successful utilization of online learning is to make sure that the online college or university is accredited. This is essential to know, because if it is not accredited then either your credits will not be transferred to another college or your degree may lack validity.

The student will have to weigh the advantages and disadvantages of online learning. For some it may be a more efficient solution to getting a college degree, while for others it may be the only way to achieve a degree. What follows is a brief discussion of the benefits and disadvantages of online learning to assist the student in finding an objective solution to meet their needs.

THE BENEFITS OF ONLINE COURSES

Online courses are cost-effective, meaning they are less expensive in non-traditional colleges and may be less expensive in traditional colleges, too, although that is not true in every case.

Online courses are convenient. You can take them from the comfort of your home, and you can study at a time that better fits with your routine. For many students, this can be a tremendous advantage because there is no travel, no competition with time and work, and fewer conflicts in establishing a semester schedule of courses. The professor posts the syllabus and course requirements online. The student must then comply with the requirements, which generally have due dates for submission or online discussions with the professor and/or with other students. In addition, there are fewer requirements of actual time slots when you must be present online. For some students who need special conditions in which to study, a home environment can be established with fewer distractions like classroom noise, questions, or activity of other students in the classroom. For some students, this equates to less stress.

Online courses are efficient. Not everyone can afford the luxury of enrolling in college and either limiting work or not working at all. Online courses allow the student to both work and go to school. For many, this means a longer time to complete a college degree. However, a degree earned in this fashion may be evidence to an employer of your desire to advance or to be better prepared in your career. One other advantage to online courses is that course sections often have lower limits for the number of students taking the course than would be the standard in a traditional college classroom. In this case, there may be another section that is online or is offered at another college and the credits can then be transferred.

Online courses permit more interactions with the professor. Online courses usually have more work that must be submitted to a professor on a regular schedule. The professor, in this case, responds to your assignments by timely answering your questions, providing critiques, and making suggestions for changes or additional work that will help clarify the learning to be accomplished. Oftentimes, professors are more accessible online (morning, noon, and night) than they are in a physical college campus setting where office hours are posted.

The student develops new proficiencies. When work is done online, the student will sharpen their computer skills. Computers are an essential tool in our daily lives, and the better we learn to navigate the computer and explore its potential, the more effective the computer becomes for us. For example, a student will learn to research course material. The computer is only as valuable as our ability to retrieve information from online search engines. There are other valuable skills utilized in online learning, such as file sharing or incorporating the many audio-visual tools that are accessed through the computer.

Online courses may allow greater specialization. Traditional college campuses have courses designed to fit into curriculums, and there is often a schema to their availability, that is, what is offered during one's freshman, sophomore, junior, and senior years. Curriculums generally allow some leeway for extra studies called electives, courses that are not required and allow students to expand their field of study. The credits from electives count toward the degree, but some online learning programs do not have electives. Instead, the program is streamlined with only required courses. In some cases, online coursework can result in very specialized degrees that are not found in traditional colleges or that are more difficult to attain because fewer students are available to take those courses. Online education then is a more efficient and effective learning experience.

THE DOWNSIDES OF ONLINE LEARNING

The downsides of online learning are typically the flipsides of the advantages.

The first is a very strong warning to the student: If you are selecting online learning, *make sure* the courses and the school offering the courses are accredited. *Do not* simply accept an online statement from the offering school that either the college or the course is accredited. Check with outside sources about accreditation. Remember, unaccredited schools and courses will result in a worthless degree, which means that you have wasted your time, your tuition money, and any other funds you may have taken out in the form of a student loan.

Online courses mean more reading and more writing assignments. This translates to greater demands on your time—more time completing these assignments than would be required in a traditional course format. It also means greater use of technology—which may not be part of the student's comfort zone.

Online courses mean little or no face-to-face interaction with a professor or other students. The student seeking a criminal justice career may be less likely to get the practical side of careers that is presented in the classroom. Online learning limits the interaction with the professor for in-depth discussions because the courses are so focused on the assignments listed on the syllabus. As you may imagine, the online environments presents more challenges in developing relationships with fellow students and professors. It is possible to communicate, but it will necessarily lack the depth of dialogue found in the physical classroom setting.

Online courses require the self-discipline necessary to schedule yourself and follow through to complete the work. In this case, you may be more responsible for locating the information you need to complete the coursework. Online courses require you to adhere to a strict schedule, and if you fall behind, it may become almost impossible to catch up.

RECOMMENDATIONS

If you decide to pursue your education online, we suggest you consider your ability to take the following steps.

- Assess the accreditation of the schools in which you are interested.
- Compare the costs of on-line and traditional schools.
- Make a calendar of necessary daily and weekly activities to assess your availability to complete online work.
- Create a space in your home that is designated just for your college work. This will help to minimize distractions. Advise others in your home that when you study, they can help by not interrupting or creating other distractions. Reading, writing, and studying are best accomplished when done at the same time every day. Consistency is the key.
- Once you enroll, make a calendar outlining your study time. Once that is established, stick to it!

- Identify resources to assist you with your online work. This includes persons with special skill sets and local sites of assistance, such as college libraries. You may also need a go-to space, such as a college library, to which you can retreat to study with fewer distractions.
- Make a post on the forum of the online class you are taking to see whether any other students live close enough to form a study group and with whom you could have face-to-face discussions about coursework.
- If professors do not post real-time office hours, ask whether they will have office hours at some location that is accessible to you. (This may be impossible for many online courses, however.)
- Internships may or may not be available with online curriculums. Further, your professors may not be familiar with specific internship opportunities in your area, and you may need to research them for yourself. You may not have the advantage of a professor who can visit the site and meet with the supervisor to ensure you are receiving the best possible experience.

SUMMARY

Online learning is good for some students but terrible for others. Each student must carefully consider whether such courses are in their best interest. While the advantages may be very attractive, all disadvantages should be carefully assessed in terms of each individual's personal abilities and style of learning for their success and goal attainment. The wrong decision can have financial repercussions and delay goal attainment, that is, obtaining the degree and beginning a career in criminal justice.

Appendix 7

Document Portfolio Checklist

(See Chapter 3 for a full explanation of each of these documents.)
    Assemble all of your "original" documents into a single file, and then use this file to assemble a set of duplicate documents for applications and interviews. Original documents should be maintained in a separate file. Never give away your original documents; if you are required to present them, make sure they are returned to you right away. Review all websites when applying for the required documents. Some important certifications may include lifeguarding, scuba diving, EMT training, CPR, or first aid. Keep your folders updated as you acquire new credentials.

_____Birth certificate
_____Social Security card
_____High school diploma
_____Firearms ID
_____College or other post-secondary diploma(s)
_____Skill certifications
_____Driver's license
_____Insurance card(s)
_____Voter registration card
_____Passport
_____Military ID
_____Selective Service registration ID
_____Awards

_____Certificates of training

_____

_____

_____

_____

_____

_____

_____

Appendix 8

Civil Service Examinations

Many jobs with local, state, and federal government agencies require civil service examinations. While civil service tests are often very similar, they are nevertheless designed to be specific to the type of position being applied for. Prep manuals[1] are available for civil service examinations, and some are available for specific tests for designated positions, such as corrections officer.

However, there are many jobs that are exempt from examination. These positions may be administrative, and the employee serves at the pleasure of the employer. Other positions that are exempt from civil service exams are part-time positions.

An excellent example of the step-by-step process for navigating civil service applications can be found on the New Jersey website for civil service (www.nj.gov/csc/). This website defines what an announcement is, and then details a nine-step process that will help the interested person to successfully complete the application process:

Step 1: Identify the job announcement.
Step 2: Review the job requirements.
Step 3: Obtain an application.
Step 4: Pay any application fees.
Step 5: Follow the application checklist.
Step 6: Review the application.
Step 7: Consider the evaluation methods.

Step 8: Review your exam results.
Step 9: Follow up after the exam.

There is a similar process in many states and in the federal government. Pennsylvania also includes a tutorial to help with the process.

CIVIL SERVICE POSTINGS

Generally, a posting for a civil service position will specify whether there is a required examination and what the applicant must do to qualify for and take that examination. Read the posting carefully. Not all postings are for jobs in which there are openings. The posting may be simply to set up an examination for future openings. You should take a few examinations for practice, even though they usually require a small fee. Each exam gives you more practice, puts you on a list, and prepares you for future tougher examinations.

The job posting will list the job title, the location(s) of the position, the salary range, minimum requirements such as education or years of experience, and other needed skills such as proficiency in certain computer software and credentials such as a driver's license. There should be a description of the job as well as a description of the specific duties the employee would be expected to perform. Prospective employees should read the posting carefully and not immediately discard it if they do not meet the education requirements, as there may be a provision to substitute experience for education or vice versa. In other cases, provisions may be made for the employee, if hired, to complete certain education requirements by a specified date. The posting may also include specific exclusions to the application process, including citizenship, such as citizenship in the United States, in the state, or in the municipality where the position is located. There usually is an application fee or a fee associated with taking the test.

COMPLETING THE APPLICATION
FOR THE CIVIL SERVICE EXAMINATION

The application for the position, in some cases, actually is the civil service examination. The applicant should be advised not to procrastinate in completing the application for the test. If your application is received after the closing date, it will, in all likelihood, be rejected. At times, there are points assigned for the date when the application is received; that is, the earlier it is received, the more points are awarded. This does not suggest you should rush and be careless or sloppy. A common mistake of civil service applicants is to attach their résumé with the assumption that it is self-explanatory of personal experience or of education. The application usually has areas for these to be filled in. *Do fill them in*, and be sure to provide the details that will allow the reviewer to understand that you have met the education or experience requirements with specificity to the tasks described. Once your application has been accepted, you will be required to provide proof of credentials (education and/or certifications) mentioned in your application. You should bring copies of these documents to your job interview.

The civil service application may be a paper application or it may be found online. In either case, be accurate, thorough, truthful, and complete. Include copies of all required documents, such as certifications, degrees, or transcripts (and check twice that you have included them—and the right copy of them). Take note—there are specific sites for taking the examination from which you must choose. Be sure to check off the one most convenient for you. The application may list various sites through the state or the nation with position openings. You must specify the places where you will accept employment and check them off as well. Many civil service applications now include a small processing fee. Take this seriously. If you write a check, make sure that there are funds to cover it. If you use a credit card, make sure you enter the correct information—check it twice—and be sure the card is not expired or overextended. Any rejection may nullify your opportunity to be considered a candidate.

CIVIL SERVICE EXAMINATION CENTERS

Whether you are filling out the application online or a paper version thereof, be sure to specify where you will take the examination. You will probably be notified at a later date when the examination will be given and where you must report for it. This may seem like simple advice, but here it is anyway: Be sure you know where the center is located. Do not assume you know. Leave plenty of time to get to the examination center—in fact, be early! If you have a mishap, make a wrong turn, get held up in traffic, or something else that causes you to be late, you probably will not be allowed to take the exam and you will have to reapply when a notice is posted again.

THE HIRING PROCESS

One of the purposes of civil service examinations is to increase competitiveness for each position. However, in many cases the employer may simply choose from the top three scores on the test. This is sometimes referred to as the rule of three. There is an exception to this rule: If an applicant has a veteran's status—that is, if he or she has served in the U.S. military—then, regardless of test score, they go to the top of the list and must be hired ahead of others. When a list is promulgated, the employer will begin interviewing. If someone does not show up for an interview, they are immediately dropped from the list. Applicants may be found unsuitable for a position because of a criminal record, substance abuse, or other conditions. Eventually, the employer will decide from the top three remaining candidates.

Your name will remain on the list for future vacancies if you are not chosen for the posted position. There is a specified length of time, however, after which a list expires. After a list expires, you must retest for the position to be placed back on the list. Your standing on a list will change over time as some are chosen for positions, some do not respond when called for interviews, or others are found to be ineligible for positions.

If you are selected, the employer will provide you with a start date. At this time, you will be scheduled for an orientation session, which may or may not be followed by training. Training is determined by the specific agency, and some positions only have on-the-job training.

JOB PROTECTION AND DISCIPLINE

Civil service appointments do provide employees with some job protection. If you are selected for a job and you complete the working test period (about one year), then you generally cannot be dismissed from a job without cause, that is, unless you do something wrong. However, disciplinary action may not mean immediate dismissal from employment. There are often steps, or what is referred to as progressive discipline, before an employee may be terminated. Progressive discipline includes steps that must be first followed, such as warnings, reprimands, suspensions (one or more days), and finally termination. So, learn your job, follow the rules, and if you do, any concerns you have about termination will be moot.

Good luck in your employment search!

Appendix 9

U.S. Federal Law Enforcement Agencies and Websites

This appendix covers federal agencies and their websites. There are many, but we have chosen to separate these from the "Important Websites" listed in Appendix 10. These websites may not seem immediately applicable to your choice of career, but we suggest that you visit some of them to familiarize yourself with other career possibilities. In addition, you may learn something new that can be applied to your chosen profession. Your future is as yet undetermined—be prepared!

U.S. Air Force Office of Special Investigations: www.osi.andrews .af.mil/

U.S. Bureau of Alcohol, Tobacco, and Firearms: www.atf.gov/

U.S. Central Intelligence Agency: www.cia.gov

U.S. Customs and Border Protection: www.cbp.gov/

U.S. Defense Criminal Investigative Service: www.dodig.mil/INV/ DCIS/index.html

U.S. Defense Intelligence Agency: www.dia.mil

U.S. Department of Homeland Security: www.dhs.gov/index.shtm

U.S. Drug Enforcement Administration: www.usdoj.gov/dea/index. htm

U.S. Federal Bureau of Investigation: www.fbi.gov/

U.S. Federal Protective Service: www.ice.gov/graphics/about/ organization/org_fps.htm

U.S. Immigration and Customs Enforcement: www.ice.gov/index.htm

U.S. IRS Criminal Investigations Division: www.irs.gov/uac/Criminal-Enforcement-1

U.S. Marshal Service: www.usdoj.gov/marshals/

U.S. Naval Criminal Investigative Service: www.ncis.navy.mil/

U.S. Postal Inspection Service: www.postalinspectors.uspis.gov/

U.S. State Department Bureau of Diplomatic Security: www.state.gov/m/ds/

U.S. Secret Service: www.secretservice.gov/

OFFICE OF INSPECTOR GENERALS

U.S. Agency for International Development, Office of Inspector General: www.usaid.gov/oig/

U.S. Department of Agriculture, Office of Inspector General: www.usda.gov/oig/invest.htm

U.S. Department of Commerce, Office of Inspector General: www.oig.doc.gov

U.S. Department of Defense, Office of Inspector General: www.dodig.osd.mil

U.S. Department of Education, Office of Inspector General: www.ed.gov/about/offices/list/oig/index.html

U.S. Department of Energy, Office of Inspector General: www.ig.doe.gov

U.S. Department of Health and Human Services, Office of Inspector General: www.oig.hhs.gov

U.S. Department of Homeland Security, Office of Inspector General: www.dhs.gov/dhspublic

U.S. Department of Housing and Urban Development, Office of Inspector General: www.hud.gov/offices/oig

U.S. Department of Interior, Office of Inspector General: www.doioig.gov/

U.S. Department of Justice, Office of Inspector General: www.usdoj.gov/oig

U.S. Environmental Protection Agency, Office of Inspector General: www.epa.gov/oig/

The Department of Justice uses an online application process. Candidates may complete and submit an application electronically through the Office of Attorney Recruitment and Management's website. Read the rules before filling out the application and submitting it. If you make a mistake, you may not be given an opportunity to correct it.

U.S. Environmental Protection Agency: www.epa.gov/oigearth

U.S. Equal Employment Opportunity Commission, Office of Inspector General: www.eeoc.gov/abouteeoc/plan/oig/index.html

U.S. Postal Service, Office of Inspector General: http://www.uspsoig.gov/investigation.htm

U.S. National Aeronautics and Space Administration, Office of Inspector General: www.hq.nasa.gov/office/oig/hq

U.S. Nuclear Regulatory Commission, Office of Inspector General: www.nrc.gov/insp-gen/invesprog.html

U.S. Office of Personnel Management, Office of Inspector General: www.opm.gov/oig/html/investigations.asp

U.S. Railroad Retirement Board, Office of Inspector General: www.rrb.gov/oig/rrboig.htm

U.S. Small Business Administration, Office of Inspector General: www.sba.gov/ig

U.S. Social Security Administration, Office of Inspector General: www.ssa.gov/oig

U.S. State Department, Office of Inspector General: www.oig.state.gov/isp/

U.S. Department of Transportation, Office of Inspector General: www.oig.dot.gov

U.S. Department of the Treasury, Office of Inspector General: www.treas.gov/oig

U.S. Treasury IG for Tax Administration: www.treas.gov/tigta/oi.shtml

U.S. Department of Veterans Affairs, Office of Inspector General: www.va.gov/oig

National Park Service Police: www.nps.gov/subjects/uspp/index.htm

www.govtjobs.com: This site publishes job listings and job resource information state by state. Links are included to municipal, city, and county government websites.

www.usajobs.gov/: This is the federal government's official one-stop source for federal jobs and employment information.

US Customs and Border Patrol: http://www.cbp.gov/: This site helps applicants locate careers in Customs and Border Patrol. It also reviews international port and immigration activities.

www.lawenforcementjobs.com/: This is a broad-spectrum website for law enforcement jobs.

Appendix 10

Important Websites

The following websites are helpful for their job announcements and career and other current information provided in specific areas of criminal justice. Individual states maintain their own websites for criminal justice agencies and employment opportunities. Interest in a specific state will take a little research to discover all websites related to that state. For example, those interested in a criminal justice career in New Jersey should review the appropriate websites in the list below. Other states and the federal government maintain similar sites. Make a list of all sites that may provide information about the career of your choice.

National Federation of Paralegal Association: www.paralegals.org; provides legal resources, professional development, and networking opportunities.

lawjobs.com: Post your résumé and investigate legal career opportunities.

The Riley Guide: www.rileyguide.com/gov; *The Riley Guide* contains job listings for government, defense, and military service in the United States. Opportunities are provided for service with the U.S. federal government, the U.S. Department of Defense, and the military service.

The Michigan Job Source: www.statejobs.com/mi; browse employers throughout the state. Government jobs are listed with the Michigan

State Civil Service, the Michigan State Police, and Michigan State University.

911 HotJobs: www.911.hotjobs.com; employment and job information on more than two thousand law enforcement departments and agencies are found at this website, as well as law enforcement job books and online practice tests.

www.quintcareers.com/researching_companies.htm: Includes information about companies that are currently hiring.

State of Michigan Vacancy Postings: www.web1.mdcs.state.mi.us/vacancyweb; locate job vacancies sorted by job title or pay.

JobBankUSA: www.jobbankusa.com; search federal government jobs and employment information.

Government Jobs: www.detroit.lib.mi.us/ceic2/jobs_gov.html; job opportunities, vacancy announcement numbers, testing dates, and requirements.

Personnel: www.state.nj.us/csc; this website identifies jobs in New Jersey that require the applicant to take a civil service examination. The site details a nine-step process for successfully completing the application. New Jersey does not have a separate Department of Personnel and this information is found under civil service.

Corrections: www.state.nj.us/corrections/pages/index.shtml.

Labor: www.html.lwd.state.nj.us/labor/index.html.

Human Services: www.state.nj.us/humanserviceswww.state.nj.us/humanservices.

Juvenile Justice Commission: www.nj.gov/oag/jjc/offices_hr_opps.htm.

Judiciary: www.NJ.judiciary.gov.USA.

New Jersey State Police: www.njsp.org/.

New Jersey Civil Service: www.nj.gov/csc/.

indeed.com

www.ezinearticles.com/?Law-Enforcement-exam-strategies-How-To-Pass-the-B-Pad

www.interstatecompact.org/: the Interstate Compact is a formal agreement between states that oversees the transfer of parolees from one state's jurisdiction to another.

www.criminaljusticeusa.com: articles cover recent events in criminal justice, such as the fastest-growing careers in criminal justice.

USA.gov's A–Z index of U.S. government departments and agencies: www.usa.gov/agencies/federal/all_agencies.

ResumeEdge.com: a professional résumé writing service.

www.usdoj.gov/oarm: there are more than ten thousand attorneys working for the Department of Justice due to the diversity of matters it must cover.

www.collegeanswer.com.

www.collegeboard.com.

www.fafsa.ed.gov/.

www.linkedin.com/nhome/: a networking site for professionals who report on their current activities.

www.Investigations.com: reference "Bo" Dietl, a retired New York detective

www.sheriffs.org: National Sheriffs Association, concerned with national security/law.

Convict Criminology: www.convictcriminology.org.

Federal Jobs Digest: www.jobfed.com.

Physical Efficiency Battery: www.nps.gov/uspp/pebstan.htm.

www.csrees.usda.gov/about/jobs_faq.html

www.opm.gov/oca/payrates/

www.nps.gov/uspp/hirproc2.htm

www.fws.gov

www.reference.com/motif/business/free-ksa-samples

www.usajobs.gov: the Federal Government's official job site.

Highlights~@bop.gov: news from the Federal Bureau of Prisons.

www.quintcareers.com/resres.html: this is a website for job-seeking assistance. It covers everything from cover letters to résumés to interviewing skills.

www.linkedin.com/job/law-enforcement-jobs/?trk=jserp_related_ searches: this website lists other websites for employment applications in criminal justice.

Appendix 11

Criminal Justice Jobs

An exhaustive list of criminal justice jobs would be too numerous to mention all or to list every title or specialty. Similarly, it is impossible to describe every position. A review of civil service bulletins for a specific state or for the federal government (found in libraries, government buildings, many college criminal justice departments, career services offices, and other places, including the Internet) will provide a listing of current job opportunities with greater specificity to the duties to be performed. This is a very short list of all possible positions. Remember that there are other lesser titles, such as assistant or deputy, that often accompany the greater titles. There are a great number of positions and a vast number of duties to be performed in each category, the point being that while one position may not be ideal, your training for it may prepare you for another position later that has the characteristics that meet your ideal for a career. While some may experience their career in a single role, there is usually a broad range of opportunities for advancement and change. These are always best prepared for through education and training.

CORRECTIONS

Commissioner: in some states referred to as a secretary
Director: oversees some aspect of the agency

Warden: also referred to as a superintendent or in some cases an administrator

Corrections officer: generally a law enforcement position, could be state or federal, juvenile, or county

Teacher: including special needs titles, such as reading or disability specialist, vocational training specialist

Business manager: could be called an accountant

Food services: a cook or a manager

Maintenance: includes supervisors and specialized staff

Architect

Grants writer

Researcher

Counselor

Social worker

Psychologist

Classification officer: a non–law enforcement title

Landscape manager or horticulturalist

PAROLE

Chairman of parole board

Hearing officer for violations

Supervisor or officer: usually a law enforcement positon

PROBATION

Supervisor or officer, state or federal: may or may not be a law enforcement position

LAW ENFORCEMENT

Police officer

Special officer: resort and summer employment

Specific types of law enforcement officers: mounted, harbor, juvenile, DARE, canine, fraud, electronic, vice, property, animal, corporate
Game warden
Public safety director
Campus or hospital police
Sheriff/deputy
Trooper/ranger

FEDERAL LAW ENFORCEMENT

TSA
FBI
CIA
INS
DEA
OSHA
ATF
Secret Service
Border Patrol
Marshal's Service
Homeland Security
Military Police
U.S. Postal Service
Other

COURTS AND LEGAL POSITIONS

Judge: federal, state, juvenile, or county
Court clerk
Prosecutor: federal or state
Defense attorney: there are specialized practices in this category
Paralegal
Legal researcher

ACADEMIC POSITIONS

Researcher
Professor
Forensics expert

OTHER POSITIONS

Crime scene investigator
Substance abuse therapist
Private investigator

Appendix 12

Private and Nonprofit Agencies and Professional Organizations

Private, nonprofit agencies and professional organizations are valuable resources for entrance into the criminal justice career path. These are not government positions. Private and nonprofit service providers operate through donations, grants, and contracts with the government. The agencies work independently and in partnership with governments performing such tasks as operating private prisons, halfway houses, community justice centers, and other services for criminal justice involvement, including offenders and ex-offenders. Private and nonprofit providers are also a valuable resource when it comes to changing careers or upon retirement when searching for a potential second career.

Professional organizations can be wonderful places to obtain career information. Some of this information could include job openings, the latest results from scientific research, changes in policy, news, organizational concerns, and more.

Please review the following private providers' listings and visit their websites for more information. Each description of an organization has been taken from its website.

BEHAVIORAL INTERVENTIONS: BI.COM

Established in 1978, BI Incorporated (BI) is a wholly-owned subsidiary of The GEO Group (NYSE: GEO), a global leader in the delivery of correctional, detention, and residential treatment services to federal, state, and local government agencies. BI provides a full continuum of offender monitoring technologies and community reentry services for parolees, probationers, pretrial defendants and illegal aliens involved in the U.S. immigration court process. BI also owns and operates an ISO-certified national monitoring center, providing 24/7 expert support supervision services exclusively to governmental agencies.

BI works closely with corrections officials to cost effectively reduce recidivism, promote public safety, and strengthen the communities they serve. BI's solutions help federal, state, and local agencies to supervise a range of individuals—from low- to high-risk offender populations. BI combines the latest in technology, expert technical and customer service, ISO-certified manufacturing practices, and evidence-based treatment and counseling programs to assist agencies to curb future crime and conserve scarce local resources.

COMMUNITY EDUCATION CENTERS: www.cecintl.com

Community Education Centers, Inc. (CEC) is a leading provider of reentry treatment and education services for adult correctional populations throughout the United States. CEC is firmly committed to partnering with government agencies to provide intensive reentry treatment and education programs that focus on changing addictive and criminal behaviors, preparing offenders for reentry, and ultimately reducing recidivism.

CORRECTIONS CORPORATION OF AMERICA: www.correctionscorp.com

In 1983, our company became the first to provide privatized prison, jail, and detention services. For more than three decades, we have strived to aid governments by reducing costs, alleviating overcrowding, and providing quality correctional care for inmates and detainees. Our approach to public-private partnership in corrections combines the cost savings and innovation of the private sector with the strict guidelines and consistent oversight of the public sector. This continues to produce proven results.

THE GEO GROUP: www.geogroup.com

GEO's International Services division provides correctional and detention services for government clients in the United Kingdom, Australia, and South Africa managing seven correctional and detention facilities encompassing approximately 7,000 beds. Through wholly-owned subsidiary and joint-venture companies, GEO's International Services division provides correctional solutions that are fully customizable and tailored to each government customer's requirements and standards.

INTERNATIONAL COMMUNITY CORRECTIONS ASSOCIATION (ICCA): iccalive.org

The International Community Corrections Association, as a private, non-profit, membership organization, acts as the representative voice for residential and other community corrections programs. As such, it expects of its members compassion, belief in the dignity and worth of human beings, respect for individual difference and a commitment to quality care for its clients. It requires of its members the professional background, research and expertise necessary to ensure performance of effective quality services delivered with integrity and competence. ICCA affirms that its primary goal is the successful re-integration of the client into the community.

THE KINTOCK GROUP: kintock.org

The Kintock Group is a private non-profit organization that contracts with federal, state and county law enforcement agencies to provide cost effective alternatives to incarcerations and reentry services for individuals transitioning from the criminal justice system to the community.

Kintock Programs provide a wide range of accredited services that encourages self-sufficiency, promotes responsible behavior, and prepares program participants to enter the workforce. Services are provided in residential and non-residential settings.

THE NEW JERSEY ASSOCIATION OF CRIMINAL JUSTICE
EDUCATORS (NJACJE): www.njacje.org

Since 1968, the New Jersey Association of Criminal Justice Educators (NJACJE) has been reaching out to academicians in criminal justice and related fields in an effort to enhance the quality of undergraduate and graduate education in the discipline. The organization was established during the early years of the Law Enforcement Assistance Administration (LEAA) as the Council of Educational Institutions for Law Enforcement (CEILE). It was formed with the support of the state's Chancellor of Higher Education to develop a Master Plan for Higher Education in Criminal Justice. One of the organizational goals was to function as liaison between the New Jersey Division of Criminal Justice (the major funding agency in the state for LEAA), and the rapidly multiplying Police Science Programs that began to develop. The Council met monthly over the years to discuss issues related to criminal justice education and to plan and sponsor numerous symposia, seminars, and workshops on various criminal justice issues. During the 1970's, CEILE affiliated with the Academy of Criminal Justice Sciences and represented the state's criminal justice educators at their meetings.

THE NEW JERSEY ASSOCIATION ON
CORRECTIONS (NJAC): www.njaconline.org

MISSION STATEMENT: To promote social justice and human dignity in the policies and institutions which govern offenders and victims of crime through educational, legislative, and rehabilitative programs.

THE NEW JERSEY CHAPTER OF THE AMERICAN
CORRECTIONAL ASSOCIATION: www.njaca.org

The New Jersey Chapter of the American Correctional Association is a non-profit professional organization that has served as a forum for corrections in New Jersey since 1983. Membership includes a wide variety of correctional employees drawing from probation, parole, institutions, community based facilities, treatments centers, schools, law enforcement, the judiciary and related governmental and private agencies. We provide criminal justice practitioners in New Jersey with educational training and networking opportunities.

THE AMERICAN CORRECTIONAL
ASSOCIATION (ACA): www.aca.org

The American Correctional Association provides a professional organization for all individuals and groups, both public and private that share a common goal of improving the justice system.

VOLUNTEERS OF AMERICA (VOA): www.voa.org

At Volunteers of America, we are more than a nonprofit organization. We are a ministry of service that includes nearly 16,000 paid, professional employees dedicated to helping those in need rebuild their lives and reach their full potential.

Through our hundreds of human service programs, including housing and healthcare, Volunteers of America touches the lives of more than 2 million people in over 400 communities in 46 states as well as the District of Columbia and Puerto Rico each year. Since 1896, we have supported and empowered America's most vulnerable groups, including veterans, at-risk youth, the frail elderly, men and women returning from prison, homeless individuals and families, people with disabilities, and those recovering from addictions. Our work touches the mind, body, heart—and ultimately the spirit—of those we serve, integrating our deep compassion with highly effective programs and services.

AMERICAN SOCIETY OF
CRIMINOLOGY (ASC): www.asc41.com

The American Society of Criminology is an international organization whose members pursue scholarly, scientific, and professional knowledge concerning the measurement, etiology, consequences, prevention, control, and treatment of crime and delinquency.

The Society's objectives are to encourage the exchange, in a multidisciplinary setting, of those engaged in research, teaching, and practice so as to foster criminological scholarship, and to serve as a forum for the dissemination of criminological knowledge. Our membership includes students, practitioners, and academicians from the many fields of criminal justice and criminology.

NATIONAL SHERIFFS' ASSOCIATION (NSA): www.sheriffs.org

Our primary goal at the National Sheriffs' Association is to preserve and protect the Office of Sheriff, so that the Sheriffs of this country can provide quality service to their constituents.

We try to achieve that goal by being a voice for the Sheriffs of this nation, and by providing resources to Sheriffs all over the country.

The 3,080 Sheriffs of the United States are very diverse and have different jurisdictional sizes and challenges of their offices. All Sheriffs share the common goal of protecting the citizens that elected us, and making the quality of life of those citizens the best it can be.

NATIONAL ORGANIZATION OF BLACK LAW ENFORCEMENT EXECUTIVES (NOBLE): www.noblenational.org

The goal of NOBLE is to be recognized as a highly competent, public service organization that is at the forefront of providing solutions to law enforcement issues and concerns, as well as to the ever-changing needs of our communities.

The objectives that are employed to implement the goal of the organization include:

An emphasis on being a competent learning organization that continuously learns from the collective knowledge of its members, and other sources of criminal justice research and data, while simultaneously working to rapidly convert this learning into action;

Working to ensure long-term organizational stability by identifying and establishing mutually beneficial relationships with corporations and other funding sources;

Recommending and executing policies, processes and procedures that recognize and pursue goals common to all segments of the community and law enforcement, with a focus on ensuring strict accountability and uncompromising integrity;

Promoting and encouraging attitudes and characteristics that permit adaptability to the changing demands placed on law enforcement, and the development of professional and communication competencies that help view, comprehend and shape appropriate responses to an ever-changing environment; and

Increasing the effectiveness and efficiency of NOBLE through a clearly defined and shared sense of purpose and commitment among its members.

INTERNATIONAL ASSOCIATION OF CHIEFS OF POLICE (IACP): www.theiacp.org

The International Association of Chiefs of Police (IACP) is a dynamic organization that serves as the professional voice of law enforcement. Building on our past success, the IACP addresses cutting edge issues confronting law enforcement though advocacy, programs, and research, as well as training and other professional services. IACP is a comprehensive professional organization that supports the law enforcement leaders of today and develops the leaders of tomorrow.

POLICE EXECUTIVE RESEARCH FORUM (PERF): www.policeforum.org

The Police Executive Research Forum (PERF) is an independent research organization that focuses on critical issues in policing. Since its founding in 1976, PERF has identified best practices on fundamental issues such as reducing police use of force; developing community policing and problem-oriented policing; using technologies to deliver police services to the community; and evaluating crime reduction strategies.

PERF strives to advance professionalism in policing and to improve the delivery of police services through the exercise of strong national leadership; public debate of police and criminal justice issues; and research and policy development.

Appendix 13

Vermont Police Academy Basic Training and Physical Fitness Training

CURRICULUM SUMMARY

	HOURS
COMMUNICATION	
Courtroom Demeanor	8
Conflict Resolution	4
Interpersonal Communication	4
Media/Police Relations	2
Report Writing	32
TOTAL	*50*
LAW	
Criminal Law	54
Motor Vehicle Law	44
Occupant Protection Usage & Enforcement	2
Hazardous Material Recognition	8
Introduction to Fish & Wildlife	2
Alcohol Services Education & Alcohol Services Act	10
Introduction to Federal Agencies	2
Juvenile Law & Procedure	8
Police Liability	4
Landlord & Tenant Law	2
Use of Vermont Statutes	2
TOTAL	*138*

INVESTIGATIVE PROCEDURES

Crash Investigation	40
Case Problems and Evidence Collection	24
Death Investigation	4
Domestic Violence Response	12
Drug Identification & Investigation	8
Interview & Interrogation Techniques	16
Sexual Assault Investigation	12
Sexual/Physical Abuse of Children	12
Hate Crimes Investigation	8
Terrorism	4
NCIC/VCIC	4
Victims Assistance Program	2
Court Diversion	2
NIMS/ICS	4
Vulnerable Adult Abuse	2
Stalking	2
Animal Cruelty	2
TOTAL	*158*

PROFESSIONAL DEMEANOR

Sexual Harassment Policy	2
Stress Management	8
Core Values & Leadership Training	4
Cultural Diversity	2
Police Ethics	8
History & Principles of Policing	6
Teambuilding & Problem Solving	14
TOTAL	*44*

PHYSICAL FITNESS

Nutrition Information	2
Physical Assessment	4
Physical Training	96
TOTAL	*102*

POLICE PATROL TECHNIQUES

Defensive Driving	24
Bloodborne Pathogens	2
Crime Prevention	2
Community Policing	6
Community Policing Project	10
Patrol Procedures Classroom:	
Preparation for Duty	3
Observation & Perception	2

Patrol Techniques	4
Radio Communications	2
Prisoner Transport	2
Scenario Safety Training	1
Arrest Paperwork	1
Unknown Risk MV Stops	4
Crimes in Progress	8
Police K9 Operations	2
Dealing with People with Mental Illness	6
Dealing with the Deaf & Hard of Hearing	2
Dealing with People with Physical Disabilities	2
Traffic Control	2
Patrol Procedures Scenarios:	
Practice Scenarios	54
Final Scenarios	32
Firearms	56
Non-lethal Use of Force	40
Impact Weapon	4
Oleoresin Capsicum Certification	4
Field Experience at Agency	16
TOTAL	*291*
OTHERS	
Administrative/Staff Time	8
Drill and Ceremony	10
FINAL EXAMINATION	2
TOTAL	*20*
TOTAL HOURS FOR BASIC TRAINING	*803*
POST BASIC INSTRUCTION	
D.U.I/DRE Enforcement	40
V.I.N. Verification	4
Basic Fingerprinting Techniques	4
Doppler Radar Operation	8
First Aid	4
C.P.R.	12
Spillman Training (optional)	12
Shotgun Training (optional)	8
LIDAR (Laser) (optional)	8
TOTAL POST-BASIC TRAINING	*100*
TOTAL HOURS FOR BASIC TRAINING	*903*

Source: www.vcjtc.state.vt.us/basic.htm

VERMONT PHYSICAL FITNESS TRAINING

Physical Assessment Minimum Standards: 40th Percentile Requirements

MALE	Flexibility	Bench Press	Sit-ups	Push-Ups	1.5 mile run
20-29	16.5	0.99	38	29	12:29
30-39	15.5	0.88	35	24	12:53
40-49	14.3	0.80	29	18	13:50
50-59	13.3	0.71	24	13	15:14

FEMALE	Flexibility	Bench Press	Sit-ups	Push-Ups	1.5 mile run
20-29	19.3	0.59	32	15	15:05
30-39	18.3	0.53	25	11	15:56
40-49	17.3	0.50	20	9	17:11
50-59	16.8	0.44	14	n/a	19:10

Physical Assessment Minimum Standards: 50th Percentile Requirements

MALE	Flexibility	Bench Press	Sit-ups	Push-Ups	1.5 mile run
20-29	17.5	1.06	40	33	11:58
30-39	16.5	0.93	36	27	12:25
40-49	15.3	0.84	31	21	13:05
50-59	14.5	0.75	26	15	14:33

FEMALE	Flexibility	Bench Press	Sit-ups	Push-Ups	1.5 mile run
20-29	20.0	0.65	35	18	14:15
30-39	19.0	0.57	27	14	15:14
40-49	18.0	0.52	22	11	16:13
50-59	17.9	0.46	17	n/a	18:05

TOTAL POST-BASIC TRAINING   *100*
TOTAL HOURS FOR BASIC TRAINING   *903*

Source: www.howstuffworks.com/framed.htm?parent=police-academy.htm&url=www.vcjtc.state.vt.us/basic.htm

Appendix 14

Paying for College

INTRODUCTION

A college education is expensive, and the costs constantly rise. Public community colleges will cost approximately $7,500 per year, and major private colleges can cost as much as $60,000 per year. Other major costs include fees, books, and room and board (although these costs may be included in the semester billing). College education for a career requires diligent planning. Debt accumulation for many is unavoidable, but you will want to manage and minimize your debt accumulation from the beginning.

Some considerations for the college financial plan include: How much are you willing to pay in cash? How much can you earn? What is your tolerance for loans? And what is your eligibility for scholarships or grants to offset the costs? Loans can take years to pay off, and they may affect your life decisions after graduating with a degree. We strongly urge you to only borrow what you need in order to avoid fiscal difficulty and long-term debt that may carry a high interest rate.

Strategies that may seem safe at the time can become a fiscal cliff, such as using credit cards to pay for tuition, books, and other campus activities. The interest rates for credit cards are prohibitive if you cannot pay them off each month. Finally, we suggest that if you have a savings account, do not raid it. It represents a safety net in case of unforeseen financial need.

Your strategies should include saving and earning as you go. To accomplish this, you will need to set up a budget, examine your spending, determine where you can reduce spending, and then keep the savings. There are Internet sites to help you with this, including Bankrate.com and Finaid.org.

PART-TIME AND FULL-TIME ATTENDANCE

If you want to finish your degree as quickly as possible, full-time attendance is the more sure strategy. Of course, not everyone can attend school full-time, and 120 or more course credits can seem like a very large number. However, remember that each course is about three credits. At three credits a course, you only need to take about forty courses to complete your degree. This may sound more manageable. Nevertheless, part-time attendance will also get you to the goal of a college degree; it will just take a little longer.

Some students may have to change their schedule from full-time to part-time, and others may feel like they need to take a break altogether for personal or financial reasons. We do not advocate taking such breaks under many circumstances, because many students fail to return. However, if a break is necessary, then try to return at the earliest possible time, preferably the very next semester. And if you must change from a full-time schedule, then we suggest other options, including the following:

- Consulting with a counselor before you leave.
- Taking one or more courses every semester to maintain continuity and enrollment at the college.
- Remembering that changing from full-time to part-time status will affect your funding for college. For example, in order to maintain Pell Grant eligibility, you must be enrolled for a minimum of twelve credits a semester. Part-time students must be enrolled for a minimum of six credits per semester, or federal assistance may be eliminated.
- Enrolling in a local college for one or more courses, if you are leaving your college campus and returning home, but make sure the course credit will be accepted at the college of your choice and count toward your degree. Do not assume that this is true because a course

has the same title as the one taught at your college. Your chosen college will probably assess the requirements and course content to be sure it is a match with its course.

- Returning to the college of your choice at the earliest possible time.

COLLEGE IS NOT FOR EVERYONE

Unfortunately, the *why* you are attending college is not always as clear to everyone as they would like to believe that it is. For some people, college is not an appropriate choice. So why are you attending college?

- Because you want to get a degree?
- Because someone else is paying for it?
- Because someone else is telling you that you should go?
- Because you have always been told that you need to go to college?
- Because you think it is the right thing to do?
- Because you don't want to disappoint someone?

These are all the wrong reasons. You should be attending college because it is what *you* want to do. You should be attending college because it will help you reach a personal goal of your own.

Some students are intimidated by the thought of attending college and by the fear that they will not do well. If this is the case, you do have options. You may take one course to try it out—you can even take it at a community college. Community colleges provide wonderful assistance to students, including counseling services, tutors, and labs to assist you with reading, writing, and math problems. These services exist to help you, and you should take advantage of them. Some professors will also extend themselves to help you get over hurdles—seek them out and let them help you.

There is also the consideration that you may discover that college is not for you. This discovery is not failure. This merely indicates a level of self-understanding that can guide you to other satisfying career decisions. We suggest that if this determination is made, then you find other alternatives to choose from, including technical and vocational schools.

STEPS TO PAY FOR COLLEGE

First, fill out the Free Application for Federal Student Aid (FAFSA) on-line at www.fafsa.ed.gov/. The FAFSA will establish your eligibility for federal financial aid. (Caution: There are other sites that sometimes come up in place of the FAFSA. These sites may charge you a small fee to fill out the form. We suggest that you avoid these sites. They are not the official site.) Among the available programs to assist you with funding are Pell Grants, Stafford Loans, and PLUS Loans. The amount you receive from each is determined by the FAFSA. The last two are loans that must be paid back. If you know someone experienced with the FAFSA ask for help, but be sure to protect your PIN. The FAFSA is a user-friendly form that allows you to go back and make changes. However, if you misplace your PIN, then the process becomes much more difficult. The FAFSA must be newly completed each year.

Second, visit your selected school's financial aid office. The office can advise you of any scholarship opportunities available through a specific school or from other sources.

Third, apply for a scholarship(s). Scholarships are not just for good students or low-income families. There are scholarships for everything, from ones for girls who are over six feet tall, to vegans, even to students with unusual last names. It takes time and effort to find them and apply.

There is an expression in football: "Go deep!" Search for scholarships in your hometown (like from the Lions Club or the Elks), college, workplace, and unions. You may spend hours searching, but if you don't quit, you will eventually find something that will help. Some scholarships only apply to students in their junior or senior year of high school. Some scholarships are for older students. There are scholarships and grants for laid-off workers or for those who are at a midpoint in their careers. Your search will only be limited by your imagination and your ability to describe yourself.

Research has made the recognition of disabilities more common. Any disability (or illness), from attention deficit disorder to classifications such as dysgraphia (a handwriting disability), may help qualify you for a scholarship or help you gain assistance at a college or university with test-taking, note-taking, and special permission to use a computer to take tests. Check for scholarships awarded by gender, ethnicity, or religion, and if you have already done something unusual, such as organizing a relief effort, or a charity, or resolved some community issue, then these may qualify you for further financial assistance.

This book is about careers in the criminal justice system, and it seems only appropriate to mention the other side of the coin—those who have offended. Young people for whatever reason may have at some point found themselves on the wrong side of the law. An education has the most potential to help people regain their footing in society. Offenses may exclude some from specified careers in criminal justice, such as law enforcement, because the offense eliminates the possibility of carrying a weapon. Nevertheless, there are jobs available in other sectors of the criminal justice profession for which a weapon is not a requirement. In fact, if the offense was a juvenile offense, the list of precluded forms of employment is considerably shorter. In some cases, there may not even be an offense but a documented problem, such as substance abuse. Such cases may be eligible for Pell Grants or even grants from agencies such as the Rehabilitation Commission. A degree is a powerful way to decrease uncertainty in your future. If there is uncertainty about this, we would suggest that the reader visit the Convict Criminology website and read the profiles of some ex-con PhD professors of criminology. (Especially be sure to visit the Convict Criminology website for information about Dr. Richards, who founded the group.)

Any of the ideas mentioned above can be entered into online search engines. Enter them, rephrase them, turn expressions around, and reenter them. Do not be discouraged—*keep searching!*

- **Check online.** Here are some easy sites that are visited regularly by students: www.fastweb.com, www.collegeanswer.com, and www.collegeboard.com. These may or may not help you find a scholarship, but they will provide a guide to what is possible and to the application process. Once you start the process, the answers you develop may apply to many scholarship opportunities.
- **Federal loans.** Realizing you need a loan can surely be an "ouch" moment—they incur debt. Loans are available to both parents and students. Be cautious of private loans from banks and other lenders. Read carefully for the interest rates and conditions, such as when they must be paid back or when interest starts to accumulate. Federal loan

programs generally offer better interest rates and terms for repayment. Many federal loans even have provisions to forgive loans if you elect to do public service after completing your degree or if you go to work for a federal agency. Another piece of good news about federal loans is that there may be deferred payment conditions in the event of a job loss.

- **State loans.** States provide loans and grants in a variety of ways. For good students, there may be in-state free tuition if you score in an upper percentile of your class. Some state universities offer free tuition to students who excel during all four years of high school. New Jersey and Georgia, for example, have the STARS program.
- **Foundation grants.** Search foundations, such as those founded by Bill Gates, George Soros, Guggenheim, and others, for special opportunities. These are sites that should be visited frequently because there are deadlines for the completion of the application processes. Application guidelines must be followed rigorously. Be thorough and do not assume. If help is needed, contact information is generally provided—use it!

Here is a list of what you should *not* do when seeking scholarships, grants and other forms of funding:

- *Do not* downplay low income or other forms of personal adversity (some of which are mentioned above). These need to be acknowledged on all applications. If you have a personal hardship, acknowledge it. If something changes at home, or if there is a job loss, medical event, or another sibling who decides to also attend school, contact your financial aid office. You may be eligible for additional financial aid or a work-study program.
- *Do not* discount a work-study program. Many colleges offer such programs. Work-study is the opportunity to work on the college campus in exchange for tuition. Some jobs are offered by the college, some are offered through a private company, or some are offered as the result of obtaining a Pell Grant. There are usually more students seeking these jobs than there are positions available, however. Even if you are advised that all current positions have been filled, though, you should ask if there is an application for you to complete in case

someone else drops out. Once you are actually on the list, the chances that you will obtain a work-study position the following semester increases greatly. After obtaining a position, you most likely will continue to be eligible in each of the following semesters as long as you participate. Work-study offers should not be ignored. This is employment that can also be placed on a résumé, and you may be able to use your supervisor as a reference to secure a future job.

• *Do not* ignore other potential sources of funding. Don't forget to compare financial aid packages and use any AP (Advanced Placement) credits, which may help you graduate sooner. Numerous websites may provide additional help, including the College Board (www .collegeboard.org/) and American Student Assistance (www.asa. org/). Also, use the various tax deductions for which you may be eligible. While paying for college, you may be eligible for some additional tax credits, such as the American Opportunity tax credit (www.irs.gov/uac/American-Opportunity-Tax-Credit) and the Lifetime Learning tax credit (www.finaid.org/otheraid/lifetimelearning. phtm).

One final note on advancing yourself toward the degree. If you have had any hobbies, interests, or other unique experiences (such as proficiency in a foreign language), you may be able to use it to get college credit. There are CLEP examinations (visit clep.collegeboard.org), and if you successfully complete them, you will be awarded college credit. Please make sure that your college will accept these credits first, and that the course(s) tested for are accepted by your college toward the degree you are seeking.

EMPLOYMENT AFTER COLLEGE

Some public employment opportunities, such as teaching or law enforcement, may offer incentives for accepting employment, such as the forgiveness of federal loans after working for a specified period of time. Completion of specified courses and advanced degrees may result in additional salary incentives.

MILITARY SERVICE, THE GI BILL,
AND OTHER SOURCES OF REIMBURSEMENT

There are opportunities for those who are still active-duty military personnel stationed stateside or abroad. College credit may be earned in several
ways. First, there are colleges and universities that provide independent
study and classroom instruction. Some of these are even offered on U.S.
military bases in other countries. Among the colleges and universities that
offer such coursework are the University of Maryland, Kaplan University,
and Pepperdine University.

Then there is the College Level Examination Program, or CLEP (visit
clep.collegeboard.org). CLEP can be valuable if you choose to do self-
preparation for your career. You can study on your own, pay a fee for
the CLEP test, and if you pass, you will be awarded college credit. Many
training programs in the military have been evaluated for college credit
by the American Council on Education (ACE). Visit www.acenet.edu
for further information. Take advantage of any training operations you
complete. Your training officer can probably advise you as to which training opportunities have been approved for college credit. In some cases,
the training may only be assessed for a few credits, whereas others may
be assessed for many credits. The author evaluated training for ACE at
one U.S. military fort, and because of the depth of training, the number
of hours of instruction, and the content of the course, he and three other
evaluators determined that that particular training was worth eleven college credits in certain course areas. ACE evaluations are paid for by the
military, and there is no charge for the men and women in the service for
this particular award of college credit.

Upon leaving the service or terminating active duty and remaining on
reserve status, there is also the GI Bill, which can help cover the cost of
college. The money from the GI Bill is used to reimburse the student for
tuition, books, and even a potential living allowance. The only catch is
that the student must pass each course with a grade of C or better. Many
colleges and universities provide a tuition discount out of respect for our
military personnel's service to their country.

Tuition reimbursement for undergraduate credits and for graduate
school may be possible if you are already on the job or in an active search
of a job. While working you should be able to continue your education.

The number of courses you elect to take will be driven by your work and personal responsibilities. If you are already working, ask whether your company/agency has a reimbursement plan. These are not uncommon in government and private nonprofit agencies, although not all may offer the program. Nevertheless, *ask!*

As a side note, this is a good interview question to ask if a potential employer asks you whether you have any questions. You may discover a little-known benefit to going to work for a particular company, *and* you will demonstrate through your question that you seek to improve yourself. Your questions about tuition reimbursement may even generate more questions from the employer, through which you can share more about yourself, your interests, and your potential skill development that would be valuable to their company/agency. Again, this is an opportunity for you to sell yourself and your value to a particular agency or company—just through this one question.

Appendix 15

Criminal Justice and Trade Publications

Publications about criminal justice fall into several categories, including magazines, journals, newsletters, and trade magazines. Each of these publications has value for the person seeking to enter the criminal justice field, someone looking to change positions within the field, or a criminal justice employee who simply wishes to remain current in the industry.

JOURNALS

The journals that are listed below are those that the student may find to be helpful when determining a career path. The vast number of journals in the field makes it impossible to list them all. Students often find journals difficult to read because they often include complicated statistics and technical language unfamiliar to the student. This is not meant to discourage or to dissuade students from reading journals—they should, especially since journals contain current research and articles about ideas that influence the field.

- *The Journal of Correctional Education*
- *The Journal of American Probation and Parole*
- *The Journal of Prisons and Prisoners*

MAGAZINES

Magazines differ from journals in that they contain articles of high inter-est, special projects and their success, notifications of conferences, job openings, book critiques, and much more. Magazines in the area of crimi-nal justice advise the reader of leaders in the field and how they came to their positions. The descriptions below have been taken from each maga-zine's website.

- *Corrections Today* **magazine**, Alexandria, Virginia, American Cor-rectional Association:

  Corrections Today magazine is a professional magazine that addresses current issues, training opportunities and needs. It is sent to every member of the American Correctional Association and provides lists of new members, associate organizations, job postings, conference listings and much more.

- *New Jersey Cops*, www.njcopsmagazine.com:

  New Jersey Cops magazine is the voice of New Jersey Law Enforce-ment and the only monthly publication that provides direct access to more than 65,000-plus Law Enforcement professionals across the state of New Jersey.

  Now in its twentieth year of publishing, we reach every police de-partment, municipality, mayor's office, county sheriff's office, state Police facility, correctional facility, federal and state law enforcement office, colleges and universities, and local offices of related organiza-tions.

  Each month, we publish industry news and events, profiles of cops and their departments, product and equipment reviews, legislative developments, and updates and advice from experts on and off the job.

  Every issue includes important information about lifestyle and leisure pursuits—such as automobiles, financial planning, real estate, education, legal, travel, and especially health and wellness.

  New Jersey Cops is recognized by state and national law enforce-ment groups as a leader in editorial coverage of important topics such as Best Practices for police work; National Police Week; National

Law Enforcement Memorial; Special Olympics; the Police Unity
Tour; police health issues.

NEWSLETTERS

Newsletters tend to focus on local criminal justice news or to be regional
in scope. That is, they may be specific to an agency, to a state, or to a
specific group. Newsletters will contain articles about the group's membership, issues that group members are currently facing, and changes in
relevant legislation, as well as advice columns and much more.

- **"The George Yefchak Quarterly Newsletter of the New Jersey
  Chapter of the American Correctional Association," www.njaca.
  org/about_us.htm:**

    The newsletter serves as the voice of the membership discussing rel-
    evant issues in probation, parole, correctional institutions, community
    based correctional facilities, treatments centers, law enforcement, the
    judiciary and related governmental and private agencies and the train-
    ing academies.

- **"The New Jersey Criminal Justice Educator Newsletter," www.
  njacje.org:**

    Since 1968, the New Jersey Association of Criminal Justice Educators
    (NJACJE) has been reaching out to academicians in criminal justice
    and related fields in an effort to enhance the quality of undergradu-
    ate and graduate education in the discipline. The organization was
    established during the early years of the Law Enforcement Assistance
    Administration (LEAA) as the Council of Educational Institutions
    for Law Enforcement (CEILE). It was formed with the support of
    the state's Chancellor of Higher Education to develop a Master Plan
    for Higher Education in Criminal Justice. One of the organizational
    goals was to function as liaison between the New Jersey Division of
    Criminal Justice (the major funding agency in the state for LEAA),
    and the rapidly multiplying Police Science Programs that began to
    develop. The Council met monthly over the years to discuss issues
    related to criminal justice education and to plan and sponsor numerous

symposia, seminars, and workshops on various criminal justice issues. During the 1970's, CEILE affiliated with the Academy of Criminal Justice Sciences and represented the state's criminal justice educators at their meetings.

- **"Prison Legal News," www.prisonlegalnews.org/:**

"Prison Legal News," a project of the Human Rights Defense Center, is an independent 72-page monthly magazine that provides cutting edge review and analysis of prisoners' rights, court rulings and news concerning criminal justice-related issues. "PLN" has a national (U.S.) focus on both state and federal prison issues, with some international coverage. "PLN" provides information that enables prisoners and other concerned individuals and organizations to gain a better understanding of a broad range of criminal justice topics, including issues related to the protection and enforcement of prisoners' rights.

- **"PoliceOne's eNewsletter," www.policeone.com/police-newsletter:**

"PoliceOne's eNewsletter" brings the latest police news to more law enforcement professionals than any other online. The newsletter is sent out three times per week to more than 150,000 LEOs. What's even better, it's free to sign up.

The "PoliceOne eNewsletter" is designed to keep all members of the law enforcement community, from chiefs to rookies, up to date on the latest news and industry trends. It covers topics such as police technology, safety and training affecting officers everywhere. Each newsletter contains exclusive columns, secure tactical tips, and videos from BluTube and PoliceOneTV.

TRADE PUBLICATIONS

Trade publications are more different in content from the other publications listed in this appendix. The trade magazine is usually specific to a trade in the criminal justice profession. Trade publications are often ignored by students, professors, and those looking for careers in the criminal justice field, although they should not be. Their recipients include practitioners who work in a specific specialty, professionals and administrators who service the criminal justice profession, and members of criminal justice organizations or associations. What makes these magazines distinct is that they offer a wide range of information. Sometimes an entire edition is devoted to a specific theme. Their value is immense because they provide information on upcoming conferences, job openings, new construction projects, new products specific to the industry, changes in philosophy, changes in legislation, changes in administration personnel, selected news articles, and so much more. One of the more peculiar and interesting features of these publications is that they will often include articles about more obscure topics that are not found in traditional textbooks or other resources. (One example might be the history of food service in prisons.) The trade publication is usually controlled by public agencies, unions, or other corporations.

- *Correctional News: Design, Construction, Operations*, San Rafael, CA, Emlen Media Corporation:

    Correctional News has been around since 1984 and addresses design, maintenance and operational issues surrounding correctional facilities. It also covers a wide range of current correctional issues.

- *Security Magazine*, **www.securitymagazine.com/**:

    Security is uniquely focused on solutions for enterprise security leaders. It is designed and written for business-minded executives who manage enterprise risk and security. *Security* provides management-focused features, opinions, and trends for leaders in business, government, and institutional sectors in print, in person and online.

Appendix 16

Codes of Ethics

INTRODUCTION

There are many codes of ethics that have been written to help guide the conduct of group members throughout the centuries. We encourage the future criminal justice professional to review the sample codes for this industry that we have included in this appendix. When you begin your first job and/or move on to other agencies, you will discover that each area of the industry, and each specific agency or department, has its own code of ethics. We refer the reader to Chapter 8 of this book, which explores the overall subject of ethics for the criminal justice employee.

AMERICAN CORRECTIONAL ASSOCIATION CODE OF ETHICS

Preamble

The American Correctional Association expects of its members unfailing honesty, respect for the dignity and individuality of human beings and a commitment to professional and compassionate service. To this end, we subscribe to the following principles.

- Members shall respect and protect the civil and legal rights of all individuals.

- Members shall treat every professional situation with concern for the welfare of the individuals involved and with no intent to personal gain.
- Members shall maintain relationships with colleagues to promote mutual respect within the profession and improve the quality of service.
- Members shall make public criticism of their colleagues or their agencies only when warranted, verifiable, and constructive.
- Members shall respect the importance of all disciplines within the criminal justice system and work to improve cooperation with each segment.
- Members shall honor the public's right to information and share information with the public to the extent permitted by law subject to individuals' right to privacy.
- Members shall respect and protect the right of the public to be safeguarded from criminal activity.
- Members shall refrain from using their positions to secure personal privileges or advantages.
- Members shall refrain from allowing personal interest to impair objectivity in the performance of duty while acting in an official capacity.
- Members shall refrain from entering into any formal or informal activity or agreement which presents a conflict of interest or is inconsistent with the conscientious performance of duties.
- Members shall refrain from accepting any gifts, services, or favors that are or appear to be improper or implies an obligation inconsistent with the free and objective exercise of professional duties.
- Members shall clearly differentiate between personal views/statements and views/statements/positions made on behalf of the agency or Association.
- Members shall report to appropriate authorities any corrupt or unethical behaviors in which there is sufficient evidence to justify review.
- Members shall refrain from discriminating against any individual because of race, gender, creed, national origin, religious affiliation, age, disability, or any other type of prohibited discrimination.
- Members shall preserve the integrity of private information; they shall refrain from seeking information on individuals beyond that which is necessary to implement responsibilities and perform their

duties; members shall refrain from revealing nonpublic information unless expressly authorized to do so.

- Members shall make all appointments, promotions, and dismissals in accordance with established civil service rules, applicable contract agreements, and individual merit, rather than furtherance of personal interests.
- Members shall respect, promote, and contribute to a work place that is safe, healthy, and free of harassment in any form.

Taken from www.aca.org/ACA_Prod_IMIS/ACA_Member/About_Us/ Code_of_Ethics/ACA_Member/AboutUs/Code_of_Ethics.aspx? hkey=61577ed2-c0c3-4529-bc01-36a248f79eba.

AMERICAN PROBATION AND PAROLE ASSOCIATION

Code of Ethics

1. I will render professional service to the justice system and the community at large in effecting the social adjustment of the offender.
2. I will uphold the law with dignity, displaying an awareness of my responsibility to offenders while recognizing the right of the public to be safeguarded from criminal activity.
3. I will strive to be objective in the performance of my duties, recognizing the inalienable right of all persons, appreciating the inherent worth of the individual, and respecting those confidences which can be reposed in me.
4. I will conduct my personal life with decorum, neither accepting nor granting favors in connection with my office.
5. I will cooperate with my co-workers and related agencies and will continually strive to improve my professional competence through the seeking and sharing of knowledge and understanding.
6. I will distinguish clearly, in public, between my statements and actions as an individual and as a representative of my profession.
7. I will encourage policy, procedures and personnel practices, which will enable others to conduct themselves in accordance with the values, goals and objectives of the American Probation and Parole Association.

8. I recognize my office as a symbol of public faith and I accept it as a public trust to be held as long as I am true to the ethics of the American Probation and Parole Association.

9. I will constantly strive to achieve these objectives and ideals, dedicating myself to my chosen profession.

Taken from www.appa-net.org/eweb/DynamicPage.aspx?WebCode =IA_CodeEthics

INTERNATIONAL ASSOCIATION OF CHIEFS OF POLICE LAW ENFORCEMENT CODE OF ETHICS

AS A LAW ENFORCEMENT OFFICER, my fundamental duty is to serve mankind; to safeguard lives and property; to protect the innocent against deception, the weak against oppression or intimidation, and the peaceful against violence or disorder; and to respect the Constitutional rights of all men to liberty, equality and justice.

I WILL keep my private life unsullied as an example to all; maintain courageous calm in the face of danger, scorn, or ridicule; develop self-restraint; and be constantly mindful of the welfare of others. Honest in thought and deed in both my personal and official life, I will be exemplary in obeying the laws of the land and the regulations of my department. Whatever I see or hear of a confidential nature or that is confided to me in my official capacity will be kept ever secret unless revelation is necessary in the performance of my duty.

I WILL never act officiously or permit personal feelings, prejudices, animosities or friendships to influence my decisions. With no compromise for crime and with relentless prosecution of criminals, I will enforce the law courteously and appropriately without fear or favor, malice or ill will, never employing unnecessary force or violence and never accepting gratuities.

I RECOGNIZE the badge of my office as a symbol of public faith, and I accept it as a public trust to be held so long as I am true to the ethics of the police service. I will constantly strive to achieve these objectives and ideals, dedicating myself before God to my chosen profession . . . law enforcement.

Taken from www.fdle.state.fl.us/Content/CJST/Menu/Officer-Requirements-Main-Page/LE-Ethical-Standards-of-Conduct.aspx.

Notes

CHAPTER 1: INTRODUCTION: WHY ANOTHER BOOK ON CRIMINAL JUSTICE CAREERS?

1. See www.smartasset.com/insights/the-economics-of-the-american-prison-system, accessed January 23, 2015.

2. See www.vera.org/files/price-of-prisons-california-fact-sheet.pdf, accessed January 2012.

3. See www.vera.org/files/price-of-prisons-texas-fact-sheet.pdf, accessed January 2012.

4. See www.detroitnews.com/article/99999999/POLITICS/80414001, accessed May 17, 2015.

CHAPTER 2: EXPLORING CAREERS IN CRIMINAL JUSTICE

1. "What works" is a specific term that refers to problem-solving approaches, that is, approaches that have been researched and found to be successful. They are also referred to as "evidence-based approaches."

2. *Dry-labbing* is the presentation of evidence, i.e., DNA, for which no test has been conducted. The Innocence Project has uncovered several instances of this that resulted in innocent persons being sentenced to prison. Fortunately, through the Innocence Project, they have been exonerated and released from prison.

3. Law enforcement agencies have Employee Assistance Programs (EAP) to help those who are struggling with personal problems. There are peer counseling

programs in many states, in which police officers generally trained as clinicians volunteer their time to assist fellow officers. New Jersey's Cop2Cop program is the only program that is mandated by state statute.

4. Robert Longworthy and Lawrence Travis, *Policing in America: A balance of forces* (Upper Saddle River, NJ: Prentice Hall, 1999).

5. Ted Conover, *Newjack* (New York: Random House, 2000).

6. Len Ward is the Director of the Division of Parole and Community Programs for the New Jersey State Parole Board. He holds a BA from Jersey City State College and a master's degree in public administration from Fairleigh Dickinson University. He began his career in the Department of Transportation and advanced to positions with the Departments of Law and Public Safety and the Department of Corrections. He is a certified instructor by the NJ Police Training Commission and certified by the U.S. Department of Justice in community-oriented policing. He is an adjunct professor of criminal justice at Fairleigh Dickinson University.

7. Dorothy Taylor, *Jump Starting Your Career: An Internship Guide for Criminal Justice, 2nd ed.* (Upper Saddle River, NJ: Pearson Education, Inc., 2005).

8. See *Seven Habits of Highly Successful People* by Stephen Covey. You may be particularly interested in the section entitled "Sharpening the Sword."

9. Matthew Sheridan and Stephen Richards, "Collateral Consequences: Felony Convictions," in *The Encyclopedia of Criminal Justice Ethics.* (Thousand Oaks, CA: Sage Publications, 2013).

10. Todd Clear, George Cole, and Michael Reisig, *American Corrections, 8th ed.* (Belmont, CA: Thompson Higher Education, 2009).

CHAPTER 3: CAREERS IN LAW ENFORCEMENT

1. Michael Di Lieto, *How to Become a New Jersey Police Officer or State Trooper* (Maywood, NJ: NJ Law Enforcement Recruit Resources, 2005–2008).

CHAPTER 4: CAREERS IN CORRECTIONS

1. Jeanne Stinchcomb and Vernon Fox, *Introduction to Corrections, 5th ed.* (Upper Saddle River, NJ: Prentice Hall, 1999).

2. Census of State and Federal Correctional Facilities, 2005, www.bjs.gov/content/pub/pdf/csfcf05.pdf.

3. Census of Jail Facilities, 2006, www.bjs.gov/content/pub/pdf/cjf06.pdf.

4. Lauren E. Glaze and Danielle Kaeble, "Correctional Populations in the United States," *Bureau of Justice Statistics* (December 19, 2014), 1.

5. Glaze, "Correctional Populations in the United States," 2.

6. Todd Clear and Natasha Frost, *The Punishment Imperative* (New York: New York University Press, 2014).

7. "The Uniform Crime Reporting (UCR) Program has been the starting place for law enforcement executives, students of criminal justice, researchers, members of the media, and the public at large seeking information on crime in the nation. The program was conceived in 1929 by the International Association of Chiefs of Police to meet the need for reliable uniform crime statistics for the nation. In 1930, the FBI was tasked with collecting, publishing, and archiving those statistics," www.fbi.gov/about-us/cjis/ucr/ucr.

8. Recidivism statistics attempt to measure some form of failure after someone has been convicted of a crime and has been incarcerated. The reader should carefully review the definition used by a researcher to ensure the correct usage of the word in that specific piece of research.

9. Bureau of Labor Statistics, *Occupational Outlook Handbook*, www.bls.gov/ooh/protective-service/correctional-officers.htm#tab-6.

10. Ibid., www.bls.gov/ooh/protective-service/correctional-officers.htm#tab-5.

11. See "Sheriff/Police Chief Salaries," at www.salary.com/Sheriff-Police-Chief-Salary.html.

12. See www.payscale.com/research/US/Job=Deputy_Sheriff/Salary, accessed May 2, 2015.

13. See www.work.chron.com/sheriff-officers-salary-5962.html, 2015. Author's Note: Salaries vary greatly between the local, state, and federal positions of sheriff officer.

14. Sheriff Joe Arpaio and Len Sherman, *Joe's Law: America's Toughest Sheriff Takes on Illegal Immigration, Drugs, and Everything Else That Threatens America* (New York: AMACOM. 2008).

15. The Constitutions of New Jersey and Pennsylvania, in 1776, required that the sheriff be elected.

16. See www.payscale.com/research/US/Job=Parole_Officer/Salary, 2015.

17. See www.payscale.com/research/US/Job=Probation_Officer/Salary, 2015.

18. Bureau of Labor Statistics, *Occupational Outlook Handbook*, www.bls.gov/ooh/.

19. See www.prisonlegalnews.org/news/2012/mar/15/electronic-monitoring-some-causes-for-concern/, accessed May 17, 2015.

20. See Stinchcomb and Fox (1999) for detailed descriptions of the work of parole and probation officers.

21. See www.bjs.gov/content/pub/pdf/ppus13.pdf, accessed January 21, 2015.

22. See www.bjs.gov/content/pub/pdf/scefy8210.pdf, accessed April 30, 2014. Author's Note: This figure does not take into account hidden costs, that is, costs that are subsumed by other state departments, such as vehicles, that in some states are located in the treasury department.

23. See www.us.wow.com/search?s_pt=aolsem&s_it=aolsem&s_chn=25&q =cost%20of%20probation, accessed May 16, 2015.

24. See www.us.wow.com/search?s_it=topsearchbox.search&s_chn=25&s_ pt=aolsem&v_t=aolsem&q=American+probation+and+parole+Association+rec ommends+a+case+load+of+50+cases+per+officer, Summer 1991.

25. See www.criminaljusticedegreehub.com/corrections-jobs/, accessed February 27, 2013.

26. See www.google.com/?gws_rd=ssl#q=Private+prisons%2C+%2C+2001, February 2001.

27. See www.Inc_Too_Good_To_Be_True.pdf, January 2012.

CHAPTER 5: THE COURTS, ITS ACTORS, AND ITS FUNCTIONS

1. See www.bjs.gov/content/pub/pdf/scefy8210.pdf, accessed June 22, 2012.

2. Johnnie Cochran, attorney to O.J. Simpson, Abner Louima, Michael Jackson, and Sean Combs, began his law career as a deputy city attorney, went into private practice, and later joined the Los Angeles County District Attorney's office as the first black assistant district attorney. He was inspired by Thurgood Marshall and the *Brown v. Board of Education* case, and later wrote, "I read everything I could about Thurgood Marshall and confirmed that a single dedicated man could use the law to change society."

3. Jeffrey Toobin, *The Run of His Life: The People v. O.J. Simpson* (New York: Random House, 1996).

4. James Inciardi, *Criminal Justice, 6th ed.* (Orlando, FL: Harcourt, Brace, and Co., 1999).

5. Courts of limited jurisdiction are federal courts set up to address specific situations (such as bankruptcy and family matters). The courts of limited jurisdiction cannot hear cases that would fall under general or other jurisdictions.

6. *Filibuster* is the use of a speech to obstruct a legislative proceeding.

7. *Cloture* is a motion to bring an end to a debate.

8. See www.noalearn.org/articles/Judge_Become_a_Judge_in_5_Steps.html, accessed May 16, 2015.

10. Abe Fortas stepped down from the Supreme Court because of ethics accusations. He is most famous for his defense before the U.S. Supreme Court in the case of *Gideon v. Wainright*. Gideon was an indigent defendant in a Florida prison who handwrote an appeal in pencil to the Court.

11. *Impeachment* is the formal process of accusation of wrongdoing (illegality) against an elected official that may lead to removal from office. There may also be civil or criminal penalties for the accused acts.

12. See www.bloomberg.com/news/articles/2014-01-13/federal-judges-in-u-s-see-25-000-more-as-salary-freeze-falls, accessed January 13, 2014.

13. See *Gideon v. Wainright*.

14 Dan T. Carter, *Scottsboro: A Tragedy of the American South* (Baton Rouge: Louisiana State University Press, 1979).

15. John Grisham, *The Innocent Man* (New York: Doubleday, 2006).

16. DNA is material contained in chromosomes that is self-replicating. DNA is considered to be unique as a material that can positively distinguish one person from another.

17. See www.recruiter.com/salaries/coroners-salary/, accessed May 15, 2015.

18. See www.bls.gov/oes/current/oes194092.htm, May 2014.

19. Jeanne Stinchcomb and Vernon Fox, *Introduction to Corrections, 5th ed.* (Upper Saddle River, NJ: Prentice Hall, 1999).

20. See www.bls.gov/oes/current/oes194092.htm, May 2014.

21. See www.bls.gov/ooh/legal/court-reporters.htm, May 2014.

22. See www.bls.gov/oes/current/oes434031.htm, May 2014.

CHAPTER 6: THE FEDERAL GOVERNMENT

1. Park police are only assigned to three cities: the District of Columbia, New York City, and San Francisco.

2. This website answers many questions about careers in the federal government, as well as questions about the application process.

3. Go to this website, www.nps.gov/uspp/hirproc2.htm, for a step-by-step process to becoming a U.S. Parks police officer. This site provides an explanation of qualifications, disqualifiers, and the Physical Efficiency Battery (PED), as well as other details about the Comprehensive Written and Psychological Examination. The website also provides several sample examination questions.

4. Visit www.fws.gov/ for job descriptions and to view some interesting videos of wardens on the job.

5. Visit www.secretservice.gov/ for a detailed job description and multiple links that explain the career and hiring process in the Secret Service.

6. Dr. Kenny held several positions as a treasury enforcement agent, including a group manager field investigator, a district director's representative (Monmouth/Ocean Counties, New Jersey), a district quality officer, a chief of advisory, and a chief of review. He earned his PhD at Rutgers University and is a tenured professor at Fairleigh Dickinson University. He is an expert in workplace violence, school violence, and domestic violence, and he has published various papers on these subjects. See his complete biography on the website.

7. See www.opm.gov/oca/payrates/.

8. See www.bop.gov/jobs/eligibility/index.jsp.

9. See www.bop.gov/about/agency/.

10. Glynco, Georgia, is the location of the Federal Law Enforcement Training Center (FLETC). This facility trains new federal employees in basic skills and other agents with advanced skills instruction. Each year the FLETC prepares more than forty thousand employees for a wide variety of duties, with more than 250 courses of instruction from fingerprinting to interview skills, to high-speed pursuits and defensive driving, to computer crimes, and more.

11. See www.fletc.gov/training-catalog.

CHAPTER 7: GETTING THE JOB, ENTERING THE FIELD, AND CAREER ADVANCEMENT

1. Headhunter: a professional human resource recruiter. They typically recruit for specific upper management positions.

2. Stephen Covey, *The Seven Habits of Highly Successful People*, (New York: The Free Press. 2004).

3. William Johnson et al., *The Criminal Justice Student Writer's Manual, 3rd ed.* (Upper Saddle River, NJ: Pearson Education, Inc., 2005).

CHAPTER 8: CRIMINAL JUSTICE ETHICS

1. Jay Albanese, *Professional Ethics in Criminal Justice: Being Ethical When No One Else Is Looking* (Boston: Pearson, 2008).

2. A Federal Consent Decree is handed down by a federal court upon finding that an agency or some function of state government is in violation of the U.S. Constitution. Upon acceptance by the specific state to be under a federal consent decree, the federal court then appoints a federal master to oversee changes in the state that will bring the state into compliance with the U.S. Constitution. Once the

federal court is satisfied that the state or agency is now in full compliance, then it will lift the federal consent decree.

3. See www.prisonexp.org/, 1999–2015.
4. Philip Zimbardo, *The Lucifer Effect* (New York: Random House, Inc., 2008).
5. Joycelyn Pollock, *Ethical Dilemmas and Decisions in Criminal Justice, 5th ed.* (Belmont, CA: Thompson Higher Education, 2007).
6. Ibid.

CHAPTER 9: LIFE AFTER THE CAREER OR "I CAN'T LIVE ON THAT!"

1. Cost of Living Adjustments (COLAs) are used to counteract the effects of inflation on Social Security, pensions, and other forms of supplementary income during retirement.
2. Richard Bach, *Jonathan Livingston Seagull* (New York: Scribner, 1970).
3. Stephen Covey, *The Seven Habits of Highly Successful People* (New York: The Free Press, 2004).

APPENDIX 1: DIRECTORY OF PROFILES IN CRIMINAL JUSTICE

1. L.E. Noel, L. E., *Voyages: Canada's Heritage Rivers* (Guilford, CT: Breakwater Books, 1995), 1.

APPENDIX 8: CIVIL SERVICE EXAMINATIONS

1. John Demsey, *Police (with Criminal Justice CourseMate with eBook Printed Access Card), 2nd Ed.* (Boston, MA: Cengage Learning, 2012); Raymond Foster and Tracey Biscontini, *Police Officer Exam For Dummies* (Hoboken, NJ: Wiley Publishing, 2011); Donald Schroeder and Frank Lombardo, *Barron's Police Officer Exam, 9th Edition* (New York: Barron's Educational Services, 2013); Donald Schroeder and Frank Lombardo, *Barron's Correction Officer Exam, 4th Edition* (New York: Barron's Educational Services, 2014).

Bibliography of References and Suggested Readings

INTRODUCTION

A bibliography usually does not contain opening remarks. This book is an exception. These are not only the books and references used to write *Exploring and Understanding Careers in Criminal Justice: A Comprehensive Guide*, but they are also informative and at times interesting sources of information about the criminal justice profession. You should review them and decide which may help you better understand the profession you wish to enter. Some are introductory textbooks, some discuss specific issues such as victimization, others are personal stories, and one proposes that we take a new look at crime and punishment.

BIBLIOGRAPHY

Albanese, Jay. *Professional Ethics in Criminal Justice: Being Ethical Ehen No One Else is Looking.* Boston: Pearson, 2008.

American Correctional Association, The, *The American Prison: From the Beginning—A Pictorial History.* The American Correctional Association, 1983.

Bach, Richard. *Jonathan Livingston Seagull.* New York: Scribner, 1970.

Bartollas, Clemens, and Stuart Miller. *Juvenile Justice in America*, 7th ed. Upper Saddle River, NJ: Prentice Hall, 2001.

Bergman, Larry W. "Corrections as a Wholistic Profession?" *The Keepers' Voice*, vol.15, no. 1 (Winter 1994): 43.

Bowker, Lee. *Prison Victimization.* New York: Elsevier, 1980.

Bureau of Labor Statistics, U.S. Department of Labor, *Occupational Outlook Handbook 2013–2014*. New York: Skyhorse.

Carlson, Peter, and Judith Garrett. *Prison and Jail Administration: Practice and Theory*, 2nd ed. Boston: Jones and Bartlett Publishers, 2008.

Clear, Todd, George Cole, and Michael Reisig. *American Correction*, 8th ed. Belmont, CA: Thompson Higher Education, 2009.

Covey, Stephen. *The Seven Habits of Highly Successful People*. New York: The Free Press, 2004.

Conover, Ted. *Newjack*. New York: Random House, 2000.

Daly, Robert. *The Prince of the City*. New York: Berkeley, 1984.

Demsey, John. *Police (with Criminal Justice CourseMate with eBook Printed Access Card)*, 2nd ed. Boston, MA: Cengage Learning, 2012.

DiLieto, Michael. *How to Become a New Jersey Police Officer or State Trooper*. Maywood, NJ: NJ Law Enforcement Recruit Resources, 2005–2008.

Foster, Raymond, and Tracey Biscontini. *Police Officer Exam for Dummies*. Hoboken, NJ: Wiley, 2011.

Grisham, John. *The Innocent Man*. New York: Doubleday, 2006.

Inciardi, James. *Criminal Justice*, 6th ed. Orlando, FL: Harcourt, Brace, and Co., 1999.

Johnson, Lee. *Experiencing Corrections: From Practitioner to Professor*. Thousand Oaks, CA: Sage, 2012.

Johnson, William, Richard Retting, Gregory Scott, and Stephen Garrison. *The Criminal Justice Student Writer's Manual*, 3rd ed. Upper Saddle River, NJ: Pearson Education, 2005.

Lewis, Anthony. *Gideon's Trumpet*. New York: Vintage, 1966.

Light, Richard. *Making the Most of College: Students Speak Their Minds*. Cambridge, MA: Harvard University Press, 2001.

Longworthy, Robert, and Lawrence Travis. *Policing in America: A balance of forces*. Upper Saddle River, NJ: Prentice Hall, 1999.

Maas, Peter. *Serpico: The Cop Who Defied the System*. New York: Viking, 1973.

Pollock, Joycelyn. *Ethical Dilemmas and Decisions in Criminal Justice*, 5th ed. Belmont, CA: Thompson Higher Education, 2007.

Schroeder, Donald, and Frank Lombardo. *Barron's Police Officer Exam*, 9th ed. New York: Barron's Educational Services, 2013.

Schroeder, Donald, and Frank Lombardo. *Barron's Correction Officer Exam*, 4th ed. New York: Barron's Educational Services, 2014.

Sheridan, Matthew, and Stephen Richards. "Collateral Consequences: Felony Convictions." *The Encyclopedia of Criminal Justice Ethics*. Thousand Oaks, CA: Sage, 2013.

Sherman, Lawrence. "Learning Police Ethics." *Justice, Crime, and Ethics*, 3rd ed. Cincinnati: Anderson, 1998.

Stinchcomb, Jeanne, and Vernon Fox. *Introduction to Corrections, 5th ed.* Upper Saddle River, NJ: Prentice Hall, 1999.

Taylor, Dorothy. *Jump-Starting Your Career: An Internship Guide for Criminal Justice,* 2nd ed. Upper Saddle River, NJ: Pearson Education, 2005.

Jeffrey Toobin. *The Run of His Life: The People v. O.J. Simpson.* New York: Random House, 1996.

Cliff Tuttle. "Juris Doctor: The Versatile Degree." *Pennsylvania Law Weekly* 18 (December 11, 1995).

Twersky-Glasner, Aviva, and Matthew Sheridan. "Police Psychologist: Gatekeeper and Ally." *New Jersey Criminal Justice Educator,* 10–11, 2005.

Walker, Samuel, and Charles Katz. *The Police in America: An Introduction,* 5th ed. New York: McGraw Hill, 2005.

Williams, Christopher, and Bruce Arrigo. *Ethics, Crime, and Criminal Justice.* Boston: Pearson, 2008.

Zimbardo, Philip. *The Lucifer Effect.* New York: Random House, 2008.

SUGGESTED READING

Some of the books we recommend for reading are already listed in the bibliography. We repeat them here because we believe that they represent significant sources of information for the student aspiring to a criminal justice career. We recognize that time is a valuable asset, and therefore we have tried to be most selective in our recommendations to provide you with reading material that provides the maximum benefit in the shortest amount of time.

Albanese, Jay. *Professional Ethics in Criminal Justice: Being Ethical When No One Else is Looking.* Boston: Pearson, 2008.

Covey, Stephen. *The Seven Habits of Highly Successful People.* New York: The Free Press, 2004.

Johnson, Lee. *Experiencing Corrections: From Practitioner to Professor.* Thousand Oaks, CA: Sage, 2012.

Criminal Justice Distance Learning, Consortium, *The Definitive Guide to Criminal Justice and Criminology on the World Wide Web.* Upper Saddle River, NJ: Prentice Hall, 1999.

Johnson, William, Richard Retting, Gregory Scott, and Stephen Garrison. *The Criminal Justice Student Writer's Manual,* 3rd ed. Upper Saddle River, NJ: Pearson Education, 2005.

Light, Richard. *Making the Most of College: Students speak their minds.* Cambridge, MA: Harvard University Press, 2001.

Pollock, Joycelyn. *Ethical Dilemmas and Decisions in Criminal Justice*, 5th ed. Belmont, CA: Thompson Higher Education, 2007.

President's Commission on Law Enforcement and the Administration of Justice. *The Challenge of Crime in a Free Society*. New York: Avon Books/Hearst, 1968.

Rafter, Nicole. "Gender, Prisons, and Prison History." *Social Science History*, vol. 9, no.3 (1985): 233–247.

Rupp, Kelly. *Police Writing: A Guide to the Essentials.* Upper Saddle River, NJ: Pearson Education, 2015.

Silberman, Charles. *Criminal Justice, Criminal Violence*. New York: Vantage, 1968.

Smalleger, Frank, and John Worrall. *Policing Today*. Upper Saddle River, NJ: Pearson Education, 2010.

Taylor, Dorothy. *Jump-Starting Your Career: An Internship Guide for Criminal Justice*, 2nd ed. Upper Saddle River, NJ: Pearson Education, 2005.

Weisheit, Ralph, and Frank Morn. *Pursuing Justice*. New York: Anderson, 2015.

Zimbardo, Philip. *The Lucifer Effect*. New York: Random House, 2008.

Subject Index

guard, viii, 51, 53–55, 95, 131, 133
Guggenheim Foundation, 256

hack, 52
halfway houses, 2, 52, 73, 239
high school diploma, 36, 41, 62, 69, 219
Holmesburg Prison, 16

Immigration and Customs
Enforcement (ICE), 93, 227–228
immigration, 93–94, 167, 228, 230, 240, 273
impeachment, 80, 275
incapacitation, 15, 30, 31
inflation, 143–146, 276
Innocence Projects, 83, 271
Institutional corrections, 52–53
insurance card, 36, 219
internal affairs, ix, 47, 58–59, 137, 165
International Association of Chiefs of Police (IACP), 132, 139, 245
International Association of Corrections and Prisons, 165
International Community Corrections Association (ICCA), 73, 138, 241
International Corrections and Prison Association (ICPA), 138
Internet, 26, 52, 116, 118, 121, 171, 207, 235, 252
internship, viii, x, xiii, 19–21, 23–26, 41, 75, 98–99, 102, 162, 165, 182, 184–185, 196, 207, 210, 217, 272, 281–282
interstate parole compact, 65–66
interpersonal skills, 39
interpreter, 78
interview, viii, x, 7, 22, 25, 34, 37–38, 56, 94–95, 99, 102, 104–105, 107,

109, 113, 119, 121–124, 162, 172, 182, 187–193, 195, 205–207, 209–2123, 219, 224, 233, 259, 276
interview preparation, 187, 190–191
interview questions, xi, 34, 38, 122, 124, 155, 187, 191–193
introduction to criminal justice, 5, 19, 21
investigative reporter, 7, 15
investigator K9 officer, 249

jail, 2, 51–53, 60–61, 83, 167, 170, 240, 273, 280
jailers, 53
job posting, viii, x, 35, 92, 103, 114, 182, 191, 222, 262
job search, 99, 105, 113, 114, 117, 120, 205–206
Jonathan Livingston Seagull, 152, 276, 279
The Journal of American Probation and Parole, 261
The Journal of Correctional Education, 261
The Journal of Prisons and Prisoners, 261
judges, ix, 1–2, 11, 12–13, 31, 61, 67, 76–81, 83, 85, 76, 87–88, 134, 137, 139–140, 237, 275
judicial branch of government, 80, 81
judicial conduct, 140
judicial decisions, 67, 80
judicial functions, 31
judicial nominating committee, 79
judicial process, 82, 89, 202, 283
juris doctor (J.D.), 75–76, 79, 281
justice of the peace, 77

keepers, 53, 279
King, Rodney, 14, 131

Name Index

About the Authors

Matthew J. Sheridan, Ed.D. Professional Profile: Over 30 years of progressively responsible experience in the criminal justice field as both practitioner and academic. Convict Criminologist, frequent presenter of papers on corrections and criminology issues. Frequent lecturer at New Jersey Colleges and Universities, professional and other interested organizations. Core areas of expertise include correctional and parole operations, correctional administration, Juvenile Justice, correctional education, and the courts. Criminal Justice Management including institutions, community residential, day treatment, and private organizations for effective responses to need. Private consultant for improving operational proficiency for compliance with state and federal standards. Conducting and reviewing. For questions please contact at msheridan@ georgian.edu

Raymond R. Rainville, Ph.D. Professional Profile: 35 years experience with government administration and higher education, including Saint Peter's University the College of New Jersey, Kean University, Brookdale Community College, and St. John's University. Core areas include: History and Philosophy of Corrections; Criminology; Community-Based Corrections; Probation and Parole; Juvenile Delinquency, Child Protection Agencies and the Law; Drugs Society and Behavior, Comparative Criminal Justice, Judicial Process; Introduction to Criminal Justice; and others. Member of Alpha Phi Sigma, the Criminal Justice National Honor Society. Past president of the New Jersey Association of Criminal Justice Educators. For questions please contact at rrainville@saintpetersuniversity.edu